ON SITE,
IN SOUND

REFIGURING AMERICAN MUSIC

A series edited by Ronald Radano and Josh Kun
Charles McGovern, contributing editor

ON SITE,
IN SOUND

Performance Geographies
in América Latina

KIRSTIE A. DORR

DUKE UNIVERSITY PRESS *Durham and London* 2018

Designed by Matthew Tauch
Typeset in Minion Pro and Trade Gothic Standard
Bold Condensed No. 20 by Copperline Book Services.

Library of Congress Cataloging-in-Publication Data
Names: Dorr, Kirstie A., [date] author.
Title: On site, in sound : performance geographies in América
Latina / Kirstie A. Dorr
Description: Durham : Duke University Press, 2018. | Series:
Refiguring American music | Includes bibliographical references
and index.
Identifiers: LCCN 2017035990 (print)
LCCN 2017041722 (ebook)
ISBN 9780822372653 (ebook)
ISBN 9780822368557 (hardcover : alk. paper)
ISBN 9780822368670 (pbk. : alk. paper)
Subjects: LCSH: Music and globalization—Latin America. |
Music—Social aspects—Latin America. | Music—Political
aspects—Latin America. | Music—Latin America—History
and criticism.
Classification: LCC ML3917.L29 (ebook) | LCC ML3917.L29 D677
2018 (print) | DDC 780.98—dc23
LC record available at https://lccn.loc.gov/2017035990

Cover art: Illustration by Favianna Rodriguez.
Courtesy of the artist.

CONTENTS

ACKNOWLEDGMENTS

In 1991, when I began working as a booking agent and tape seller for the pan-Andean band Markahuasi, I never imagined that the social and sonic arenas of cultural and economic (re)production they introduced me to would become the focus of my intellectual life for over twenty years—first as my senior thesis, then as my dissertation and eventually, as this book. This project was indelibly shaped by, and is eternally indebted to, the cohort of Latina/o cultural workers who made San Francisco's Mission District a nexus of immigrant-of-color activism through the early 1990s. Carlos Lara Yupanqui and Freddy Franco deserve particular recognition for the many overnight car rides they spent teaching me to hear, sense, and interpret the intricacies of Andean song. The artists and activists of La Peña del Sur, among them Alejandro Stuart, Galo Paz, and Samuel Guia, gave their time and energy to help me to reconstruct its history. The collective creative of work of these cultural workers and their comrades endures as an illuminative example of the power of sound and performance to shape and transform place.

From my early years in community college through my doctoral education, I was fortunate to have remarkable advisers and mentors. Carlos Córdova introduced me to interdisciplinary scholarship at the City College of San Francisco and encouraged me to think about transferring to a four-year university. At the University of California, Berkeley, I was honored to have Julio Ramos direct my undergraduate thesis; his mentorship was integral to my decision to continue in the academy, and his unflagging support for my work has continued through my graduate and postgraduate years. Gina Dent cultivated my interest in popular culture generally, and greatly enriched my knowledge about Black popular culture. José Saldívar was an enthusiastic sounding board and a careful reader, as well as an adviser and ally. Ruthie Gilmore taught me why space *always* matters and modeled what scholar activism at its best looks like. And Craig Gilmore coached me through the formidable book-pitching process. I continue to learn from this group of extraordinary intellectuals, and I am honored to count them as close friends.

A project such as this requires years spent abroad. A Tinker Research Grant from the UC Berkeley Center for Latin American Studies, a Hellman Foundation Fellowship, and a UC San Diego Faculty Career Development Grant provided the financial support that enabled me to travel. My time in Peru was graced by scholars and cultural workers who enabled this project to take shape. First and foremost, I am eternally indebted to the Barrueto and Ayllón families for being amazing teachers, hosts, and kin, and especially to Charo Barrueto and Pasqual Ayllón, who, in addition to being talented performers, haven proven to be lifelong friends. I was also fortunate enough to call the late Rafael Santa Cruz a friend and colleague. May this intrepid scholar, talented musician, and gifted performer rest in power; his influence certainly permeates these pages. Octavio Santa Cruz and Susana Baca were generous collaborators, sharing their wealth of knowledge about Afroperuvian history and culture. The amazing *hermanas* Robles have been engaging and thoughtful interlocutors, introducing me to feminist and queer iterations of these traditions.

During my time at the University of California, San Diego, I have been part of a number of invigorating and nourishing intellectual communities. Shortly after arriving to Southern California, I was invited to participate in the Sound Studies working group funded by the UC Humanities Research Institute. Reading and thinking alongside feminist sound studies powerhouses Inés Casillas, Roshanak Kheshti, Shana Redmond, and Deborah R. Vargas made this book immeasurably better. Their collective scholarship has defined the field of feminist and queer approaches to the study of race and sound, and I am honored to call them my comrades. The Department of Ethnic Studies is full of intelligent and committed colleagues, all of whom I have benefited from teaching and learning with. In particular, Curtis Marez has been the most generous, helpful, and encouraging mentor that one could hope for, as well as being a marvelous friend. My work on Afroperuanidad and the Black Pacific have been greatly enriched by UCSD's Black Internationalisms, Transnationalisms, and Diaspora working group and the Black Studies Project. I'm grateful to my BIT coconveners, Dayo Gore and Jessica Graham, for helping to build desperately-needed intellectual community, and to the UCSD Center for the Humanities for the financial support that made the working group possible. A Center for the Humanities faculty fellowship also allowed me time to write, revise, and share work with an impressive cadre of faculty from across campus.

The publication process is formidable and at times, unnerving! But I was incredibly fortunate to work with a fantastic cadre of experts at Duke University Press. I am forever grateful to Ken Wissoker for shepherding the project through every step, from proposal to publication; to Olivia Polk and Christi Stanforth for handling all production details large and small; and to the two astute, rigorous, and generous readers, whose engagement with the work made it immeasurably better. Favianna Rodriguez's willingness to work with me to customize the cover art was an unexpected gift from a long-admired artist.

It goes without saying that academic work can be isolating. I feel graced every day to have the unwavering community and support of my lifelong friends and sisters—Jessica Delgado, Jennifer Hamelburg, Emily Leys, Heather Murphy, Erica Steiner, and Vanessa Zelenak—as well as the Goetcher/Rivers/Valentine clan. My sojourns in the San Francisco Bay Area, Ohio, Illinois, and San Diego have yielded a number of exceptional friends and interlocutors. Asha Nadkarni, Renu Cappelli, and Mrinalini Chakravorty have been allies through thick and thin, and across many cities. My colleagues at the University of Illinois, particularly Ruth Nicole Brown, Karen Flynn, Soo Ah Kwon, Mimi Nguyen, and Fiona Ngo, made the cold climate infinitely more hospitable. In Southern California, Maylei Blackwell, Sara Cassetti, Erica Edwards, Arianne Miller, Alanna Aiko Moore, Leila Neti, Marcia Ochoa, and Shelley Streeby have proven that you still can make amazing new friends in middle age. Colleagues in the field who have become dear friends and inspiring interlocutors—Eva Hageman, Christina Hanhardt, Jennifer Kelly, Marisol LeBron, Christina León, and Ivan Ramos—have made conference travel something to look forward to. Felicia Lynch traveled cross-country to have insightful conversations over folded laundry and chicken dinners. My parents Kathleen and Richard and my brother Scott have staunchly stood by me as I've transitioned from small-town school kid to professor and have cheered me on through many an obstacle. My partner, Sara Clarke Kaplan, has been my closest interlocutor and fiercest advocate for nearly two decades, and has believed in me and my work even when my own faith wavered. Her passion, brilliance, and love are equal parts invigorating and sustaining, and it is sharing my life with her and Miles Martín that makes everything worthwhile.

INTRODUCTION

Thinking Site in Sound

"You can't have a revolution without songs." It was below a banner emblazoned with this popular slogan that Chilean Socialist Party leader and populist activist, Salvador Allende Gossens, greeted cheering throngs of thousands to declare his victory in the nation's contested 1970 presidential elections.[1] In his subsequent inaugural address to the Chilean parliament, Allende again roused the attention of aural publics by concluding his speech with "Venceremos!" (We Shall Overcome), referencing his campaign song that was popularized by the leftist coalition, Unidad Popular. Through a practiced deployment of sound and staging, the Allende camp acknowledged its indebtedness to Chile's burgeoning Nueva Canción movement, a pan–Latin American ferment that mobilized regional "neo-folklores" to promote anticapitalist and anti-imperialist commentary and to foment alliances among the nation's student, labor, and indigenous populations.[2] Indeed, Nueva Canción cultural workers were among Allende's most ardent supporters, among them acclaimed artist Victor Jara, who had written and performed new lyrics to "Venceremos" as part of his ongoing support for the Unidad coalition. Already the soundtrack for Allende supporters, "Venceremos" flooded the radio airwaves in the months following Unidad's victory, arguably becoming the unofficial anthem of Chile's revolutionary government. Yet, less than three years later, as the Allende administration fell to the U.S.-backed military coup that placed infamous dictator Augusto Pinochet in power, the sound and text of this militant march would evoke in its audiences both defiance and despair. For, the words to "Venceremos" would be the very last uttered by Victor Jara following his capture, torture, and public murder by Chilean military officers.

In the same year that "Venceremos" sounded the Unidad Popular's electoral victory in Chile and heralded the spread of socialism throughout Latin America, another notable South American ballad found its way to the international stage. During a European tour in 1965, renowned U.S. singer/songwriter Paul Simon met South American folkloric group Los Inkas at the Parisian nightclub L'Escale.[3] Intrigued by the band's instrumental interpretation of "El Cóndor Pasa," a melody first arranged by Peruvian folklorist Daniel Alomía Robles in 1913, Simon brazenly elected to record his own version of the song layered over Los Inkas' LP.[4] With Simon's awkward English lyrics superimposed, "El Condor Pasa (If I Could)" was released to U.S. and European audiences in 1970 to become a celebrated hit—one for which Alomía Robles was neither credited nor compensated. Presaging the world beat movement by nearly a decade, the haunting ballad topped charts in the United States, Germany, Holland, Belgium, and Spain, and helped to land Simon and Garfunkel's *Bridge over Troubled Water* a Grammy for "Album of the Year." Following several lawsuits and few apologies, Simon's appropriation of "El Cóndor Pasa" would later become one of world music's most infamous origin stories.

I open with the apposition of these seemingly dissimilar soundtracks for several reasons. First, each of these sonic flashpoints recalls a pivotal juncture within the itineraries of what I describe throughout this book as "South American musical transits." The thematic anchor of *On Site, In Sound*, this term references the genealogy of interconnected musical actors, aesthetics, texts, and practices whose modes of circulation are hereto examined.[5] As an organizational frame, it is deliberately capacious and intentionally strays from the conventional rubrics that most often inform musical study in the Americas. Rather than relying on nation or genre as an organizational principle, South American musical transits connotes an analytical framing of the sonic that straddles the particularism of geographic emplacement and the dynamism of cultural travel. In other words, it is a conceptual rather than descriptive term that, eschewing fixed or stable notions of sonic origin or musical destination, contemplates the alchemic capacity of aural transmission to produce, contest, or reimagine individual and/or collective perceptions of social space—its commonsense contours, ambits, and borders, as well as its fundamental abstractions, contradictions, and exclusions. Here and throughout, South America is invoked not as a fixed or stable regional location, but rather as a spatialized claim to relative and relational modes of creative production.[6] Musical transit registers how such claims are negotiated in and articulated through the dynamic interaction of performance practice, circulation process, and geohistorical context. This emphasis on cross-national and cross-regional circulations, conversations, and influences enables me to develop a primary argument of this book: that sonic production and spatial formation are mutually animating processes. Moreover, it allows me to narrate the rich if understudied geohistory of three musical moments that—owed to the racial-regional designs of academic disciplines, nationalist imaginaries, and generic conventions—are most often discussed as politically discrete, geographically bounded, and aesthetically disparate: Música Andina, Nueva Canción, and Música Afrosudamericana.

Second, these sonic flashpoints both mark moments of profound transformation within the geopolitical history of South American musical transits. The competing ideological and economic trajectories that these musical milestones foretell—the birth of a regional grassroots cultural politics rooted in anti-imperial socialist activism on the one hand, and the advent of a global culture industry steeped in uneven relations of race and capital on the other—aptly index the complex amalgam of structural forces and ideological struggles that form the contextual backdrop of this book.[7] These geohistorical conditions can be recapitulated in brief as four correlative realms of social conflict that have profoundly shaped South American cultural politics over the past century: early centurial nation-building projects that, through the state-sponsored "folklorization" of regional indigenous musics, ambitioned the generation of detectably modern yet singularly domestic aural canons and listening publics; a subsequent era of leftist pan-American musical activism that since its emergence in the 1950s, has advanced various regional and international populist agendas via grassroots strategies of promotion and political education;[8] a surge in campaigns of foreign-backed militarism and state terror that violently repressed these socialist movements, often via the detention, torture, and "disappearance" of prominent cultural workers;[9] and finally, the hemispheric imposition of neoliberalism as a global market integration strategy that bolstered the entrenchment of global culture industries oriented toward capital accumulation in the global North and resource extraction from the global South. Although rarely discussed in concert, the juxtaposition of Paul Simon's rise to world music fame and Victor Jara's violent murder poignantly illustrates a central exposition of this book: that the musical cultures of América del Sur have figured as a central node for the material-discursive expression of these struggles over political governance, economic vision, and cultural representation.

Third, I lead with these sonic flashpoints because they effectively allegorize the salient theoretical positions and evidentiary accounts that often ground popular and academic debates concerning Latina/o American musical migrations—conversations that have served as the theoretical point of departure for this book. Over the past three decades, Latina/o and Latin American studies scholars have effectively established a rich subfield of popular music studies scholarship, detailing the protean economic imperatives and political stakes that undergird relations of sonic production and exchange within and between the global Southern and global Northern Americas. The contributions of feminist of color sound studies scholars including Frances Aparicio, Deborah Pacini Hernández, Raquel Rivera, María Elena Cepeda, Licia Fiol-Matta, Deborah R. Vargas, and Alexandra Vasquez, among others, are particularly instructive, as they cogently elucidate the inextricability of musical relations from those of race and ethnicity, gender and sexuality, economy and class.[10] *On Site, In Sound* extends this scholastic trajectory by introducing a third analytical dimension to its contemplation of how the social and sonic intersect and overlap: the spatial. To date, a few noteworthy exceptions notwithstanding, the constructed and contested nature of social space remains remarkably undertheorized within discussions of musical circulation, both within the field of Latina/o sound studies and within popular music studies more generally.[11] Read together, Victor Jara's regionalized musical activism and Paul Simon's internationalist musical appropriations also offer an illustrative indexical contrast of two salient yet uninterrogated premises concerning interrelations of space and sound that commonly inform studies of musical circulation within the Americas.

The first of these narratives might be described as the uncritical celebration of "music in place"—that is, the extolment of sonic practices that are viewed as, and thus valued for, their ostensible aesthetic invariability and geographic autochthony. This approach to the study of popular music, which emphasizes rootedness and continuity over movement and dynamism, has informed much of the existing ethnomusicological scholarship about the artists and texts discussed in this book.[12] This privileging of "local" musical geographies such as Jara's electoral activism over global aural circulations such as that of "El Cóndor Pasa" is often leveraged in order to critique the deleterious effects of mass mediation. While critiques of capitalist mediation are crucial, the South American musical transits narrated herein effectively demonstrate that this particular analytical maneuver is problematic for several reasons. First, it speciously presumes that music's capacity to express political designs or enact solidarity practices is arbitrated by its static entrenchment in bounded, circumscribed spatial typologies such as community, region, or nation. Consequently, social space is understood and represented as static and unproblematic rather than unstable and contested, and the crucial role of performance in sounding competing geographic imaginaries and arrangements both within and beyond these typologies is effectively occluded and disavowed. Next, the "music in place" premise tends toward geopolitical framings of sonic practices and practitioners that fracture rather than foment internationalist solidarities. As a result, musicians such as Jara are viewed as national icons rather than international activists, and popular sonic movements such as Nueva Canción are historicized according to their national and regional variations rather than the hemispheric political ties and crosscurrents that they enabled. Finally, as I will soon expound upon in greater depth, such static conceptions of space and sound tend to sustain rather than unsettle the most suspect of cultural binarisms, including distinctions between traditional and modern, authentic and corrupted, high and low.

The analytical foil of the "music in place" narrative is represented in the second flashpoint—a proverbial, cautionary tale about the perils of sonic globalization. Coded as abstraction from a proper geographic domain and alienation from authentic aesthetic origins, the globalization of sound, it has often been argued, inevitably reproduces uneven relations of culture and capital between global South and global North.[13] Indeed, transactions of musical appropriation touted as the "rescue" of far-flung cultural traditions have catapulted the careers of white global Northern artists such as Paul Simon. Such cynical examples of so-called sonic partnerships thus merit trenchant scrutiny as they veritably reinstantiate material inequities via imperial relations of nostalgic consumption.[14] However, scholars of popular music studies often anchor such criticism in the erroneous presumption that the commodification or depoliticization of musical forms is the inevitable result of exogenous circulation, or, when "local roots" travel "out of place."[15] In this instance, "the local" is offered as a spatial metaphor for the ostensibly culturally and geographically fixed or static landscapes of the non-West, while "the global" is narrated as the dynamic, agential (albeit usually malign) forces of the West.[16]

Taken together, then, these sonic flashpoints reference the entangled structural forces and ideological stakes that propel South American musical transits as well as the correlative analytical premises that most often frame their study. As such, I offer these as a point of departure from which to stage the interwoven inquiries of *On Site, In Sound*. The questions that shape this book emerge from conjoint thematic interests and theoretical pursuits. Conceptualized at a time when the burgeoning world music industry was matched by a boom in scholarship on globalized pop, *On Site, In Sound* developed out of my interest in tracking South American musical transits and geographies of aural circulation that defied the putative cultural imperialist model of global Southern musical dissemination: extraction, abstraction, and resignification. In the shadow of new media technologies and neoliberal markets, I was instead curious about those transregional and –national itineraries of South American musicians and musics that had never been "discovered" or endorsed by industry promoters yet were crucially sustained through globally dispersed networks of sonic production, distribution, and consumption. What geohistorical conditions, political and economic strategies, and creative artistic practices have enabled these alternative modes of bodily and cultural transit? How might such histories be tracked, what unheard stories do they harbor, and what might they teach us about grassroots cultural struggle and quotidian practices of life making amid the dystopic conditions of neoliberal globalization?

This shift in scholarly attention from South American "world music" to the politics of South American "musical worlding" prompted a thorny yet provocative theoretical conundrum: how to *emplace*—within existing literature reviews, field debates, and analytical claims—an unruly set of globalized musical practices and transregional cultural landscapes that stubbornly refused submission to the conventional "in" or "out of place" contextual framings that dominate ethnic, area, cultural, and music studies scholarship. Popular and academic discourse concerning transnational musical migrations has routinely examined and debated how relations of mediation and routes of travel transform musical texts and practices.[17] These conversations have engendered compelling models of aural interaction—from "soundscapes" to "contact zones" to "glocalisms."[18] Yet, despite a common predilection for spatial metaphors, such accounts fail to amply or adequately consider the dynamic relations of space and place that musical production necessarily entails.[19] While contentious, these conversations are oft rooted in a common misconception: that while sonic cultures are constantly on the move, the places from, to, and across which they travel remain constant, intact, uncontested. This fictional premise has dissuaded scholars of popular music from taking seriously the spatiality of sound—the ways in which music is "linked to particular geographical sites, bound up in our everyday perceptions of place, and a part of movements of people, products, and cultures across space."[20] It is to the inverse logics and implications of this site-sound relationship that this book turns its critical attention. It argues that an integrated analysis of space, sound, and difference unfolds a neglected path of scholarly inquiry: the agential force of musical poetics and practice in shaping social relations of embodiment, mobility, and coalition.[21] It asks: how have South American cultural workers negotiated the constraints of global culture industry relations by activating grassroots practices of sonic siting, staging, and transmission to pursue their creative endeavors? What unique types of performance geographies have such modes of spatialized cultural activism engendered? And if, as feminist, antiracist geographers have persuasively argued, the construction of place is dynamic, ideological, and contested, then how have the material contours and ideological coherence of dominant geopolitical regimes of sociality, activism, labor, and commerce been transformed by these nonconventional modes of musical circulation?

These are some of the primary political concerns that animate this inquiry. Convening the theoretics and vocabularies of space, sound, and difference, *On Site, In Sound* examines four geographies of South American musical transits from the 1960s to the present. Each of its chapters offers a case study of aural cultures and migrant "musicking" practices that circulate via quotidian, minor, or nonconventional modes of transmission such as street performance, piracy networks, underground nightclubs, and other extralegal transactions.[22] In charting these dispersed yet connected sonic networks, *On Site, In Sound* necessarily questions and complicates modes of analysis that situate musical texts and cultural workers as singularly or universally "in" or "out of place." Rather, it interrogates the politics of musical emplacement itself, arguing that the invention and maintenance of these performance sites and circuits have relied upon tactics of "sonic transposition"—that is, the (re)configuration of place through the practice of sound.[23] Put differently, it advances that global Southern cultural workers who are unable or unwilling to access industrialized structures of musical production and promotion in the global North have alternatively relied on informal and/or improvisational networks of communication, exchange, and promotion to forge and sustain sonic relationships. These alternate forms of aural "franchise" have most often required the material and discursive transformation of social space—a reconfiguration of the boundaries between public and private, commercial and residential, labor and leisure, and so on—through the practice of sound.[24]

The South American musical transits examined herein complicate dominant itineraries of musical globalization by demonstrating how state-sponsored research and knowledge production, regional and international media networks, and nonconventional modes of sonic transmission have all forged concurrent and competing pathways of aural circulation. Blurring rather than bolstering diametric framings such as the local and the global, the rooted and the mobile, the homogenous and the hybrid, these geographies of musical transit emanate from grassroots modes of popularization, follow dynamic itineraries of cultural and bodily migration, and illustrate creative negotiations of neoliberal globalization. They have occasioned the analytics and approaches deployed and developed throughout this book, which are meticulously attentive to the spatial work of sound, the sonic politics of place, and the generative material and imaginative potentialities realized in quotidian geographies of performance.

SETTING THE TERMS

Sound and space—however one defines these terms—are phenomenologically and ontologically intertwined. Sounds, after all, are always in motion; they emanate, radiate, reflect, canalize, get blocked, leak out, and so on.
—ANDREW J. EISENBERG, "Space"

Attention to the dynamic interplay of sonic production and spatial formation figures as a central preoccupation of this book. To think the spatial and the aural together, it argues, is to enliven registers that, through their subordination to the (purportedly) animate corollaries of the visual and temporal, have often suffered a common fate: relegation to static and/or abstracted domains such as Euclidean backdrop or reflective node.[25] Within cultural criticism, the spatial and the sonic are often discussed as the mere scenery or scrim upon which the agential forces of the visual or temporal are staged. In this sense, the deadening of space and the muffling of sound operate somewhat analogously, in that the effective capacities of each have been eclipsed by a narrow focus on their representational or mimetic functions. Against such tendencies, *On Site, In Sound* aims to enliven the study of the spatial and the sonic by investigating the dynamic, mutually defining relationship between musical circulation and geographic formation.

THINKING SITE

From the early 1970s through the mid-1990s, the intersection of 24th Street and Mission Ave. figured as a public transport nexus designed to shuttle San Francisco's segregated Latina/o population to various outposts of low-wage factory, sweatshop, and reproductive work. In July 1993, on an unusually sunny late afternoon that punctuated the city's notoriously frigid summer weather, the Andean music ensemble Markahuasi set up their generator-fueled sound equipment opposite the Bay Area Rapid Transit (BART) stop's entrance and exit escalators to play a few sets. Their improvisational performance soon attracted an enthusiastic crowd of Mission District denizens who paused their daily routines to listen. Thenceforth, random individuals were hailed as a collective aural public forged through shared rituals of musicking: listening and singing, clapping while dancing, shouting out song requests or hollering "¡Otra! ¡Otra!" (Encore! Encore!). Deploying quotidian technologies of siting and sounding, Markahuasi effectively converted a subway station into a performance venue, one representative of what Chicana literary critic Mary Pat Brady has aptly described as a "counter-cartography": a place that reimagines dominant arrangements of racial capitalist space and/or narratives of how social space can or should be understood, organized, and occupied.[26] Markahuasi's improvisational sonic event demonstrates the power of performance to transform a site designed to facilitate racial capitalist relations of labor and commerce into a place of cultural production and community congregation, collective respite, and sensory pleasure. Moreover, it reveals how technologies of performance can serve to interrogate and denaturalize the constructedness of social space itself—

specifically, the ways in which its seemingly immutable material organization and ideological scripts are in fact unstable, contested, and susceptible to respatialization.

In her recent meditation on the significance of the geographic imagination, Doreen Massey advances a compelling definition of space: "the product of interrelations" that recounts "a simultaneity of stories-so-far."[27] Here, Massey proposes a conceptualization of the spatial that encompasses both the infinite totality of organic social relations and ongoing contests over how such relations are imagined and made sense of. In doing so, she challenges perceptions of space as fixed, static, or unproblematic, instead highlighting its fluidity, relationality, and heterogeneity. Following Massey, *On Site, In Sound* proceeds from the premise that spatial formation is an ongoing social process that materializes, in both immediate and far-reaching contexts, *differential* experiences of proximity, mobility, attachment, regulation, and containment. In accordance with Katherine McKittrick and Linda Peake's persuasive contention that difference must be conceptualized through "socially produced markers (such as race, class, gender, and sexuality) *and* their attendant geographies," it understands the social construction of space and the social construction of difference as co-constitutive.[28] For racialization, gendering, and class formation are spatialized practices of material emplacement and ideological abstraction that encompass no less than what Ruth Wilson Gilmore has described as the "death dealing displacement of difference into hierarchies that organize relations" within and between contested sites, scales, and landscapes.[29]

The extent to and urgency with which the spatial is engaged throughout this book are incumbent upon the structural imperatives of its contextual purview: global transformations in capital accumulation and production landscapes, the emergence of new media technologies, the entrenchment of neoliberal modes of governance, and the proliferation of multiscalar social movements. Within social and cultural theory, such processes are often discussed as the "deterritorialization" of production, finance, and technology, and correspondingly, as the abstraction or erosion of geographic registers. Such postulations, however, fail to consider the extent to which these transformations have in fact entailed comprehensive geopolitical reorderings. As Massey and others have shown, contemporary processes of global (dis)-integration signal not the death or neutrality of space, but rather, its constructedness, its materiality, and its dynamism.[30] And, it is precisely through charting the spatial politics of such transformations that we can make material sense of how relations of power and difference are territorialized in and reproduced through ongoing, contradictory processes of spatial formation. We can investigate, for example, how flexible modes of accumulation such as free-trade zones require state-funded infrastructural emplacements such as transportation networks and public works, yet are staffed by workers who often live without such amenities; how neoliberal trade agreements and transnational corporatism have renewed nationalist attachments, spawned regional vigilantisms, and entrenched border militarism;[31] or, how culture industries and information technologies have in turn produced new regimes of interconnection, deepening digital divides, and crises of copyright and intellectual property protections.[32] These and other multiscalar processes of spatial formation have continually structured both the contexts of struggle and the conditions of possibility that have propelled the South American musical transits discussed throughout this book.

To invigorate engagements with the spatial, human geographers have developed a language of geographic differentiation. Two conceptual terms that emerge from this body of work are frequently used herein: "place" and "scale." "Place" is a term that indexes a particular intellectual shift: challenges to the "subordination of space to time" popularized by political geographers beginning in the 1970s, and subsequently, the introduction of innovative models for capturing the processes by and through which the temporal "takes place."[33] Here, I use place to connote an ensemble of social relations given meaning through geopolitical designation.[34] My discussion of musical emplacements and transpositions presumes an understanding of place as sensory, ideological, and relational. Place is sensory to the extent that it assumes social meaning via multiple sensory registers, from the visual and the sonic to the olfactory and the tactile. Place is also relational, as it references geographic arenas produced through interaction with wider, overlapping, and or competing social relations, divisions, and tensions. Finally, place is ideological, in that it announces particular epistemologies of orientation, expanse, connection, and affiliation. These premises underpin the interventions that I have introduced thus far, which are developed and detailed throughout this book: that sonic cultures neither can nor should be understood as inherently "in" or "out of place," and concomitantly, that the dynamic and contested (re)-production of place is indelibly shaped by relations of musical transit.

That all places are constructed and contested does not mean that some places are commonly viewed as especially "natural," "universal," or "necessary." To give name to such places and their constitutive role in coordinating relations of capital, geographer Neil Smith proposed a typology of spatial differentiation that he dubbed nested "scales." Smith defined scale as "the geographic resolution to the contradictory social processes of competition and cooperation."[35] For Smith, geographic scales such as home, urban, region, and nation represent sedimented modes of spatial organization that both orient and naturalize capitalism as a mode of production and a mode of life. Smith's language of scale is useful because it draws critical attention to the ways in which seemingly ubiquitous or stable modes of geographic division, or *scales*, involve ongoing material and ideological struggles to fix boundaries between different locations, places, and sites of meaning.

Analyses of scale, then, set the stage for the discussion of South American musical migrations that follows in that it provides a descriptive rubric of the conventional spatial orderings that configure industrial regimes of aesthetic expression, dominant production landscapes and exchange networks, and sanctioned modes of political dissent. And, it sheds light on the political stakes and oppositional potential of acts of sonic transposition. For, given that the cartographic practice of enclosure is most often imagined and explicated through grammars of racial, gender, sexual, and class difference, it follows that to challenge structures of racism and heteropatriarchy is to question the integrity of seemingly natural geographies of containment, access, or empowerment. And, conversely, to expose the constructed nature of social space is to expose the spatial organization of difference.[36] The chapters that follow engage in such a project by highlighting nonconventional scales of movement and constraint, including hemispheric and diasporic formations. In doing so, they unfold stories of musical transit that expand the geographic imagination to include sites and modes of spatial contest that exceed Smith's typology of scale. Concurrently, they exact pressure on the tendency within ethnomusicological scholarship to adopt colonial mappings of the world, particularly "the local," which is most often coded as provincial and isolated, traditional and static, feminine and nonwhite.

THINKING SOUND

The study of musical cultures has long provided for scholars of race, gender, and sexuality a rich archival index of the enmeshed relations of labor, difference, and desire that inhere in particular geohistorical landscapes. Yet, the "transnational turn" within ethnic, area, and cultural studies research has dramatically shifted how musical cultures are contemplated. Arguably, this is in no small part owed to the ways in which the proliferation of new global media structures, technological innovations, and international cultural flows have accelerated the disorderliness of musical circulation and, accordingly, have highlighted the inadequacy of conventional geopolitical frames of musical study. For example, as the South American sound studies scholar Ana María Ochoa Gautier has astutely observed, contemporary shifts in global relations of technology, sociality, and exchange have generated new typologies of sonic codification, platforms for promotion, and methods of dissemination: "Today it has become normative that the circulation and marketing of musical genres historically considered under the aegis of folklore or intangible heritages occur side by side and/or is interspersed with what historically has been considered mass music, classical music of the Western world."[37] For Ochoa Gautier, these shifts can no longer be reduced to the dialectics of "retraditionalization" and "hybridization" but, rather, necessitate "a fundamental reconceptualization on the role of the temporal and spatial dimensions of the sonic and their existential and epistemological significance under the changing technological and social conditions of a globalized world."[38]

In the introduction to their 2003 anthology *Musical Migrations: Transnationalism and Cultural Hybridity in Latin/o America*, volume 1, Frances Aparicio and Cándida Jáquez anticipate Ochoa Gautier's keen observations, arguing that the intellectual challenges posed by the study of transnational circulations of sound, rhythm, and performance have effectively "transform[ed] traditional methodologies and theoretical frameworks that have defined music and music making primarily through discrete categories such as national identity and musical genre."[39] In the decade that has passed since the publication of this field-shaping collection, many of these interventions have been posed by scholars of sound working within my home fields of critical race, gender, and ethnic studies, and the political import and institutional impact of their labors cannot be overstated. Significantly, this work has shifted the subject/object relationship that has traditionally structured ethnomusicological inquiry, offering instead antiracist, feminist, and queer analyses of how musical practice figures in the production of historical memory and cultural canons; how aural imaginaries reflect and refract contested, cross-cutting social relations; and how the sonic offers unique practical and aesthetic repertoires for the expression of solidarity and formation of community.[40] *On Site, In Sound* aims to contribute to these conversations, and shares their political and intellectual commitment to thinking about the sonic as a critical realm of social conflict and a productive site for imagining and activating alternative social possibilities.

The burgeoning field of sound studies has equipped scholars of ethnic, area, and cultural studies with valuable theoretical and methodological tools for engaging popular music as a unique mode of sensory signification, interpretation, and practice. In the words of scholar Jonathan Sterne, "sound studies is a name for the interdisciplinary ferment in the human sciences that takes sound as its analytical point of departure or arrival."[41] Among its many contributions, the emergent field of sound studies has prompted productive conceptual breaks with and reconfigurations of the logo- and ocular-centric tendencies of critical race and gender studies, insisting upon new theoretical frames for and methodological approaches to the study of the aural.[42] This turn toward the sonic has often entailed, for example, the embrace of listening as a critical practice; attention to the polyphonic technologies and textualities of song, including rhythm, instrumentation, vocality, and sensuality; and the positioning of the auditory as a unique yet imbricated sensory index of political labors, uneven relationships, and unwritten stories. In my examination of the dynamic interplay of the spatial and the sonic within South American musical migrations, I integrate three conceptual frames developed by scholars of race, gender, and sound: "listening," "musicking," and "performance."

In the most immediate sense, the practice of listening advanced here can be described as a method of cultural "reading" that takes seriously the unique representational capacities and material functions of sound. Such a method is necessarily multipronged. As Ana María Ochoa Gautier has astutely argued, perceptions of the aural and practices of listening have deep and contested genealogies that are inextricably enmeshed in the social relations and "audible techniques" that have constituted them.[43] At stake in her work, as well as my own, is attention to how legacies of colonialism, Eurocentrism, anti-Black racism, and capitalist modernity in South America can be traced in the competing epistemologies of sound and their attendant textual and taxonomic registers.[44] I address these issues at length in chapters 1 and 3, as each explores how the emergence of state-sanctioned "folklores" and "heritage cultures" in the early and mid-twentieth century generated sociopolitical contest over how Peru's national past has been narrated and memorialized through the creation of what Ochoa Gautier has dubbed "aural public spheres."[45]

Like other forms of textual analysis, listening is a multisensory hermeneutic that requires "the deliberate channeling of attention" toward the interplay of sensory content, form, and context.[46] I take seriously Alexandra Vasquez's contention that in the case of southernized musics, "listening in detail" proffers a critical methodological antidote to the tendency within Western ethnomusicology to reduce the work of Latin American artists to a univocal anthropological gaze. Following Vasquez, this book aims to provide "an experience with rather than an account of" South American musical transits, periodically pausing to attune aural attention to the aesthetic richness and ingenuity that defined the texts and performances discussed herein.[47] Yet, this book likewise heeds Deborah R. Vargas's call that we "listen for" performative affirmations, negotiations, and disruptions of social norms and structures, musical canons, and modes of cultural analysis.[48] Hearing such "dissonances" requires "listening against" presumed narrative, aesthetic, generic, and technical registers and hierarchies: purported distinctions, for example, between high and low, authentic and hybrid, prodigious and amateur, and so on.[49] Mindful of these insights, *On Site, In Sound* deploys a method of listening that integrates attention to sonic aesthetics, musical canons, practical scenarios, and historicogeographic contexts. My aim is to capture some of the understudied and unanticipated ways in which South American cultural workers have mobilized musical performance and practice as a means of negotiating and even transforming the spatial arrangements of power and difference that conspire to silence or subdue their ongoing struggles against emplacements of raced, gendered, and classed vulnerability, violence, and exploitation via the articulation of new modes of cultural and economic reproduction and political participation.

A second important conceptual tool that has enabled my attention to the interplay of musical text and spatial context is an analytic that sound studies scholar Christopher Small has dubbed "musicking." For Small, to music "is to take part, in any capacity, in a musical performance, whether by performing, by listening, by rehearsing or practicing, by providing material for performance (what is called composing), or by dancing."[50] Musicking is important to this project's queries and interventions for several reasons. First, by questioning the primacy assigned to musical works over musical performances, this analytic disrupts many of the racial-colonial presumptions that have framed dominant approaches to the study of music: that musical texts can be read as singular, objective transcripts of a unidirectional conversation between performer and listener; that performance plays little to no role in the creative process of music making; and that social interaction and context are irrelevant to the interpretation of musical works. Conversely, by conceptualizing music as action rather than object, musicking enables an engagement with the sonic that bridges the common interpretive gaps that *On Site, In Sound* aims to address: between artist and audience, between the political and the aesthetic, and between text and context. In doing so, this conceptual optic avows the performative dimension of musical interactions, which are necessarily enmeshed in and productive of a broad array of social relationships, meaning-making practices, and material contexts.

My interest in exploring musicking as a dynamic mode of social (and as I will soon detail, spatial) interaction has necessarily prompted my engagement with a third conceptual frame: "performance." As performance studies scholar Diana Taylor has argued, the former is a vexed term as it simultaneously connotes "a process, a praxis, an episteme, a mode of transmission, an accomplishment, and a means of intervening in the world."[51] Following Taylor, performance is engaged here as both optic and object of analysis. My use of performance as an analytic tool draws upon the insights of Taylor and other scholars such as VéVé Clark, Joseph Roach, and Celeste Fraser Delgado and José Esteban Muñoz that take seriously performance as a technique of action/embodiment that effectively negotiates, interprets, and potentially reshapes social texts, relationships, and environments.[52] For example, chapter 2 takes interest in how creative modes of siting that strategically leverage public and semipublic space as places of musical activity have enabled unique modes of immigrant sociality and cultural and economic reproduction. Similarly, chapters 3 and 4 examine the creative mobilization of theatrical practices such as staging and choreography—as well as embodied actions such as musicking, gesture, vocality, and audience engagement—to examine how South American cultural workers have strategically emplaced nonconventional geographies of musical circulation, economic activity, and political convocation.

Each of these conceptual frames—listening, musicking, and performance—encourages the contemplation of sonic cultures, social relations, and geohistorical contexts as inextricably linked and mutually defining. As such, they both stipulate and ground my integrated approach to thinking site and sound.

THINKING SITE IN SOUND

Analysis of site and sound as synchronous processes brings focus to an important yet neglected dimension of musical study: the *effective* work of musical production and circulation. Scholars of sound have importantly demonstrated the elusive power of song to convene audiences, forge attachments, mobilize publics, market lifestyles, enact fantasies, sell commodities, (dis)articulate registers of social meaning, and so forth. Yet few have considered how sound's *affective* labor is alternately enabled by and generative of its effective capacities.[53] *On Site, In Sound* takes interest in one such capacity—sonic transposition—and the political and economic work it performs and accomplishes. Through an examination of quotidian South American musical transits, it theorizes the constellated practices of imagination and performance that transform street corners into sound stages, sidewalks into vending stalls, private patios into public nightclubs, or living rooms into theater venues. It argues that such sonic emplacements effectively reorganize and potentially challenge dominant conceptions of place, practices of convocation, and methods of cultural and economic exchange. And, it takes interest in contemplating how such grassroots cultural tactics might be productively mobilized in other geographies of struggle against colonial, racial capitalist, heteropatriarchal designs.

On Site, In Sound deploys "performance geography" as both a theoretical framework for and methodological approach to the exploration of these questions. I extend this fertile concept introduced by Caribbean feminist geographer Sonjah Stanley Niaah to describe the range of situated and imagined places at and through which the collective cultural task of materialization—including embodiment, mobility, attachment, and speculation—collides with the physical and ideological constraints of context.[54] Performance geography proffers a conceptual frame for apprehending the ever-evolving conjuncture of sonic and spatial intra-action.[55] It approaches the practice and circulation of musical performances as at once *in situ*, or "intelligible in the framework of the immediate environment and issues surrounding them," and *in flux*, or perpetually (re)shaping the very function and meaning of their contexts of elaboration. In this sense, performance geography is a mode of analysis rooted in performance cultures rather than capitalist scales, positing the site/sound relationship as an entangled negotiation between dispossession and embodiment, displacement and territoriality, muting and sounding.

As the term suggests, performance geography highlights points of convergence within the fields of performance studies and human geography, demonstrating how the methods and vocabularies of each might be productively combined. Scholars of performance and performativity have persuasively demonstrated how social categories are constituted and consolidated through performance acts. This work largely coheres around an examination of how the materiodiscursive reproduction of subjected (gendered, raced, sexualized, classed) bodies has become so routinized as to appear natural or inevitable.[56] Similarly, political geographers aim to expose the constructedness of seemingly natural or immutable political territories such as bodies, as well as the broader social relations and modes of differentiation that organize them.

Given the shared political stakes of these intellectual endeavors, spatialized approaches to performance are particularly productive, as they offer nonreductive tools and frames for materializing, and thus amplifying, analyses of the interplay of performance, text, and place. For example, against the tendency to understand performativity as a social process that occurs at the scale of the abstract individual subject and in isolation from (rather than in interaction with) broader scales of social meaning, a territorialized approach to performance politics enables a reconceptualization of performativity as "a dialectical operative that makes connections between labor, work, and the practices associated with the material production of everyday life and with imaginative work as a means of engaging in political action and resistance."[57] In other words, performativity can be understood as a multiscalar entanglement of space and practice that links embodied acts to broader realms of social meaning and contest. Thus, rather than locating the agential force of performance within individual bodies or conduct, we can expand our attention to the ways in which collective improvisations within scripted social encounters "can expose the fissures, ruptures and revisions that have settled into continuous reenactment."[58]

In co-convening these registers, then, performance geography is an analytic that enables the address of three interrelated areas of theoretical and thematic neglect within contemporary studies of musical circulation. First, it foregrounds the materiality of performed sound: the realms, distances, and surfaces within, across, and through which sound travels; the mechanisms of its production, amplification, and mediation; and sound's contextual relationship with other modes of cultural production and signification. Next, performance geography emphasizes the dynamic relations of space and place that animate media circulation patterns and emplacements, thereby interrogating the dominant racial capitalist landscapes within which global Southern sounds are most often (de)localized and (de)valued. And finally, it emphasizes the spatial dynamism of sonic work: the ways in which artists and activists use performance as a means of confronting the constraints of their physical and discursive containment and/or abandonment, and conversely, how they creatively manipulate social space to enable new modes, relations, and venues of performance.

On Site, In Sound examines four performance geographies of globalized South American cultural production from the 1970s to the present: informal economies of Andean musical fusion, iconic circulations of worlded "Latin" music, cultural production in Peru's Black Pacific, and an urban neighborhood *peña* in the United States.[59] In each of these case studies, I examine how spatialized practices of musicking—from the use of creative staging techniques, to the construction of informal economies and improvisational performance venues, to the activation of transnational musicians' networks—have enabled South American cultural workers to negotiate the social and spatial circumscriptions of extant racial capitalist landscapes. As critical, creative responses to uneven processes of neoliberal encroachment, long-standing structures of anti-Black and settler colonial racism, and revanchist anti-immigrant public policy, each of these performance geographies indexes how expressive cultures can challenge and, potentially, transform the dominant raced and gendered mappings of place that configure production regimes, inform disciplinary frameworks, and structure regimes of aesthetic and affective expression and consumption.

Chapter 1 sets the historical stage for my analysis of South American musical transits by chronicling the "worlding" of Latin American "folklore" vis-à-vis the example of the well-known ballad "El Cóndor Pasa." In it, I examine the mobilization of this traveling melody in three distinct geohistorical contexts: nation-building processes in early twentieth-century Lima, migrant musical communities in mid-century New York, and the nascent world music industry of the 1970s. Combining archival research with musicological and cultural analyses, I argue that these protean recontextualizations of "El Cóndor Pasa," initiated by artists ranging from Peruvian ethnologist Daniel Alomía Robles, to Quechua chanteuse Yma Sumac, to U.S. folk artist Paul Simon demonstrate how the strategic deployment of a seemingly transparent artifact of national folklore can work to instantiate, consolidate, or destabilize geopolitical formations such as the local, the national, or the global, and/or extant geopolitical boundaries between public and private, rural and urban, political and aesthetic.

Chapter 2 examines the sociospatial politics of contemporary indigenous migrant community formation in California through an examination of what I term the "Andean music industry": the extensive—and, at times, extremely lucrative—U.S.-based informal economy of Andean musical production that has operated as parallel to, and at times in competition with, the world music industry over the last several decades. The birth of this industry can be traced to the early 1980s, when, rather than appealing to world market promoters for corporate sponsorship of "import" recording projects, dozens of Indigenous Andean musicians chose immigration to global Northern metropoles as an alternative option for their economic and aesthetic pursuits. The result was the creation of an extensive network of Andean performance that relocated the spatialized processes of cultural production, mediation, and consumption to everyday public spaces: commercial venues, such as subway stations, street corners, and shopping malls; and, more recently, virtual platforms such as Facebook and YouTube. Drawing upon critical race studies, popular music studies, and political geography, I argue that attention to the unique relations of culture and capital born of this industry demands an important retelling of dominant narratives about world(ed) music and musical worldings—one attentive to prior histories of migration and displacement, to ongoing regional and national revanchisms, and to the oppositional potential of strategic appropriations of physical and virtual public space.

Chapter 3 charts a vibrant geohistory of Black women's cultural activism in Lima from the mid-twentieth century to the present. Combining the analytics and vocabularies of sound studies, critical race and gender studies, and feminist geography, it examines convergences within the transnational, cross-generational work of five Black women performers—U.S. artist Katherine Dunham and Afro-Peruvian artists Victoria Santa Cruz, Susana Baca, and sisters Peta and Kata Robles. I argue that despite differences in content and form, and at times even approach and aspiration, their collective work as political activists and cultural producers can be understood as both formed by and formative of "performance geographies of feminist diasporicity." Through a geocultural reading of their performance texts and pedagogical practices, I detail how the artist-activists have mobilized spatialized expressive practices such as siting and staging and as spatial imaginaries such as "the coastal," "the Pacific," and "the Afro-diasporic" to advance deprovincialized manifestations of the historical continuities, transnational ties, and internationalist impulses that connect otherwise localized and specific stories of diasporic cultural formation in the Black Americas.

I argue that these Black feminist geographies of political colloquy and communion imagined and activated by these Afroperuana artists are instructive for several reasons. First, they articulate powerful, nuanced critiques of and responses to the commonsense geographies of race, gender, and place that have physically and ideologically contained Black cultural production and political struggle in postcolonial, postmanumission América del Sur. Next, they highlight important convergences among three sociocultural movements that are rarely coexamined: Peru's mid-century Black Arts Revival, Black liberation struggles in the United States and continental Africa, and internationalized forms of Latin American musical production such as Nueva Canción. In doing so, they not only amplify transatlantic mappings of the African diaspora; they also reveal a vital if neglected history of Afro-Latino participation in the region's pan-Americanist social movements of the 1960s–1970s. Finally, the contours of these Black feminist performance geographies effectively challenge and recalibrate the dominant racial-regional designs that most often inform popular and academic discourse on Blackness and indigeneity in the Southern Americas.

Chapter 4 returns to the Mission District of San Francisco, where I use the case study of La Peña del Sur—a grassroots cultural organization that operated there for nearly a decade—to examine the dynamic role that a spatialized cultural politics can play in processes of transnational, multiracial community formation. Founded in 1992 by South American immigrant artists, and located in the rented basement apartment of queer Chilean artist and activist Alejandro Stuart, La Peña del Sur was a unique institution— cooperatively founded and sustained, commercially unlicensed, and community funded. Drawing into conversation sound and performance studies, critical geography, and queer of color critique, this chapter examines three vital elements of La Peña del Sur as a performance geography. First, it offers a queer reading of the *peña*'s improvisational spatiopolitical structure, which productively troubled commonsense geotemporal boundaries between public and private spheres, aesthetic and political practice, and labor and leisure time. Next, it surveys the multiscalar political work performed through La Peña's conceptual imaginary of "Southernness," which positioned the organization as both locally situated and transnationally oriented. Finally, it reflects upon La Peña's ongoing confrontation with debates concerning competing conceptions of sustainability as they relate to the limits and possibilities of institutionalization. I argue that, taken together, these defining features of La Peña—and the ongoing sociosonic negotiations that produced them—enrooted a vital venue for otherwise unlikely encounters among Mission-area residents, which in turn enabled creative coalitional responses to issues ranging from California Proposition 187 to the Zapatista revolution to the gentrification of San Francisco's neighborhoods of color.

To conclude my discussion of performance geographies of hemispheric South American musical circulations, I turn to a contentious trend within current sonic worlding practices: *piratería*. Through a case study of Lima, Peru's most established and notorious pirate market, El Hueco, I contemplate the questions of sonic debt and musical futures heralded by its unauthorized relations of media reproduction, mediation, and consumption. Located on the fringes of Lima's *centro histórico*, El Hueco boasts over four hundred venders that traffic in the unauthorized manufacture and sale of tens of thousands of audio and video recordings, sourcing both local and transnational distribution networks. El Hueco's extralegal economic activities are in keeping with Peru's broader landscapes of musical exchange, as the BBC recently reported that 98 percent of all music transactions in the nation occur in the black market. The International Intellectual Property Alliance, a private-sector coalition of seven trade associations representing U.S. producers of content and materials protected by copyright laws, has commissioned several investigative reports condemning the significant scope and international reach of Peru's unlicensed digital media trade, and has urged Peruvian authorities to crack down on centers of contraband dissemination such as El Hueco.

Against U.S. culture industry narratives that cast El Hueco as a marker of global Southern "incivility," "disorder," or "corruption," however, I suggest an alternative reading of Lima's piracy networks. El Hueco has served as a primary archive for *On Site, In Sound*, as it, alongside its elder twin Polvos Azules, constitutes one of the largest sonic collections in the nation. In the absence of state infrastructure and public services such as libraries and research centers, pirate markets such as these function as important sites of collective knowledge production, digital curation, and artistic registry. I argue that small-scale piracy practices such as these have, since the advent of the audiocassette, accomplished critical modes of popular archival work that sanctioned sites of knowledge production are unable or unwilling to perform. Pairing my discussion of El Hueco with other examples of informal or unlicensed modes of aural circulation discussed throughout the book, I interrogate the U.S.-centrism of dominant popular and academic debates concerning the politics of artistic and author protections.

I conclude *On Site, In Sound* with a bold argument: that the settling of musical debts (such as practices of appropriation) via the expansion of U.S. culture industries and international copyright law demands both access and capitulation to the political logics and economic structures of neoliberal capitalism in ways that will not, and indeed cannot, serve the interest of global Southern musicians. Here I question, for example, the effects of leveraging such "protections" via the vulgar conversion of collective musical texts and practices into singular commodities with individual owners and quantified economic value. I close by posing the question of what it would mean to rethink questions of musical appropriation and debt in a manner that decouples the valuation of creative work and capitalist determinations of value. I ask, how might we create and sustain venues for musical production and exchange—a sonic commons—that refuses current structures of private property protection and regulation? I argue that such musical futures will most effectively be pursued via multiscalar organizing agendas that, rather than capitulating to legislative models of individualized economic redress, pursue the eradication of vulnerability, exploitation, and encumbrance via collective investments in infrastructure, services, and opportunities.

By staging unlikely disciplinary, thematic and geopolitical couplings, *On Site, In Sound* endeavors the encouragement of critical dialogue between the fields with which it communes: ethnic, area, feminist and queer studies; cultural, performance, and sound studies; and political and cultural geography. To do so, it proceeds with productive engagements with the theoretical and thematic strengths and gaps in each. First, by modeling an approach to spatial inquiry that centralizes race and gender as modalities through which capitalist landscapes are produced and experienced, this book highlights how ethnic studies methods can enrich geopolitical analyses of culture-capital relations. Next, by coupling frames of critical race and gender studies with geographic grammars, *On Site, In Sound* also argues for the need to territorialize, and by extension, materialize analyses of transnational, post-national, and diasporic cultural practices. Finally, by modeling materialist approaches to popular music studies, it emphasizes the political stakes and imaginative possibilities enabled by nonconventional geographies of world musicking. Ultimately, in integrating the seemingly divergent analytics, methods, and vocabularies of these fields, *On Site, In Sound* aims to draw critical attention to sounded sites of struggle, solidarity, and possibility.

1

SOUNDING PLACE OVER TIME

On the Sonic Transits of "El Cóndor Pasa"

In 1913, Peruvian ethnologist, musician, and composer Daniel Alomía Robles arranged the orchestral score "El Cóndor Pasa," an eight-part musical accompaniment to the eponymously entitled zarzuela that promoted patriotic unification as an antidote to imperial interventionism.[1] Knitting together a variety of regional aesthetics, rhythms, and instrumentations, the artist anticipated that the ordered aural amalgamation of popular traditions designated as "folklore" could be exploited to foment a collective if tiered sense of Peruvian national belonging. A century later, following a sundry of improbable musical transpositions and transits that Alomía Robles and his cohort could hardly have predicted, world music promoters and listeners have lauded "El Cóndor Pasa" as the South American sonic "crossover" par excellence. This dubious designation stems from the song's overwhelming commercial success, as to date it has received far more radio airtime, recording attention, and media renown than any other song from the Andean region. While many readers may not recognize this popular tune by name, most would recognize it by ear. For, the Peruvian National Institute of Culture estimates that between 1933 and the present no fewer than four thousand versions of the ballad—deemed "Peru's second national anthem"—have been recorded worldwide.[2] Although the earliest copyrighted renditions of the melody were instrumental, over three hundred lyrical arrangements of it have been documented. Today, over 250 sonic variations of "El Cóndor Pasa" are available for download on iTunes,[*] interpreted by artists ranging from the Mariachi Masters, to Perry Como, to the Philharmonic Orchestra of London.

Both an archive and artifact of Peruvian national folklore, "El Cóndor Pasa" has "traveled" for nearly a century, traversing the boundaries of geography and genre, audience and aesthetics, language and signification. This chapter proffers a travelogue of sorts, charting three salient destinations among the ballad's innumerable geohistorical transits: the esteemed urban stages of early twentieth-century Lima; South American migrant musical communities of mid-century Paris and New York; and the nascent world music scene of the early 1970s. Tracking the dynamic interplay of cultural text and spatial context within each of these performance geographies, I advance several interrelated claims. In contradistinction to methods of musical inquiry that search for and/or valorize fixed, unproblematic geographies of sonic origin, I contend that processes of musical circulation differently and differentially produce, complicate, or reimagine collective perceptions of social space—from its commonsense ambits, contours, and borders, to its fundamental abstractions, contradictions, and exclusions. The enmeshed tales of musical transit examined herein effectively evidence how a single musical score can be effectively rearticulated across space, time, and genre to sound competing spatial imaginaries, social emplacements, and affective attachments. Given this, I propose reading "El Cóndor Pasa" as a geographic story—that is, a text that, through ongoing processes of aural transmission and transit, comes to sound both an emplaced and abstracted accumulation of political sensibilities, aesthetic encounters, and ideological claims. Lending an assiduous ear to the aural textures of instrumentation, arrangement, rhythm and artistry, I detail how "El Cóndor Pasa" has been mobilized by artists and promoters in distinct geotemporal contexts to imagine, consolidate, or destabilize social relations within different places, such as the nation, region, or hemisphere, as well as between different kinds of places, such as rural and urban, public and private, global North and global South. In so doing, I demonstrate how performance geography proffers a nonreductive method for apprehending the alchemic relations of space, sound, and difference that inhere in quoditian relations of musical production and circulation.

"TODOS SOMOS CONDORES": INDIGENISMO, AND
NATIONAL CULTURE IN EARLY TWENTIETH-CENTURY PERU

At the dawn of the twentieth century, *limeño* playwright Julio Baudouin published a polemical two-act zarzuela condemning the exploitation of Andean miners by U.S.-owned corporations.[3] Premiering at Lima's distinguished Teatro Mazzi on December 19, 1913, the dramatic production promoted national unification via an appeal to the paternalistic sympathies and anti-imperialist fervor of the city's *criollo* intelligentsia.[4] Set in the fictional highland mining settlement of Yápac, *El Cóndor Pasa* narrates the valiant travails of protagonist Frank, a mestizo miner critical of his "gringo" bosses for the physical and economic abuses they exact upon indigenous laborers. Frank's exploration of his hybrid cultural identity and the emergence of his anti-*yanqui* political consciousness allegorized for Peru's urban classes both the challenges to and benefits of constructing a modern, autonomous republic in the New World.

The operetta opens with a haunting chorus sung from the wings, accompanied by a mournful melody played by a wandering Andean shepherd on his bamboo *kena* (a notched, straight-ended flute):[5]

Ya en la nieve de las cumbres
comienza a brillar el Sol,
y el día, la luz del cielo
para nosotros no son;
que cuando raya la aurora
nos manda la esclavitud
sepultarnos en la tierra
huyendo del cielo azul . . .

In the snowcapped mountains
the Sun has begun to shine
yet the day, the light of the heavens
are not for us;
for when the dawn breaks
our enslavement requires us

to bury ourselves in the earth
fleeing the blue sky[6]

In keeping with Western theatrical traditions, *El Cóndor Pasa*'s offstage chorus sounds the central polemic of the play, revealing insights of which the audience is presumably aware but the characters have yet to learn. Its poignant verses presage the unpopular views of Frank, an outspoken, light-skinned miner who publically decries the exploitative practices of the foreign-owned Cerro de Pasco Corporation. Known by el moniker *el indio rubio* (the white Indian), the protagonist's fervent incriminations are met with distrust by fellow indigenous coworkers who, in stark contrast, are depicted as meek and servile. During a casual conversation in the first scene, Native miners Tiburcio and Félix express their distrust of Frank owed to both his unusual appearance and his lofty ideals. In response to Frank's fervent assertion that "the masters treat us like beasts," Tiburcio dismissively replies, "This is how it should be, Frank. The masters were born to order, and us to obey them."[7] When Frank then insists, "There is something in my mind that tells me that life shouldn't be this way," Félix crisply retorts, "You would think that the same blood as our imperious master burns in his veins."[8]

Raised by indigenous parents María and Higinio, Frank's paternal roots have long been the speculation of Yupac's denizens, including his own father, who alludes to a possible affair between his wife and his boss: "The last condor that passed through here, I saw him flying above my hut one evening, losing himself in the heavens. . . . Mr. Mac King was inside, your mother, María was there too . . . but I do not know if that condor took our love with him on that tragic flight."[9] But Frank balks at his father's suspicions, postulating that his fair hair and complexion are not the product of his mother's indiscretions, but rather, a physical manifestation of his political beliefs: "The red hair on my head is a reflection of the burning hatred that is in my blood. . . . I hate the masters, because from the moment they bought the mines they also bought us as their beasts of burden."[10]

However, following a heated confrontation with the company's head, antagonist Mr. King, Frank learns from his cohort the shocking truth about his heritage: the ruthless "yanqui" coproprietor of the foreign corporation, is, indeed, his biological father. Amid this revelation, community tensions mount. At a wedding that takes place shortly thereafter, a drunken Mr. King physically and emotionally brutalizes Higinio, who retaliates by following his boss home and crushing him to death with a large boulder. A shepherd who witnesses the incident informs the other miners, who fear physical and economic reprisal. Mr. Cup, the other owner of Cerro de Pasco, arrives soon thereafter and threatens Higinio and his comrades at gunpoint. In a final act of selfless heroism, Frank faces off with the mine owner and kills him in self-defense. Tiburcio and Félix are stunned by this dramatic turn of events, as is María who sobs inconsolably for the loss of her yanqui lover. Yet apprehensions are quelled and spirits lifted with the sudden, auspicious sighting of a condor in flight—the first to be glimpsed since the establishment of Cerro de Pasco in the region. A long-standing symbol of Andean power and resistance to Spanish colonization, the miners greet the revered bird in song. Frank joins the chorus, and together the miners proclaim in jubilant unison, "todos somos condores" (we are all condors).

A critical reading of this social drama reveals the strategic portrayal of a heterogeneous republic that, buttressed by the bonds of a shared biocultural past, encounters a common destiny in the expulsion of foreign influence and capital.[11] Baudouin's zarzuela thus echoed the political strategies and narrative tropes of early twentieth-century Peruvian *indigenismo*, a cultural movement that debated questions of socioeconomic modernization and national belonging in relation to what social critic José Mariátegui dubbed "the Indian question"—the marginalization of indigenous populations within the national imaginary.[12] Through its empathetic portrayals of an exploited "Indian other," *El Cóndor Pasa* promoted a vision of postcolonial unification rooted in an asymmetrical geotemporality of national belonging.[13] In it, Peru's exploited yet guileless indigenous peasants of the rural highlands come into consciousness via contact with their heroic mestizo counterpart, Frank. Frank represents indigenismo's ideal national subject, one that embraces a uniquely American model of social and economic development that seamlessly integrates the mythical past traditions of the indigenous countryside with the modern political thought that predominates in Peru's urban coastal capital. It is Frank who is conscious and critical of entrenched colonial hierarchies, and it is he alone who possesses the courage and reason to defy and ultimately defeat Misters King and Cup—characters who symbolize foreign influence and exploitation.

With its *indigenista* ethos and anti-imperialist directive, *El Cóndor Pasa* held enormous appeal for Lima's largely criollo-identified middle and upper classes. Critics lauded the social drama's artful capture of a unifying "mestizo spirit" born of the "energetic dreams, voices, and characteristics" that coalesced in the "forging a 'New Homeland.'"[14] The overwhelming domestic popularity of the drama is well documented. Debut attendee Juan Sixto Prieto, an established historian and critic of Peruvian theater, affirmed that "[El Cóndor Pasa] was a true success," noting that its social commentary regarding Peru's provincias (rural provinces) deeply affected Lima's urban audiences.[15] The cultural historian Jorge Basadre Grohmann estimated that in the five years following its release, the operetta was performed over three thousand times by more than three hundred theater companies.[16] Indeed, El Cóndor Pasa would eventually become Peru's most frequently interpreted national drama, and Baudouin a celebrated architect of national culture.[17] In the words of literary critic José Vallarnos, El Cóndor Pasa would come to represent "a classic drama of the indigenismo genre or, better yet, of new Peruvian theater."[18]

Interestingly, numerous critics have argued that El Cóndor Pasa's domestic sensation was owed in no small part to its auditory allure.[19] Arranged by composer, musician, and folklorist Daniel Alomía Robles (figure 1.1), the drama's musical score echoed Baudouin's indigenista orientation, exposing urban audiences to an orchestral adaptation of little-known rhythmic traditions from Peru's highland regions.[20] Alomía Robles was an avid student and compiler of indigenous musics, and was anxious to introduce these to Lima's cosmopolitan classes: "At that time, Italian music predominated [in Lima]," Alomía Robles retrospectively recalled. "There was absolutely no familiarity with Native music."[21] Alomía Robles's sonic script lent an "authentic" air to the social drama while demonstrating how indigenous musical traditions could be effectively "modernized" through the introduction of European instrumentation and symphonic arrangements. This bold aural experiment was "enthusiastically received" with "repeated ovation" by Lima's urbane public, and celebrated in the popular media as "prodigal art."[22] As its press coverage emphatically intones, Alomía Robles's "El Cóndor Pasa" sounded for many a uniquely Peruvian modernity—one that looked to ostensibly "disappearing" indigenous lifeways as the raw materials for the construction of an "autochthonous" yet modern national culture.

A century later, Baudouin's revolutionary drama continues to command national repute as a key literary contribution to Lima's early twentieth-century indigenista movement.[23] Yet, remarkably, its sensation and circu-

1.1 Portrait of
Daniel Alomía Robles

lation have been utterly eclipsed by Alomía Robles's musical score, which has remained in exhaustive international transit since the 1930s. To date, the celebrated play has only ever appeared in Spanish, and remains relatively obscure among non-Peruvian audiences. Fragments of *El Cóndor Pasa*'s musical score, in contrast, have enjoyed innumerable stylistic and lyrical arrangements, interpreted and popularized by artists throughout the globe. In 2004, the homonymous ballad was designated a "national cultural patrimony," and it continues to be celebrated by domestic and international listeners alike as a hallmark of Peruvian cultural production.

As an aural icon of both Peruvian patriotism and of world music, how does this musical text—an overdetermined amalgam of geohistorical traces, ideological mobilizations, and aesthetic significations—index multiple, overlapping interrelations of place, sound, and difference? And, what can we learn from tracing "El Cóndor Pasa"'s numerous geographies of transit? I begin the subsequent section by contextualizing Alomía Robles's arrangement of *El Cóndor Pasa*'s musical score within a broader discussion of two related historical trends: first, the invention of folklore as a nationalist proj-ect of modernity in Latin America; and second, the emergence of what Ana María Ochoa Gautier has called "an aural public sphere" across the southern continent.[24] I then turn to the controversy that surrounds Alomía Robles's sonic work in order to tease out the relations of coloniality, race, and nation that informed the positioning of indigenous cultural production in Peru as a national resource infinitely available for extraction and abstraction. Finally, I turn to "El Cóndor Pasa" itself, reading the aural logics that informed its strategic transformation from symphonic score to nationalist anthem. Here, I foreshadow how Alomía Robles's early twentieth-century practices of mu-sical worlding set the stage for internationalist appropriations of Peru's re-gional soundscapes.

EL CÓNDOR PASA, TRACK ONE: NATIONAL WORLDINGS AND "EL PERÚ DE MAÑANA"

The introduction of Alomía Robles's acclaimed musical score to Lima's ur-ban public coincided with the centennial eve of Peru's postcolonial sover-eignty. This was a significant moment of national reflection for the artist and his contemporaries. Despite a near-century of independence from the Spanish Crown, the combined effects of governmental and economic in-stability, civil and interregional armed conflict, and provincial fragmenta-tion thwarted the effective institutionalization of political agendas popu-larized during the independence wars.[25] Moreover, Peru's settled oligarchy remained remarkably intact. In lieu of fostering economic independence, this smattering of patrician families continued to broker neocolonial ar-rangements that, as dramatized in *El Cóndor Pasa*, privileged foreign invest-ment over national development, and foreign corporate interests over those of the domestic proletariat.[26]

By the early twentieth century, however, Lima's burgeoning class of ed-ucated mestizo artists and intellectuals began to challenge this established social order, condemning U.S. and European interventionism and calling for the creation of national infrastructure and industry. This emergent co-hort of nationalist pundits discussed and debated the future direction and management of domestic development in relation to Peru's extremely dis-persed and stratified national populace. The so-called "Indian question" fig-ured at the center of these deliberations.[27] How might national unification be achieved if four-fifths of the populace consisted of non-Spanish-speaking indigenous communities residing in remote areas of the Andes and Amazonia? Could the cultural differences between the cosmopolitan capital and the rural countryside be reconciled? Would the integration of the indigenous peasantry into the national polity threaten political and economic modernization? Was such a sociocultural reordering to be desired?

This sustained public debate over future strategies of national development inevitably provoked questions concerning the very boundaries and meaning of nation itself. For the mestizo Peruvian artist and intellectual of the early twentieth century, the relationship between national "development" and the construction of an autonomous national identity became a central preoccupation.[28] These self-designated architects of the postcolony deemed national unification an urgent if formidable task that would require the creation of popular symbols that could be rendered legible across Peru's extreme ethnic, linguistic, and geographic divides. Such symbols, they argued, must promote the modernist ideologies of the intellectual and economic bourgeoisie while also appealing to the "traditional" aesthetic sensibilities of Peru's popular classes. The effort to address these contradictions led nationalist artists to embrace an academic phenomenon that was sweeping Latin America's emergent postcolonial nations: folklore.[29]

As cultural theorists William Rowe and Vivian Schelling have argued, "folklore was 'discovered' in Latin America in the early twentieth century, when modernizing states were seeking ways to achieve a partial integration of those rural populations which a weak capitalist economy could not fully incorporate," and was thereupon adopted by the postcolonial state "in order to bring about national identity."[30] Considering the cultural, ethnic, and regional heterogeneity of postcolonial Latin American republics, it is easy to imagine how folklore was espoused as a strategic solution to what Anne McClintock has aptly described as the temporal paradox of nationalism: the necessity of simultaneously "gazing back into the primordial mists of the past" while maintaining an eye toward "an infinite future."[31] Indeed, folklore provided cosmopolitan cultural workers with a geotemporal framework for the envisagement of national unification: those texts and practices deemed antithetical to national development could be rearticulated as national folklore—fragments of a shared cultural past that would be institutionally honored as such—while the project of modernity, namely, "cultural" and economic development, could be counterposed as the nation's inevitable future. Accordingly, folklore figured as a prevalent topic of concern and debate for the "modern" Latin American intellectual of the early twentieth century.[32]

At the XXVII Congreso Internacional de Americanistas of 1938, the Peruvian intellectual Frederico Schwab delivered an impassioned speech that placed folklore at the center of the (Latin) Americanist political agenda: "It is not a coincidence that, among all of the International Congresses of Americanists, the present XXVII is the first to consider, among other signaled topics, folklore. Today one can observe, throughout South American countries, a growing interest in this field of study. . . . This interest in folklore demonstrates . . . that South American and Central American countries are consolidating themselves ethnically and socially . . . in them a national consciousness is awakening . . . a new concept of nationality that allows them to understand the culture of their people."[33] The clear link that Schwab draws between the production of popular folklore and the project of national unification was echoed throughout early twentieth-century Peru as nationalist artists adopted folklore as the discursive field through which the development of a national cultural imaginary would be elaborated. In texts ranging from Ricardo Palma's *Tradiciones peruanas* to Julio de la Paz's *El Cóndor Pasa*, distinctive regional indigenous cultural texts and practices were recast as national folklore—the proposed geohistorical and cultural link between Peru's diverse citizenry.[34] A new class of artist-intellectuals, including Alomía Robles, emerged as the self-elected curators of those cultural texts and practices collapsed within the nation's territorial purview. Sponsored by a newly formed Ministry of Education, they were enlisted to cull, assess, and preserve those "remnants" of the nation's dignified yet distant indigenous past. Adhering to prevalent neocolonial discourses of cultural and biological *mestizaje*, these intellectual statesmen studied and systematized *lo folclórico* as a crucial component of the *patria*'s unique cultural evolution, one that began with the imminently "disappearing traditions" of rural indigenous communities and ended with the hybridized forays of cosmopolitan mestizo classes in the coastal capital.

The pivotal role of parochial or "folkloric" musics within the construction of a modern national culture in postcolonial Peru cannot be understated. As sound studies scholar Ana María Ochoa Gautier has persuasively argued, the emergence of folkloric studies in Latin America during the 1880s through 1920s prompted the constitution of an "aural public sphere" that, through the production and institutionalization of sonic hierarchies, enacted modes of social differentiation in national and regional contexts.[35] In contrast with Western "imagined" national communities defined by the interaction of capitalist imperatives and print culture, Peru's low literacy rates, extreme economic stratification, and uneven development meant that aural media such as radio, records, and recitals functioned as particularly potent pedagogical tools for nationalist instruction.[36] It was through practices of what Ochoa Gautier has dubbed "sonic recontextualization"—that is, the introduction of a particular text or trope from one context to another—that folklorists such as Robles designated regional song and sound as public resources to be mined for the construction of uniquely American nationalist forms and genres.[37] Often, these intellectuals not only documented and studied indigenous musics, but also held important public posts in government, academe, cultural institutions, and communications—positions in which "their role was to mobilize folklore for specific political and aesthetic ends within early twentieth century processes of nationalization."[38] Such was the case in postcolonial Peru, where, through the calculated invention and management of a national culture, uneven relations of race, ethnicity, gender, and capital, as well as competing and contradictory localisms, found shady resolution in Western folkloric studies' evolutionary logic and ethnographic gaze. It was in this context that Robles's "El Cóndor Pasa" found its earliest conception.

ON NATIONAL FOLKLORE

In both popular and academic circles, significant debate surrounds the origins of Alomía Robles's operatic score. Prior to his collaboration with Baudouin, the dedicated folklorist had spent over fifteen years touring remote regions of the Ecuadorian, Peruvian, and Bolivian highlands.[39] During his travels, a commitment to the compilation and "preservation" of Andean "folklore" drove Alomía Robles to record and transcribe over six hundred popular songs.[40] While few have challenged his academic acumen, the extent to which this archive influenced the folklorist's subsequent creative work—and most specifically, his arrangement of "El Cóndor Pasa"—remains a matter of public contention. Peruvian musicologist Rodolfo Holtzman diplomatically describes this controversy in the following terms: "While some celebrate his compositions without reservation . . . others see [Alomía Robles] as a compiler *par excellence* of autochthonous wind [music] and negate his creative capacities.[41] As I will soon detail, challenges to Alomía Robles's authorship of "El Cóndor Pasa" are rooted in the charge that significant portions of the musical score are remarkably similar, if not identical, to two popular Andean ballads that date back to at least the nineteenth century. Some defenders of the folklorist claim that "El Cóndor Pasa" was merely "inspired" by his research on Quechua and Aymara folksongs. Other apologists concede that while sonic "borrowings" indeed occurred, Alomía Robles's modern arrangement and instrumentation of "disappearing" traditions constituted venerable creative authorship. Critics, however, allege that Alomía Robles willfully appropriated melodies composed and popularized by indigenous musicians whose race and class position precluded the claim to or copyright of their creative work.

Was Robles an accomplished artist or unprincipled academic? A mestizo born and raised in the highland city of Huánuco, was he merely a composer who imagined himself a modern extension of and ally to Andean communities?[42] Or, did he deliberately appropriate indigenous traditions in the name of patriotic ardor and national order? These questions are elusive and remain difficult to answer. And their political stakes become even more profound if we are to consider the unforeseen future of "El Cóndor Pasa"'s many transits. But I want to bracket concerns over Alomía Robles's *intentions*—the terms in which this debate is most often framed—to consider a broader set of interrelated polemics that merit deeper consideration. What are the political stakes involved in the introduction of indigenous "popular" sonic forms—collectively (re)authored and (re)arranged over time, often part of a dynamic, shared repertoire of common expression—into networks of commodity exchange? As we shall soon see, the uneven practices of aesthetic extraction, curation, and dissemination that inform contemporary world music relations are often inflected by earlier moments of sonic recontextualization.[43] In other words, the archive of the Latin American folklorist—culled, catalogued, and interpreted in accordance with the logics of Western knowledge production—has often effectively albeit unwittingly facilitated subsequent methods and forms of regional and international worlding. At the same time, however, alongside these practices of aural appropriation and commodification exist continued commitments to collective ownership, coalitional convocation, and other modes of dynamic expression. As I will demonstrate, indigenous and African-descended cultural workers have often exploited the methods and archives of ethnologists such as Alomía Robles to remake dominant social and aesthetic scripts and to adapt them to new sites and contexts. Thus, I want to suggest that tracing the circulation of "El Cóndor Pasa" provides an apt point of departure for examining how the politics of artistry and authorship converge with relations of labor, emplacement, and value. It is to these complex entanglements that I now turn.

SOUNDING THE LOCAL, HEARING THE NATIONAL

Silence is shattered with the sharp, piercing cry of the Andean *kena*. Its effortless flight across space and scale could as convincingly signal climax as commencement. Alone, it sounds an imposing call: audience, attune your ears to the musical story to unfold. It begins with a slow and melodic *yaraví*—a mestizo musical genre derived from the highland mourning practice of *harahui*.[44] This prelude's lento tempo and minor notes invoke sentiments of loss or longing. It is both elegant and oppressive, an antipodean invitation to linger and escape. Escape ultimately arrives in the form of transition, as unhurried melody abruptly becomes measured march. Here, the score bridges into *pasacalle*, an upbeat rhythm European in origin associated with the *peninsular* and later *criollo* communities of the northern Peruvian and Ecuadorian coasts.[45] The beat grows louder, tighter, faster. Woodwind notes are now rushed and clipped, as if fleeing the percussive force that threatens to overwhelm them. The tension that builds is frenetic, as if a collision is near. Reprieve arrives under the *charango*'s command, as its lively *rasgueos* (rhythmic strums) provide rhythmic escort toward a much-anticipated finale.[46] Suddenly, woodwinds, strings, and drums erupt in harmonious concert. Again, the rhythm shifts: the first beat is stressed, followed by two short taps. Pasacalle gives way to *kashua*, precursor to the most ubiquitous of Andean rhythms: *el huayno*. Both popular dance and revered song, *el huaynito* summons movement. The melody loosens, hands begin to clap, feet begin to tap. As "El Cóndor Pasa" nears its end, individual listeners become collective participants. We are reminded of Baudouin's final words . . . "Todos somos condores."

The instrumental text that domestic and international listeners would come to know as "El Cóndor Pasa" includes only three of the eight segments that made up Robles's original operatic score.[47] These were abridged then fused into a trinary medley released by Lima's Disquera Víctor in 1917.[48] Under Alomía Robles's direction, the ballad was interpreted by Orquesta del Zoológico, an ensemble named for a concert venue located in the zoological garden of Lima's Parque de la Exposición. Strikingly, the content, progression, and instrumentation of this version varied significantly from the one debuted at Teatro Mazzi only four years earlier. Arranged for popular musicians and instruments rather than genteel symphonists of an orchestra, these aesthetic adaptions arguably endeavored broader public appeal and wider political reach.

The listener unfamiliar with the immeasurable variance in South American sonic and rhythmic configurations might not capture the aesthetic innovation that was clearly legible to Alomía Robles's Peruvian compatriots. In the nation's Andean and coastal regions, rhythm functions as a central organizational logic within musical production. It alternatively, or at times, simultaneously connotes genre, affect, event, and gesture.[49] For music scholars such as Alomía Robles, rhythm likewise functioned as a sonic index of temporal and geographic emplacement. In the case of the former, it connoted a particular moment within calendars of work, leisure, and worship, as well as historical position within genealogies of musical form. In the case of the latter, it territorialized particular racial/ethnic groups into distinctive regional geographies. What is unique about Alomía Robles's 1917 version of "El Cóndor Pasa" is that it both deploys and explodes this logic of sonic particularism by merging three distinct rhythmic traditions—*yaraví*, *pasacalle*, and *kashua*—into a single compilation. This aural entwinement of mestizo, European, and indigenous genres—simultaneously sounding parochial difference and harmonious inclusivity—effectively reordered temporal fragments and geographic localisms into a single sonic opus representative of a broader spatiohistorical configuration: the nation.

The logic of aural entwinement that informed Alomía Robles's rhythmic arrangement was echoed in the instrumentation of the score, which also mirrors this triadic structure. String instruments of European origin, such as the violin, were blended with those of the New World, such as the *charango*, to form the cadenced *rasgueo* of the score.[50] Precolonial bamboo wind instruments such as the *kena* and *siku* provided the text with its melodic contours and transitions.[51] Through this repeated, ternate fusion of indigenous, European, and mestizo traditions, Alomía Robles's popular recording of "El Cóndor Pasa" sounded an idealized hybridization of Peru's distinctive racial, ethnic, and regional geographies. Employing the sonic prose of rhythm and instrumentation, Alomía Robles effectively fabricated a hybridized musical text that appealed to an emergent national public across Peru's messy cultural and linguistic divides. In this way, "El Cóndor Pasa" performed a simulated transculturation of sonic localisms that could be sounded at the national scale.

In describing Alomía Robles's musical arrangement as a simulated "transculturation," I reference both the import of Fernando Ortiz's neologism as well as the inherent limitations of its application. Coined by Ortiz in his seminal 1940 study, *Contrapunteo cubano del tabaco y el azúcar*, "transculturation" challenged the colonial underpinnings of the concept of "acculturation" by offering a distinct model of cultural evolution that linked the independent Cuban nation-state to its colonial past. Against the notion that the colonial encounter resulted in the absorption of an "inferior" culture by a dominant one, transculturation emphasized the dynamic relationship of contradiction and synthesis that emerges from cultural interaction. Ortiz's work posed an important critique of modernist nationalist discourses in Latin America that disavowed the cultural presence of the indigenous and Black peasantry.[52] Similarly, Alomía Robles and his folklorist cohort sought to highlight the breadth of indigenous traditions that shaped mestizo life and culture in New World urban centers. However, the subsequent adoption of transculturation as a nationalist discourse effectively privileged "mestizaje" as the biocultural ethos of New World modernity, thereby positioning indigenous actors and cultural workers as always already traditional, historical, and disappearing.[53] In the case of early twentieth-century Peru, the deployment of transculturation as a nationalist discourse staged what Aymara feminist Silvia Rivera Cusicanqui has dubbed a "successive wave of recolonization"—that is, a technique of neocolonial reordering that entwined practices of geohistorical differentiation with the project of biocultural assimilation and erasure. In other words, as indigenous Andean autonomy was deemed antithetical to national development, the violent subjection of highland peoples and land through processes of state intervention and management was represented within nationalist circles as "transculturation"—the benevolent unfolding of corporeal, territorial, and cultural integration rather than the decisive erosion of indigenous sovereignty. As subaltern studies scholar John Beverley has argued, the deployment of transculturation as a nationalist discourse within the Latin American postcolony has consistently been betrayed by a "hidden agenda of race and class anxiety" that stems from the fear that "racial and class violence from be-low will overturn the structure of privilege inhabited by upper class liberal intellectuals."[54]

It was precisely this dissimulative deployment of transculturation as a colonial-national project that characterized the institutionalization of folk-lore by Peru's early twentieth-century intellectual bourgeoisie. Moreover, it was toward this end that Alomía Robles's creative musical arrangement was quickly appropriated by Lima's criollo nationalists and cultural apologists. Indeed, while the popular press was attentive to Baudouin's theatrical ex-position, media coverage of Alomía Robles's unique ballad was both syco-phantic and extensive. Preeminent newspapers ranging from *La Crónica* to *El Comercio* lauded the score as an unprecedented national musical achieve-ment: "The public—which, in matters concerning national texts is the best judge—has demonstrated through their interminable ovations that this mu-sic is theirs . . . and from our [Peruvian] musical soul master Robles has created a sensation of sagacious harmonization."[55] Such glowing reviews in the popular news media were mirrored in Lima's academic and intellectual circles, as "El Cóndor Pasa" was mobilized as a potent ideological tool for managing the race and class anxiety that Beverley describes. The "sagacious harmonization" of "El Cóndor Pasa" lauded in the popular press was in-deed an opportunistic interpretation of Alomía Robles's musical project. It was in this way that the song came to function as a nationalist folkloric text par excellence, precisely because it introduced a literal sonic harmony that could stand in for the cacophony and contradiction of Peru's many local-isms: grievances over regional development and distribution of resources, racial divides and ethnic parochialisms, and so on. Tellingly, "El Cóndor Pasa" was memorialized in the national newspaper *Revista La Opinión Na-cional* as "a text crafted with a love of all things national . . . rich in the ma-terial of Incan music, but harmonized with great art."[56] Owed to his com-bined training in folkloric and Western musical traditions, Alomía Robles was lauded in the national press as "the author of Peruvian folklore" and would eventually be named director of the Fine Arts Branch of the Ministry of Education in Lima.[57]

Shortly after its successful release to Peruvian audiences in 1917, "El Cón-dor Pasa" was introduced to audiences abroad, during a fourteen-year stint (1917–1933) that Alomía Robles spent living and traveling in the United States. Although the artist and his large family struggled economically during this sojourn, newspaper records reveal that his musical arrangements were performed by a variety of renowned musicians and in a number of elite venues. For example, on the evening of July 24, 1930, a "program of Peruvian music" prepared by Alomía Robles was interpreted by the Goldman band on the New York University Campus. The *New York Times* reported that the well-attended musical event featured original "compositions . . . based on ancient Inca melodies," including the *kashua* portion of "El Cóndor Pasa."[58] The song was also heard across the radio airwaves of wjz in New York as part of the "Evening of Peruvian Music" show assembled by Alomía Robles.[59] Strikingly, it was through this small-scale radio and concert programming of the folklorist's arrangements that pan-Andean regional sonic forms were further codified as national music.[60] Publicity for Alomía Robles's musical work in the United States echoed the discursive tropes of Peru's indigenista movement, advertising it as contemporary "national music" based in "ancient Inca melodies." That the folklorist's repertoire in fact "borrowed" from contemporaneous indigenous musics was again disavowed, while these "borrowings" further elevated him to the status of patriarchal curator of Peru's national past and future.

At first glance, this chain of South American musical transits, first from the rural Andean highlands to the urban port city of Lima, then from a national stage of the global South to an international stage in the global North, might seem coincidental or inconsequential. However, read through a lens attentive to the intersections of the spatial and the sonic reveals that these performance geographies in Peru and then the United States can in fact be understood as an archive of aural abstraction, musical worlding, and sonic recontextualization that predate the U.S. world music industry by nearly a century. We see that as "El Cóndor Pasa" circulates across an array of sites and spheres, its various deployments differently and differentially perform the work of place making, be it the aesthetic undertaking of imaging homeland, the ideological work of securing sensory attachment, or, as we shall soon see, the material manifestation of an (inter)national division of musical labor.

Prior to his return to Peru, perhaps in order to raise money for his family's return voyage, Alomía Robles sold a piano arrangement of "El Cóndor Pasa" to the Edward B. Marks Musical Corporation, who registered it with the U.S. Library of Congress as "Danza Inca" on May 3, 1933.[61] The ballad was recorded for the first time in the global North shortly thereafter, covered by none other than the United States Marine Band.[62] However, the composition did not reach the apex of its international renown until it was appropriated and reproduced by a U.S. artist several decades later.

During a 1965 European tour performance at the Théâtre de l'Est Parisien in Paris, renowned singer/songwriter Paul Simon had a chance encounter with performers from the South American folkloric group Los Inkas. The band's Argentinian and Venezuelan members, who, incidentally, learned to play Andean music in Paris, were the product of another geohistory of South American musical transits. According to ethnomusicologist Fernando Rios, Los Inkas' musical style and repertoire were deeply influenced by Southern Cone folkloric groups such as Paraguay's Los Guaranís that had arrived in Paris twenty years earlier.[63] From these migrant musical groups Los Inkas learned and performed pan–Latin American folkloric staples popularized in the Southern Cone during the 1940s—among them, Alomía Robles's version from 1917 of "El Cóndor Pasa." Simon was intrigued by the band's instrumental interpretation of ballad both for its haunting melody and unique instrumentation. Learning little of the song's origin other than its designation as "Peruvian folklore," Simon paid Los Inkas a nominal fee to produce and record a musical arrangement of the ballad. With the addition of his English lyrics overlaid, Simon's "El Condor Pasa (If I Could)" was released to U.S. and European audiences in 1969 to become a celebrated hit—one for which Alomía Robles was not credited, despite the copyright filed in 1933 with the U.S. Library of Congress.

While Simon's artistic contribution to the 1969 ballad lies solely in the English lyrics that he introduced to Los Inkas' instrumental score, the musician has received numerous professional accolades for the ostensive "musical innovation" that was "El Condor Pasa (If I Could)." In a *New York Times* review of Simon and Garfunkel's Grammy-winning *Bridge over Troubled Water*, music critic Don Heckman lauds Simon's "charming translation of an 18th century Peruvian melody."[64] Over the past several decades, subsequent press coverage of Simon's independent career has been equally laudatory. An article in the *New York Times* from 1993 credits the artist with "reshaping music from various fringes into forms that please a wider public" while along the way "help[ing] to move his sources and collaborators into an international spotlight."[65] Similarly, a 1997 article in *Grammy Magazine* praises Simon's "use of Latin American polyrhythms" and credits his 1971 recording of "El Condor Pasa" as "presag[ing] the World Beat movement by over twenty years."[66]

In a recent interview, Simon recalled the fluke timing and circumstance that made possible his reinvention of "El Cóndor Pasa" for audiences in the global North: "I was roaming around Europe by myself, doing folk stuff. It was there that I met Los Inkas. . . that was the first time that I had ever heard South American music. They gave me an album of their stuff and 'El Condor Pasa' was on the album. The Simon and Garfunkel record of 'El Condor Pasa' was recorded over that preexisting track. . . . the notion was if I liked the music, if it sounded good to me, it was popular. For me there was really no distinction between one culture and another."[67] As the above interview so poignantly elucidates, despite a complete unfamiliarity with the sonic and rhythmic intricacies of Andean musical traditions—to the extent that Simon and Garfunkel's "El Condor Pasa" was recorded over a portion of a preexisting musical track—Simon unabashedly celebrates his willful appropriation of the musical work and repertoire of Los Inkas. Moreover, through a crude discourse of international multiculturalism, Simon retrospectively remembers his re-presentation of "El Cóndor Pasa" as an ideal manifestation of musical "crossover," uncritically lauding his ability to bring fetishized difference to the global stage while disavowing the economic relations of power and ideologies of difference that make such casual and unequal "collaborations" possible.

Ironically, Simon and Garfunkel's international release was reexported to Latin America in the 1970s with the popularization of the folk revival movement Nueva Canción. While Nueva Canción was a cultural movement of "Pan-American solidarity not with, but against the United States," ethnomusicologist Eric Zolov has argued that "El Condor Pasa" was partially responsible for the commercial success of the 1970s folk resurgence in Mexico as well as other parts of Latin America.[68] In a telling interview, Mexican author Luz Lozano recalled: "I have thought for a long time, 'How did that folkloric thing get started?' And I would say that it was with that song ["El Condor Pasa"]. Or at least, it contributed a lot. It was the image that we had of [Simon and Garfunkel]. It was more than just them, like a triangulation: them, the Andes, and here, us. . . . I didn't know the song [before they recorded it]. I think that after that, the [movement] started to emerge here."[69] Interestingly, it was both the international circulation and the perceived national displacement of "El Cóndor Pasa" that helped to reinforce the anti-imperialist stakes of the Nueva Canción movement in sites outside of Peru. As Zolov argues, the internationalization of Latin American folk music in the United States and Europe inspired awareness throughout the global South concerning the extent to its cultural forms were converted into yet another source of raw materials for industrial production in the global North. Indeed, several renowned Latin American artists recorded interpretations of "El Cóndor Pasa" in the early 1970s, plausibly in response to Simon's uncritical, uninformed popularization of the ballad. For example, in 1971 Cuban vocalist Celia Cruz recorded a mambo-esque arrangement of the song under the direction of Tito Puento.[70] "El Cóndor que Pasa" featured original lyrics that accentuated the Andean condor as an enduring, anti-imperial symbol of peace and freedom throughout Latin America. That same year, famed indigenous Peruvian exótica singer Yma Sumac released an experimental version that featured the soprano's vocal interpretation of Alomía Robles's 1917 instrumental version. Sumac's career, which I will soon discuss in greater detail, entailed its own history of transits and worldings. But before I turn to how indigenous Andeans have responded to "El Cóndor Pasa"'s numerous aural abstractions and sonic recontextualizations, I want to first address the political significance of Simon's first foray into the emergent musical world of world music.

Significantly, Simon's dubious appropriation of "El Cóndor Pasa" came to function in the international sphere as a model for transnational artistic projects in which musical giants such as Simon have intervened to "save" purportedly dying musical traditions of the global South by popularizing them in the global North. Ry Cooder's partnership with Cuban musicians of the Buena Vista Social Club offers a salient example of this phenomenon, as Cooder has repeatedly been celebrated in the international media for his heroic efforts in "discover[ing] musical treasures that the [Cuban] nation itself had overlooked."[71] Of course, as George Lipsitz, among others, has cogently argued, a key element of such projects is their intentional obscuring of the unequal relations of power between Western artists and their third world sources of inspiration.[72] The relations of power and difference that such projects represent—most notably neoimperialism and imperialist nostalgia, racist love and racial violence—are lost on Western audiences whose enthusiastic consumption of world music made "El Condor Pasa (If I Could)" a top hit for Simon and Garfunkel in the United States and Germany, and in Ry Cooder's case, earned *him* a Grammy, rather than earning one for the musicians with which he recorded.[73] Ironically, the musical score that was intended to articulate a vision of a multiethnic postcolonial Peru united in combating the violence of U.S. and European interventionism has come to symbolize precisely that which it was designed to counter: the facility with which neoimperialist projects expropriate material and cultural resources of the global South for the economic and political benefit of the global North.

Nonetheless, projects such as Simon's and Cooder's have been continually celebrated in the international media as an ideal variety of global community formation made possible by globalization's rapid technological innovations and territorial integration. PBS, for example, recently described musical partnerships such as the Buena Vista Social Club as the creation of a "musical borderland where distinct traditions could collide, meld and produce a third language—a democratic language, in which all the participants are on equal footing."[74] Such uncritical reviews of these transborder "collaborations" disavow a central contradiction of contemporary economic restructuring. On the one hand, globalization processes have resulted in the diversification of markets in the global North via the increased flow of goods across its permeable borders. These processes, however, have likewise included an increased militarization of northern borders, a proliferation of U.S. and European interventionism, and the implementation of structural adjustment policies throughout the global South. Such encounters between the "first" and "third" world have engendered devastating effects in nations such as Peru—particularly for indigenous and African-descended communities—including civil war, poverty, displacement, and death.[75]

Simon's definitive and unapologetic adoption of "El Cóndor Pasa" and its repeated reproduction in the United States and Europe by artists ranging from Perry Como to Zamfir signaled a structural irony that was not lost on contemporary Peruvian cultural nationalists.[76] In April 2004, the long-standing efforts of Peru's Instituto Nacional de Cultura (National Institute of Culture, or INC) to reclaim "El Cóndor Pasa" culminated in the designation of Alomía Robles's score as a national *patrimonio cultural.*[77] In addition to advocating for this national honor, the INC has launched a comprehensive research project designed to assemble a national archival collection to memorialize the popular ballad and its "original" musical arranger. Entitled Proyecto Cóndor Pasa, the project's stated goal is the education of a national and international public on matters related to the composition. These include the pivotal role of "El Cóndor Pasa" in twentieth-century Peruvian national cultural formation; its fraught and complicated journey to the global stage; and, of course, its authentically Peruvian musical roots.

Interestingly, while Proyecto Cóndor Pasa offers a vehement condemnation of Simon's musical appropriation, its uncritical celebration of Alomía Robles's musical venture fails to acknowledge some of the troubling similarities between Alomía Robles's nationalist cultural project and Simon's neo-imperialist one. Not the least of these similarities is the appropriative practices themselves—his progressive intentions aside, Alomía Robles never credits the previously unpublished vernacular traditions that constituted what is now known as "El Cóndor Pasa." Nor does Proyecto Cóndor Pasa acknowledge the extent to which Alomía Robles's ethnographic project was appropriated by mestizo nationalists to deploy transculturation as a dissimulative alibi for institutionalized neocolonial technologies of material and ideological differentiation, expropriation, and extraction. Equally troubling, both Simon and Alomía Robles embrace nostalgic notions of indigenous essentialism, albeit for different purposes. By marketing his musical collections as cultural artifacts from the global South, Simon leverages Western "imperialist nostalgia" for the "discovery" of "exotic" cultural forms.[78] In doing so, the global Northern artist "pioneered" a model of musicking that mimicked extant "world system" relations, namely a racial-colonial international division of labor. As was common among members of his indigenista cohort, Alomía Robles was likewise limited by his strictly anthropological gaze; for the mestizo nationalists of the era, the introduction of Andean aesthetics to the arena of high culture could be understood solely in terms of the need to preserve and curate the "vanishing culture" of Peru's Indians.[79] Strikingly, *Proyecto Cóndor Pasa* conveniently disavows the ways in which Alomía Robles's project of "preservation" completely displaced the central role of the highland female vocalist, thus dis-placing her from the public stage of national development. Simon completed this cycle of gendered violence with his own linguistic overlay, shrouding any trace of her dislocation. Finally, Proyecto Cóndor Pasa fails to address the extent to which both Robles and Simon garner legitimacy for their own work by emphasizing their faithful representation of ostensibly "authentic" indigenous traditions. In the end, while both are engaged in projects of cultural representation—that is, drawing attention to the richness of Andean musical practice in national and international circles respectively—neither musical "collaboration" makes a move toward political representation—addressing the profound inequities of wealth and power that structure the relation between mainstream artist and popular sources of inspiration.

TRACK THREE: THE PERUVIAN SONGBIRD

Between the bookends of Alomía Robles's nationalist crusade and Paul Simon's internationalist expeditions falls another story of South American musical transits, albeit one that has garnered considerably less scholarly attention. Alternatively remembered as the "Peruvian Songbird," the "Incan Princess," and the "Queen of Camp," Peru's Yma Sumac was a multifaceted artist whose body of work boldly straddled the bounds of popular folklore and experimental art, Andean nationalism and self-exoticism, vocal virtuosity, and operatic outlandishness.[80] During the course of a near sixty-year career, Sumac's voice would traverse geographic continents, musical movements, and creative media, all the while defining and defying various aesthetic, generic, and disciplinary classifications. Yet, despite her undisputed vocal prowess and decades of international popularity, Sumac's coverage in the U.S. and European media was consistently animated by what would become world music's familiar tropes of the exotic and the erotic, the aberrant and mysterious, the unexplored or untamed. This was in no small part owed to her complicated position as an indigenous woman artist within the movement that ethnomusicologist Heather Sloan has called "the other world music": 1950s "Exotica." Drawing upon feminist of color hermeneutics, I "listen against" these putative narratives, instead "listening in detail" to the complexities and contradictions that defined Sumac's career.[81] Focusing on her significant role in promoting contemporary Andean song, what follows recounts three aspects of Sumac's critical sonic work: first, her role in popularizing Andean song in Latin America; next, her negotiation of the Exotica movement in the United States; and, finally, her recording in 1971 of "El Cóndor Pasa."

Shortly after Alomía Robles's return to Peru and rise to government office, another artist of Andean "folklore" roused considerable public attention. But this time, it was primarily among Lima's expanding class of indigenous migrants fleeing political and economic instability in the highlands. In 1942, Zoila Augusta Emperatríz Chavarrí del Castillo—a fifteen-year-old Quechua girl from Ichoacán, Cajamarca—made her radio debut in Peru's capitol.[82] She had recently moved to the city to live with an elder sister; in the year prior, a government official stunned by her solo performance at the religious winter solstice festival Inti Raymi had arranged for the budding singer to study on scholarship in Lima. While taking university extension courses, Chavarrí del Castillo had secretly joined the preeminent Compañía Peruana de Arte, a pan-Andean ensemble comprising forty-six musicians and dancers. This membership was against the wishes of her devout parents, who deemed secular performance an unfit career for a respectable young woman. To hide her deception, the aspiring young artist assumed the Quechua stage name Imma Sumack. Why she adopted this name, which roughly translates as "how beautiful," is uncertain. Perhaps, it was out of respect for or even in defiance of her mother, the formidable Ima Sumac Emilia Atahualpa Chavarrí del Castillo. Or maybe it was to honor the notable personage, Ima Sumac, who appears in the precolonial Incan drama *Ollantay*.[83] What is clear is that the teenage artist was "an overnight sensation," garnering the troupe extensive public attention and accolades. Radio audiences were stunned by the untrained singer's vocal acrobatics—her ability to toggle between piercing high and rich low registers, her incredible five-octave range, and her uncanny vocal aptitude for imitating various musical instruments.[84] Within weeks, the Compañía would receive invitations to travel throughout the Southern Cone, and within eight years Yma Sumac became a hemispheric phenomenon, introducing audiences throughout the Americas to contemporary Andean song.

Sumac's career abroad began in April 1942 with a live performance over Radio Belgrano in Buenos Aires. Like the Lima debut, the broadcast was a huge success. Sumac's sweet yet haunting voice flooded radio airwaves, and the Compañía soon received invitations to appear in distinguished venues throughout Latin America. Shortly thereafter, Sumac wed the Compañía's director, *ayacuchano* folklorist Moisés Vivanco, and with the blessing of her parents launched her first international tour.[85] In the interests of efficiency and economy, Vivanco dismissed nearly two-thirds of the original group, reducing it to the more manageable size of fourteen members. Nearing the end of 1942, the new troupe, now called Imma Sumack y el Conjunto Folklórico Peruano departed for their first concert tour, which included bookings in Peru, Bolivia, Brazil, Argentina, Chile, and Mexico.

El Conjunto Folklórico spent a considerable portion of their tour headlining in the vibrant *peña* scene of Buenos Aires, where pan–Latin American *música folklórica* had been cultivated among leftist youth since the 1930s.[86] There, the group was overwhelmingly successful, in no small part owed to the intrigue surrounding Sumac's unique voice. A performance review in 1943 of El Conjunto Folklórico's appearance in Ta-Ra-Bis—"the number one nightclub in Buenos Aires"—reported: "Señorita Sumack is a topliner and it's her voice (which can imitate any of the Inca instruments played) that provides high spot. [Sumac's voice] has an unusually high, piercing sweet quality which helps much to lend unusual quality."[87] Later that year, Sumac recorded her first album with El Conjunto in Argentina under the Odeon label. Titled "Yma Sumac," its track list featured eighteen of Vivanco's original compositions and artistic arrangements of popular huaynos, pasacalles, and danzas. Sumac interpreted these primarily in Quechua, accompanied by instrumentation representative of the regional variations and specificities of indigenous Andean song. Between this acclaimed album, a full appearance calendar, and considerable critical recognition, El Conjunto Folklórico played a crucial role in the mainstream popularization of Andean song in South American urban centers such as Buenos Aires.[88] Indeed, it was in that city in the wake of El Conjunto's tour that Los Guaranís learned their *música andina* repertory, which would travel with them to Paris in 1951 and, ultimately, inspire the formation of Paul Simon's contracted musicians, Los Incas. Although it is impossible to confirm, we can speculate that Sumac's performances with El Conjunto in Argentina were crucial to introducing a young generation of artists to Andean music, and subsequently, to promoting the transit of South American song from metropolitan cities in the Southern Cone to the stages of bohemian western Europe.

El Conjunto's inaugural Latin American tour culminated in their most prestigious appearance to date: an invitation from Mexico's President Camacho to perform in the renowned Palacio de Bellas Artes. On the tail of this career high, the troupe set their sights on traveling to New York City. U.S. media accounts typically frame the group's northbound journey as a natural or inevitable step toward the pursuit of fame and financial success. However, the troupe had already achieved both of these, and interviews with the artists suggest that it was in fact the desire to learn and incorporate new aesthetic influences that drew them to the global city of Manhattan. Sumac was a self-proclaimed lover of jazz, and was interested in further honing her love of vocalese and improvisation. Vivanco aspired to expand his musical career to include soundtrack composition and other multimedia projects. In short, despite the ethnocentric presumptions of U.S. media pundits, the artists seemed to be less interested in pursuing the milestone of "commercial success in America" and more interested in growing artistically through exposure to new aesthetic traditions and techniques.

In order to facilitate their move abroad, Vivanco again restructured the group, this time reducing it to a simple trio: the director, who would play guitar and other accompanying instruments; Sumac (figure 1.2), who would sing lead vocals; and her cousin Cholita Rivero, who would dance and sing contralto.[89] Now named Inca Taki Trio (in Peruvian dialects of Quechua, *taki* translates as both "song" and "dance"), the threesome arrived to Manhattan in early 1946. There, they settled in a tiny, three-room walkup on Perry Street in Greenwich Village. Like their compatriot Alomía Robles, who strained to make a living as a musician in the United States, the group struggled to launch a professional career. Their overwhelming success throughout Latin America did not translate into public recognition in the United States. For the first several years following their arrival in Manhattan, the bulk of their bookings were limited to one-night stands or opening acts. According to a 1951 feature in *Collier's* magazine, the group's engagements varied from a real estate convention at the Commodore Hotel to a regular gig at "Prudencio Camacho's La Parisienne Delicatessen in New York's Greenwich Village, in a back room richly blanketed with the aroma of pickled herring, salami, and liverwurst."[90]

Whereas Alomía Robles presented the U.S. public with musical arrangements tailored to the familiarities and tastes of a mainstreamed ear, the Inca Taki Trio represented a wholly different experience of South American music. These were indigenous Quechua musicians that U.S. audiences would hear live rather than experience in curated abstraction, performing in Quechua and Spanish rather than English and utilizing Andean as well as Western instruments. While Robles's professional training and accolades earned him near immediate recognition within "high art" scenes in the metropolitan East Coast, the raced and gendered "foreignness" of Inca

1.2 Yma Sumac. Photo by Peter Stackpole.

Taki Trio" marked the band as both visually and aurally illegible to main-stream U.S. audiences. For four years the group survived from one gig to the next, finding work wherever possible. Sumac supplemented the group's income by singing in New York jazz clubs as well, and even performed with Louie Armstrong's band; although these invited engagements provided lit-tle monetary compensation, the singer was moved by the collaboration and expressed an admiration for Louis Armstrong's work that dated back to her early career in South America.[91] But the group's financial situation was dire, and by the end of the 1940s members began to discuss the possibility of returning to South America or accepting one of the many invitations that they had received to enter the vaudeville circuit. Neither of these contin-gency plans came to pass, however. Inca Taki Trio's professional fate radi-cally changed in 1950, when the group unexpectedly landed a record deal with the prestigious label Capitol Records. Capitol, a lead promoter of the emergent genre "Exotica," took interest in the group's "unusual sound." The recording contract approved the artist's proposed track list and, in an un-usual move, agreed to Sumac's desire to sing in Quechua accompanied by Andean instrumentation. However, the label also assigned renowned Exot-ica producer Les Baxter to codirect the album with Vivanco in order to give it a more "Hollywood lounge" style and feel.[92]

In the words of ethnomusicologist Heather Sloan, the term "Exotica" refers to "an entire genre of exotic lounge music, a kitschy Western-centric pop music that relied heavily on percussive instruments to evoke images of mysterious, far-away places."[93] It emerged amidst the confluence of several geopolitical events: the return of U.S. soldiers deployed in the South Pacific during World War II; the increased leisure travel of white, middle-class couples and families to Latin American locations deemed "exotic" by tourist industry promoters; and the aesthetic pursuits of mainstream white male composers in the United States in search of new aural (re)sources. The result was the formation of a musical movement that emphasized the use of instruments atypical to Western orchestral norms of the era—conch shell horns, bamboo flutes, chimes made of shells, goat-skinned drums, and so on—to create for a white Western audience audible fantasies of travel, exploration, and conquest.[94] Albums such as *Ports of Paradise* and *Ports of Pleasure* promised listeners the opportunity to aurally partake in adventurous excursions to fictitious locations in the non-West—locations rendered legible not through geohistorical detail, but rather, through colonial tropes of cultural primitivism, sexual excess, and untamed landscapes. As Roshanak Kheshti has argued, relations of world music listening are always gendered and sexualized; in the case of mid-century Exotica, these relations were defined by aural fantasies of masculinist pleasure and escape.[95]

Sumac's fit within the mid-century Exotica movement was disruptive at best. Whereas albums produced by the genre's famed composers such as Les Baxter and Martin Denny relied on the globalized abstraction of place— aural conjurings of a mythical, "untouched" paradise—Sumac's work was dynamically embedded in regionally specific sounds. Her vocal fame pivoted around an uncanny ability to emulate the sounds of her youth, from the throaty warble of a songbird to the piercing cry of the Andean kena. Moreover, Baxter, Denny, and others rarely partnered with female artists, and certainly not those with an established name, career, and following. For Exotica composers, the curated presence of "unfamiliar," that is, non-Western, sounds within conventional musical scores was intended to signal for white global Northern listeners spontaneous yet safe experiences of imperial exploration and industrial escape. This musical movement was guided by the discovery and exhibition of seemingly "exotic" sounds and instruments, not the promotion of global Southern musicians, as was the case with late twentieth-century world music enterprises. Proponents of the

Exotica genre had little to no interest in co-collaborating with global Southern cultural workers, nor in taking seriously what might be learned from or about their established aesthetic vocabularies, scripts, and techniques.

Nevertheless, Capitol executives opted to market Inca Taki Trio's first recording, *Voices of Xtabay*, as an Exotica project. While the group was granted considerable artistic leeway in the production of the album, Capitol argued that, given the risk that they were assuming by signing this "unusual" group, the label should take charge of creating a public image for the musicians that would link them to the already popular Exotica movement. It was at that moment when the "Incan princess" was born. Almost overnight, Sumac—by all accounts humble and shy if proud and forceful—was transformed from a Quechua migrant musician into the fictional exotic mistress, Xtabay. In the form of Xtabay, Capitol press materials converted Sumac's indigenous singing body into a racialized, sexualized object of colonial desire to be visually and aurally consumed by U.S. audiences. *The Voices of Xtabay* liner notes touted that "the Xtabay is the most elusive of all women. You seek her in your flight of desire and think of her as beautiful as the morning sun touching the highest mountain peak. Her voice calls to you in every whisper of the wind. The lure of her unknown love becomes ever stronger, and a virgin who might have consumed your nights with tender caresses."[96] Press releases for the trio were equally disturbing, as Capitol promoters spun increasingly fantastic yarns about the chanteuse's heritage, childhood, and talents. As one journalist put it, "Yma was not only presented to the American public as an Incan princess, a sun worshiper and a Golden Virgin or Chosen Maiden dedicated to the sun—it was even implied that some 30,000 Indians rose up in protest against her departure from the mountains."[97] So fantastic were Inca Taky's Trio's promotional materials that even Capitol conceded that they had gone too far. Upon admitting that promoters had unnecessarily "sweetened up" Sumac's biography, label executive Walter Rivers stated in 1951: "We have learned our lesson. Next time, we'll give her a more dignified presentation."

Such lush embellishments were met by Sumac with an admixture of humor, pity, and contempt. Within a year the artist blew through nine managers and agents due to frustrations with their attempts to portray her as primitive, exotic, and sexually available rather than refined, talented, and deserving of professional recognition. While some U.S. media pundits charged that Sumac's over-the-top self-commodification damaged her reputation and career, none have addressed the structural racism and sexism that the singer confronted in her dealings with U.S. promoters and audiences. In fact, Sumac was quick to dispel the ridiculous rumors surrounding her Exotica caricature—no, there was no riot prior to her departure from Ichoacán. And no, she was not considered to be Incan royalty. But those who knew and respected her did characterize her persona as unusually poised and dignified. Described by her peers as a "regal, haughty-type dame" that could rectify the "moth-eaten party manners" of even the boldest of Broadwayites, Sumac was regarded as the consummate professional.[98] That is, until she felt underestimated or disrespected, in which case she would erupt in caustic tirades in Quechua. Such was the case when Sumac was rejected for a role in an MGM-sponsored Clark Gable film because, according to the casting team, she did not "look like an Indian." With a cynical laugh, Sumac asked if she could have the part if she were to braid her hair, wrap herself in a blanket, and hop about grunting "how." She then reportedly concluded the audition with some choice words in her native tongue.

While critics and listeners discussed and debated the polemics surrounding Sumac's promotional materials, most conceded that the young artist's vocal prowess was truly formidable. Her ability to sing contralto, mezzo-soprano, soprano, and coloratura—and more particularly, to transition with liquidity across registers—was extremely rare in any artist, much less one so young and untrained. In 1950, Glenn Dillard Gunn of the Washington, DC, *Times-Herald* wrote, "There is no voice like it in the world of music today," while renowned music critic Albert Goldberg of the *Los Angeles Times* stated: "To hear her is at last to experience something new in music."[99] Still, as a young immigrant indigenous woman in the public eye, Sumac also garnered considerable unsolicited advice and professional disesteem. Within the opera community, many condemned her lack of vocal specialization and warned that her constant shuttling between registers would destroy her instrument. It was suggested that the talented yet untutored young Sumac should pursue professional training in Europe. Within the popular music industry, critics often zoomorphized the signature scants and vocal stylings of the Quechua chanteuse. *New York Times* columnists alternately described Sumac as "adept at making nearly supersonic humming sounds and at producing rhythmically startling woofs and barks from her middle range," and as possessing "an uncanny ability to imitate exotic bird and animal calls."[100] Such rhetorical framings of the artist and her work as primitive, coarse, and unrestrained were both animated by and animating of the scientific racism of the era. In 1950, *Collier's* magazine reported that Dr. Hollace E. Arment, head of the music department at Auburn University "ventured the theory that Yma's voice may be a throwback to a more primitive era." According to Dr. Arment, "before our written present musical scale came into being . . . voices of much greater range than is common today were taken for granted." He has suggested that Sumac's "unusual" voice may be "a peephole into the past."[101] Scientists at an Argentinian university seemed to share Dr. Arment's hypothesis, as they subjected the artist's throat and vocal chords to numerous anatomical studies. Despite these ongoing antagonisms, however, Sumac remained based in the United States, eschewed "professional" training, and continued to wield her instrument and artistry as she pleased.

In the twenty years that followed her Capitol debut, Sumac would record an additional seven albums, which stylistically ranged from experimental Andean folk, to Mambo, to lounge, to psychedelic rock. This generic promiscuity, rare among her contemporaries, often stymied conventional critics and listeners, who expected stylistic consistency among their favored performers. Sumac biographer Nicholas E. Limansky observed that "reviews of her appearances in contemporary newspapers and periodicals were . . . diverse and indeed perplexing, reflecting . . . general confusion as to exactly what kind of performer she was. Not knowing whether to categorize her as a popular singer, folk artist, semi-classical artist, or ethnic performer with eccentric musical tastes, most reviewers simply left out any comment on that very important aspect of her persona." However, this failure to decode or capture Sumac's artistic ingenuity was likewise owed to the artist's stubborn transgression of the raced and gendered geographies of productive labor, public performance, and Western repertories that made no room for indigenous migrant performers in general, and indigenous migrant women performers in particular. In other words, as an artist, Sumac was difficult for U.S. audiences and critics *to place* precisely because of her ongoing refusal *to be emplaced* in singular or discrete geographies of home, work, and creativity.

As a young performer, Sumac rejected her parents' desire to restrict her singing engagements to religious festivities and venues—a cultural form of reproductive labor typically performed by indigenous women that, although communally valued, was unwaged. Bucking the heteronormative conventions that psychically and aurally circumscribed women within private/domestic spheres, Sumac embraced the public spotlight and actively pursued opportunities to travel—particularly after she divorced Vivanco for the second (and final) time in 1965. Despite the efforts of Capitol promoters, Sumac's fit within Exotica was tenuous at best because both her art and artistry defied the geohistorical abstractions of the genre. And as an early icon of world music, Sumac playfully satirized or outright scorned attempts to commodify or essentialize her indigeneity. And although her work was deeply indebted to indigenous traditions, she ignored the mandates of those who discouraged her from experimenting with Western aesthetics, instruments, and genres. Thus, rather than remembering Sumac according to the mythical monikers that attempted to fix her within particular geographies of sound—the "Peruvian Songbird" of Andean radio, the "Incan Princess" of Exotica, or Hollywood's "Queen of Camp"—I want to suggest that Sumac is best understood as what Deb Vargas has in another context referred to as a "dissonant diva."[102]

For Vargas, the reclaimed figure of the "diva"—that raced and gendered subject rumored to be or represented as "too much, too dramatic, too demanding"—might be productively listened to for the "dissonances" that she sounds; that is, we can view and hear her ostensible promiscuities, rarities, or excesses as performative disruptions to, or reconfigurations of, normative conventions of embodiment, practices of archiving, and conceptions of the politicoaesthetic. The deployment of "diva dissonance" as a feminist, antiracist, queer hermeneutic equips scholars of sound with a much-needed method for apprehending the inherent political work of textual performance. In this case, we can read the many "dissonances" of Sumac's lengthy career as a traveling indigenous musician—her refusal to be physically bound by gendered codes of domesticity and privacy, her disregard for the condemnation of critics and colleagues regarding her generic promiscuity or vocal excesses, her refusal to be cast as a nameless, faceless artist of what is marketed as "traditional" or "national music—as a series of productive disruptions of the dominant social norms and epistemological practices that effectively sanction or silence the audibility of particular sound artists and aural cultures within music industry structures, media accounts, and public memory.

An excellent example of Sumac's diva dissonance at work can be found in her psychedelic rock album, *Miracles* (1971). Released a year after Simon and Garfunkel's award-winning *Bridge over Troubled Water*, Sumac's final studio album made its mark for both its acclaim and its controversy. While its psychedelic rock arrangements of ballads embellished with Sumac's signature scats has made it a cult classic among aficionados of the experimental and improvisational, *Miracles* also gained public notoriety when it was pulled from record stores after an "accidental release" in 1971, then permanently withdrawn shortly after its rerelease in 1972. According to Sumac, this was due to an ongoing dispute with Les Baxter, who wrongfully claimed credit for the album's concept and production. Critics and listeners have widely debated how and why this "blizzard of litigation and acrimony" between artist and producer arose—often, in a predictably racist and sexist manner that condemns Sumac's betrayal of Baxter, who is credited with "discovering her" and "making her career."[103] Yet this focus on the album's eccentricity and embroilments has overshadowed what could arguably be deemed Sumac's most boisterous, most blasphemous recorded response to decades of racist masculinist imperial incursions: a rendition of "El Cóndor Pasa" that can easily be read as an ironic, intertextual conversation with suddenly "Latinized" U.S. folk artists of the era—most specifically, Paul Simon.

The final track on the artist's ill-fated final studio album, Sumac's "El Cóndor Pasa" was a flop among most critics. It boasted none of the Latin American folkloricism associated with Los Incas director Jorge Michelberg's arrangement. Reviewers such as Nicholas Limansky charged that Sumac's overly "busy" and "uninspired" interpretation missed "the inherent simplicity of the original piece." Limansky goes on to compare Sumac's track to "other native instrumentalists" [*sic*] whose renditions of this "traditional Peruvian song" he seems to prefer.[104] Still, a handful of Sumac's loyal fans have lionized the unusual track, which they have alternately (and indeed, aptly) characterized as "space-age," "psychedelic," and "lounge." Such descriptors respectively conjure the familiar scenes and sounds of modernity, transgression, and excess of the 1970s. What is interesting to consider, however, is how these sonic tropes are dissonant with those used to describe the sonic script of Simon's "If I Could"—traditional, static, and simple. Following Vargas, I want to suggest that these "dissonances" can be heard as a powerful intervention into the racist masculinist discourses and practices of a midcentury U.S. culture industry that coded sonic interaction in racial sexual terms: the uncritical cooptation of non-Western musics by white men such as Simon was celebrated by audiences and critics as a laudable example of innovative discovery and sensual mastery. The experimental art of indigenous singers such as Sumac, however, was condemned as misguided generic promiscuity, both socially and aesthetically inappropriate. But, what if we are to listen against the grain of this dichotomy . . . if we privilege attention to the disobedience, dissonance, and departure that inform the psychedelic arias and baritone warbles that comprise the aural script of Sumac's "El Cóndor Pasa"?

With requisite flourish the song begins. Sumac's operatic vocalese flawlessly emulates the most proficient of kena soloists. Her unearthly, improvisational notes flutter increasingly skyward, soaring to perilous heights. They mockingly compete for auditory attention with their companion instruments: a seemingly possessed xylophone and an ethereal-sounding synthesizer. These "space-aged" accompaniments are reminiscent of television soundtracks of time travel or other aural representations of temporal transformation. Certainly, they defy the notions of stasis, tradition, and primitivism that have long characterized mainstream Western assessments of indigenous Andean song. Suddenly, this strained convergence gives way to "El Cóndor Pasa"'s familiar opening melody. Sumac tackles this hallmark verse with a stretched, low register warble that is reminiscent of the kena's longer, lower-pitched relative, the *kenacho*. She expertly captures its magnificent vibrato—a stylistic technique that requires considerable mastery among flautists. Electric guitar and bass now accompany her melodizing, following a steady rhythm that significantly departs from the slow and stretched beat of the conventional yaraví. The result is a song that is equal parts euphony and sass. As the song builds, it veers from the anticipated rhythmic bridge of pasacalle, instead introducing the abrupt punctuation of an Andean harp then leaping into the culminating rhythm of huayno. Here, Sumac's "El Cóndor Pasa" becomes increasingly improvisational and unruly. Spectacular phonic riffs sound in rapid succession, exhausting the ear of a listener who desires culmination and closure . . . finally, it ends, with Sumac's signature scants fading so slowly that it is hard to discern if or when they have finally become inaudible.

To bookend a recording career that spanned nearly three decades, Yma Sumac chose "El Cóndor Pasa" as her archival swan song. Interestingly, it was never mixed or edited; the entire album was recorded during a single studio session. Its dissonances, then, are raw and candid in both content and form. It has been said that Sumac was dissatisfied with the album, perhaps owed to battles over artistry and authorship that surrounded it. But she continued to perform versions of the above arrangement of "El Cóndor Pasa" throughout the remainder of her career, which extended well into the 1980s. While Sumac never confirmed that her unusual cover of the ballad, released only months after its popularization in the United States and Europe by Paul Simon, was a response to the colonial hubris of the New York folk artist, given the timing of its production, the artistic choices that Sumac made, and her frustration with white masculine authority in the industry, we can certainly read her text as such. For example, whereas Simon required hired musicians to record and perform his version of "El Cóndor Pasa," Sumac effortlessly tackled its Andean instrumentation via her own vocal virtuosity, paired with her own hired soundtrack of "space-aged, psychedelic rock." We might read Sumac's "El Cóndor Pasa," then, as a disruptive performance of antimasculinist mastery-in-reverse: on the one hand, Sumac addresses the absence of indigenous women among musicians in internationalist circles by inserting a vocalese arrangement of Andean instrumentation; on the other hand, she disrupts the static geotemporal imaginaries of "authentic indigeneity" that have most often informed the ballad's deployment.

As I have previously argued, folklore has been used as a technology of nation building for the postcolonial nation-state, a means of institutionalizing indigenous expressive culture as merely a remnant of the historical past. Yet, as William Rowe and Vivian Schelling have cogently argued, throughout Andean history "the cultures referred to as folkloric have upheld their own ideas of nationhood capable of challenging the official state. In these circumstances, the idea of folklore breaks down, since the phenomena it refers to challenge the legitimacy of the society voicing the idea itself."[105] While the authors' claim focuses on Andean cultural politics at the national scale, given the cultural and economic processes of late twentieth-century global capitalism, it becomes increasingly important to now address the extent to which similar struggles for historical and political sovereignty have been advanced at the intersection of local and global scales. In my view, we can read Sumac's bold reappropriation and satirical reinterpretation of "El Cóndor Pasa" as an example of such interventions at work. If, as the case of "El Cóndor Pasa"'s innumerable transits so vividly illustrates, Andean musical cultures have been appropriated for the projects of nationalist modernity and international imperialism, then they have likewise been reframed as a fluid repository of knowledges, texts, and practices that shift and adapt to the material and aesthetic concerns of the indigenous immigrant artist.

ON SOUND AND TRAVEL

What can we learn from "El Cóndor Pasa"'s circuitous itinerary of musical transits, particularly when its authorship and origins remain elusive? Arguably, attention to the reproduction of this mythical ballad across sonic and linguistic as well as spatial and temporal boundaries points to critical fissures within the theoretical and methodological frameworks through which globalized cultural production is often addressed. Indeed, as the Latin American Subaltern Studies Collective has cued, and as the myth-making around "El Cóndor Pasa" dramatically illustrates, the turbulent contest through which archives and canons are constituted—be they linguistic, sonic, or performed—makes impossible a singular, absolute, or unbiased representation of the past. Thus, as cultural critics who read and deploy sonic, literary, and visual texts as critical supplements to institutionalized "evidence" and hegemonic historical narratives, *we too* must cautiously avoid subscribing to a search for "authentic" or "fixed" origins, be they cultural or geographic. For even when deployed as a means of marking the violence of capitalist homogenization and colonial erasure, the unifying and essentializing logic of geocultural authenticity can only be narrated through modernity's twin linear tropes: temporal progress and primitive loss. Given this, rather than gauging the extent to which a particular cultural form maintains its aesthetic and political integrity in the face of worlding—in this case, seeking to measure the legitimacy of Simon's "El Condor Pasa" against that of Alomía Robles's arrangement or Sumac's interpretation—might it not be more productive to address how a cultural text—a song, a melody, even a rhythm—can be enlisted at different moments, in distinctive forms, in the service of divergent political projects?

A significant—if often underemphasized—aspect of the material and ideological work of cultural performance is its constitutive role in the production of place—that is, the construction of spatial categories that give meaning to a particular, articulating ensemble of social relations.[106] Within cultural studies, the historical and contemporary globalization of musical practice has most often been read through a discourse of coercive "travel"—that is, of capitalist extraction and ideological reconfiguration, and its attendant reconstitution of the *content* and *form* of cultural practice. However, as geographers Cindy Katz and Neil Smith have observed, this approach operates on the implicit assumption that while cultural practices change over time, the material and ideological geographies on which they "take place" remain constant or static.[107] Conversely, I have suggested that it is equally fruitful to question how traveling cultural practices in general, and musical practices in particular, can be mobilized to alter, and in fact produce, distinctive conceptions and relations of space and place. This alternative method of cultural inquiry—performance geography—argues for the contemplation of expressive practices as not only *transformed by* processes of travel, exile, and displacement but, in fact, *transformative of* the discursive and structural constructions of "place" with which they come into contact.

The performance geographies of "El Cóndor Pasa" hitherto examined reveal the crucial political stakes that inhere in the imbricated processes of sonic production and spatial formation. A critical function of Alomía Robles's original score was its capacity to both imagine and garner support for a reconstituted, multicultural Peruvian nation-state—one in which the transition from indigenous to Spanish to mestizo was both seamless and purged of the attendant violence of recolonization. And as the violence of neocolonial expansionism was elided, the fact of African chattel slavery was decisively disavowed. In Gramscian terms, Robles's score was a crucial part of the construction of a national popular that, in the sounded service of neocolonial state-led developmentalism, glossed over divides of gender, class, ethnicity, race, and region.

While perhaps less immediately evident, Simon's reappropriation of "El Cóndor Pasa" was equally enmeshed in processes of sociospatial construction. As a foundational recording of the world music industry, Simon's material and cultural exploitation of Los Inkas' instrumental track explicitly lauded an emergent geography: the "global village" of late twentieth-century capitalism, which emplaced then naturalized an international division of musical labor under the abstracted rubric of "world music." Simon's "El Condor Pasa (If I Could)" can be read as an allegory for the artistic relations that defined this sonic formation; his facile overlay of lyrics over Los Inkas' track both relied on and leveraged conceptions of the global South as the ultimate primitive resource—perpetually located in the past and infinitely available for expropriation. Global Northerners such as Simon, in turn, were positioned as both creative entrepreneurs and consuming publics.

Conversely, by migrating throughout the global South and later, to the global North, in order to control the production and distribution of her music, Yma Sumac's performing body and body of performed work carved out a distinctive performance geography of musical transit, one in which the erasures of postcolonial nationalisms and the neocoloniality of world music globalisms were boldly negotiated. Straddling rather than suturing the seemingly stable or static boundaries between popular folklore and experimental art, indigenous nationalism and self-exoticism, vocal virtuosity and campy crooning, we can read the dissonances and excesses that defined Sumac's art and artistry as productive interrogations of geopolitical structures of differentiation and abstraction that could contain neither her traveling body nor her soaring voice.

CONCLUSION

Through a critical juxtaposition of three distinct performance geographies constituted by and through "El Cóndor Pasa"'s musical transits, I have historicized the ways in which a single compilation has been rearticulated across space and over time to generate mutually animating texts and contexts. In doing so, I have illustrated how "El Cóndor Pasa"'s circuitous journey might encourage us, as critical readers, to embrace an analysis of cultural production as historically and geographically *dynamic*, as well as situated.

Such a theoretical shift, I contend, might allow for new ways of imagining the politics of globalized cultural practice, as the (re)production of fluid and contingent texts through which the sociopolitical processes of ideological negotiation and mediation "take place."[108] Toward this end, I have introduced performance geography as a useful framework for theorizing dynamic relations of musical, social, and spatial formation. Within the fields of Latina/o studies and American studies specifically, greater attention to sociospatial production challenges the long-standing limitations of area studies models—most particularly their static conceptions of space, place, and culture. Latina/o studies has long been at the forefront of alternative approaches to spatial politics, particularly in the last generation of work on border thinking. From the *nepantla* of Gloria Anzaldúa's "borderlands," to José David Saldívar's "borderthinking," to Mary Louise Pratt's "contact zones" or Mary Pat Brady's "double-crossings" of "*la frontera nómada* and other "spatial urgencies" of Chicana writing, this scholarship has encouraged us to rethink the subject produced at the limit of the United States' material and ideological Southern Border.[109] Today, the current U.S. political climate post-9/11 has demonstrated the facility with which a state-in-crisis can instantaneously produce multiple border zones—from airports and waterways, to hospitals and elementary schools, to state lines that divide mountains from desert. How, then, can we go beyond our own tendency to confine our spatial analysis to the territorialized southern boundary of the United States without reducing its structural and discursive significance? A key point of departure, I argue, is to increase our attention to the role of culture in both producing and making meaning of contemporary spatial formations; that is, to interrogate how cultural products and processes either facilitate or constrain the quotidian reproduction of material and ideological borders, from bodies to communities to nations. By following a single ballad through its geographic, technological, and ideological displacements, I have provided an illustration of how spatialized thinking might usefully be applied to analyses of musical production and circulation. In so doing, I have offered an alternative perspective on our own role as cultural critics and audience members—one in which we are not merely lone consumers, but rather collective subjects forged through music that we make and to which we listen.

2

PUTUMAYO AND ITS DISCONTENTS

The Andean Music Industry as a
World Music Geography

If your music isn't World Music, where in the world are you?
—BARBARA BROWNING, *Infectious Rhythm*

For many musicians around the world, "the popular" has become a dangerous cross-roads, an intersection between the undeniable saturation of commercial culture in every area of the human endeavor and the emergence of a new public sphere that uses the circuits of commodity production and circulation to envision and activate new social relationships.
—GEORGE LIPSITZ, *Dangerous Crossroads*

In 1975, Dan Storper, a recent graduate of Washington University's Latin American studies program, opened the doors of his two-hundred-square-foot boutique craft and clothing store in Manhattan's Upper East Side. Named "Putumayo" after the Amazonian tributary that wends through the Andean valleys of Colombia's southern border, Storper's tiny storefront ped-dled a miscellany of artisanal wares from throughout the Southern Ameri-cas and the Caribbean. Within a decade, Storper's experimental outfit grew from a single retail store stocked with inventory stored in the garage of his parents' suburban home to a multi-million-dollar corporation that sourced "ethnic inspired" clothing and art to over six hundred retail stores throughout the United States. Storper began playing music of the Andean region over the speakers in his stores as a sensory tool designed to create "an environment that made you feel as if you were escaping the city and traveling to South America."[1] As the apocryphal story goes, following the "extraordinary response" to these compilations,"[2] Storper established Putumayo World Music in 1993—a label oriented toward "introduc[ing] people to other cultures through great world music."[3] Over the past two and a half decades, Putumayo has released over eighty thematic compilations, each billed as "meticulously researched and curated musical journeys" that are "guaranteed to make you feel good." Through retail partnerships with companies ranging from Starbucks to Whole Foods, and online storefronts such as Amazon and iTunes, Storper's Putumayo has become one of the most internationally recognized and financially lucrative world music businesses in the world.

This chapter is not about entrepreneur Dan Storper, nor is it about his ubiquitous world music label. However, Putumayo's self-promoted origin story proffers an apt opening for this chapter for several reasons. First, it both supports and extends a central claim advanced in the previous chapter: that Andean musics have been an animating aesthetic force within the rise and development of world music projects in the global North as well as the "aural imaginaries" that such projects continually (re)produce.[4] For if "El Cóndor Pasa" can be read as an aural archive of a near-century of South American musical transits and the contested relations of sonic appropriation and recontextualization that animate them, then the making of Putumayo—with both its acknowledged indebtedness to Andean sound and its unacknowledged indebtedness to Andean-based modes and networks of cultural circulation—can be read as a continuation of that story. Indeed, Putumayo represents an archetypical example of the contemporary world industry regimes that emerged out of colonial-capitalist relations and structures that date back to the early twentieth-century processes of South American musical worldings, from the nationalization and subsequent canonization of folklores throughout Latin America, to the mid-century emergence and popularization of commercially driven musical genres such as Exotica, to the marketization of asymmetrical, antipodal aural "partnerships" such as the one Paul Simon established with Los Inkas.

Next, as the interviews reveal, Storper's strategic deployment of Andean sound within his retail stores not only increased clothing and craft sales by enhancing the sensory experiences of white middle-class consumers. It likewise prompted the establishment of an "international music" label that penetrated a crowded industry by introducing a unique, low-cost model of advertising: "lifestyle marketing." Defined by media mogul Vivek Tiwary as "the introduction of your music into another area of a person's life" through advertising "that appeals to their activities, interests, and opinions," lifestyle marketing is unique in that it entails "creative and unique promotions at non-music outlets . . . such as coffeeshops, skateshops, clothing stores, smokeshops, tattoo parlors, nature shops, gyms, danceclubs, bars, etc." Media advertising executives such as Tiwary contend that lifestyle marketing is particularly effective "because you can directly target a specific type of consumer who will most likely be a fan of your specific genre of music."[5] Mutually beneficial corporate partnerships such as these have since been adopted by an ever-growing number of world music industry players.[6] Chris Fleming, cofounder of the world music department at the Virgin Megastore in Times Square and head of media acquisitions for the New York Museum of Natural History gift shop contends that "Putumayo single-handedly revolutionized the whole [world music] genre," adding "they brought [non-Western music] out of the archives, made it more accessible."[7] Storper concurs, arguing that the beauty of the "lifestyle company" model is that it integrates the "promotion of world understanding" with the monetary success. "I always felt business could be a force for positive change,"[8] Storper avers.

The Putumayo "lifestyle" label, then, represents a novel iteration of previous world music formations. It is one that marries imperial heteromasculinist narratives of exploration, rescue, and curation—of "distant lands," "dusty archives," and "undiscovered cultures"—with an uncritical celebration of individual capitalist entrepreneurship via the creative pursuit of emergent markets alongside the cultivation of new listening publics. In this sense, Putumayo's brand of lifestyle marketing and its promotion of "conscious capitalism" are wholly predicated upon the abstracted notions of place, sound, labor, and value that this book assiduously critiques.[9] Despite a proclaimed commitment to educational and social justice agendas, the Putumayo label both models and narrates static, universalist patterns of musical circulation that entrench rather than challenge global Northern corporate interests, aesthetic registers, and racial fantasies. Musical flows, we are told, follow a linear course from artist to entrepreneur, from rural to urban, from global South to global North. Eclipsed by such narratives are the ways in which aural texts and spatial contexts are fluid, contested, and mutually animating. What of those musical flows that predate late twentieth-century globalization, that follow itineraries of labor migrations, or that are popularized through noncommercial and/or grassroots circuits of dissemination?

In what follows, I explore a current of South American musical transits that both unsettles and challenges these master narratives about and dominant mappings of "world music" circulations. Rather than center exemplars of corporate world music industry relations, this chapter understands Putumayo and its ilk as the structures that haunt world musicking practices in the global North, but do not fully constitute them. For even as world music brokers narrate themselves into being as discoverers, saviors, and curators of "disappearing local musics," the obscured and appropriated subjects, relations, and practices of musical creation, transmission, and exchange on which such racial-colonial projects built their financial success and cultural renown remain vibrant, heterogeneous, and contested sites of spatial and cultural production that are too often overlooked by narrow attention to the corporate world music regimes.[10]

To address this "other" world of world music, this chapter eschews conventional approaches that position world music's significance and function through contrary conceptual claims—integration versus opposition, endurance versus transformation, aesthetics versus politics—to straddle the genre's contradictions, offering instead an analysis of both the productive possibilities and potential limitations enabled by two performance geographies of world "musicking": street performance in the global city of San Francisco, and more recently, sound performance on digital platforms such as YouTube.[11] Specifically, what follows offers a spatiohistorical reading of the ongoing development of what I term the "Andean music industry": the extensive—and, at times, extremely lucrative—international informal economy of Andean musical production that has operated as parallel to, and at times in competition with, the world music industry over the last several decades. The birth of the industry can be traced to the early 1980s, when, rather than appealing to world market promoters for corporate sponsorship of "import" recording projects, dozens of indigenous South American musicians chose immigration to global Northern metropoles as an alternative option for their economic and aesthetic pursuits. Within a few short years, these artists established a hemispheric network of Andean performance that subverted the world music industry's established geoeconomic order by relocating the spatialized processes of cultural production, mediation, and consumption to the everyday public spaces of subway stations, street corners, and shopping malls.

Like the world music industry, the Andean music industry (AMI) was born of and at the intersection of multiple geohistorical forces, from global economic restructuring and technological innovation to hemispheric migrations and aesthetic circulations. Yet, an account of the AMI's unique relations of culture and capital demands an important retelling of dominant geohistorical narratives about world(ed) music and musical worldings—one attentive to prior patterns of migration and displacement, to ongoing regional and national revanchisms, and to the oppositional potential of strategic appropriations of public and virtual space. Arguably, the AMI's most unique and creative features—its informal economic logic, its improvisational public stages, and its self-produced artistic merchandise—each represent a creative manipulation and/or circumvention of the world music industry's institutional trammels. Whether by bypassing entrenched routes of musical migration, adopting nonconventional modes of production, or carving out new sites for self-promotion and product dissemination, the industry's political logics and economic scaffolding offer a powerful critique of and response to the modalities of social abandonment and spatial constraint that typically mark global Southern musicians' initiation into commercial music industry circuits.

Given this, this chapter takes Browning's provocative query quite literally, addressing this unique musical project through an analysis of the intersubjective politics of social and spatial emplacement. Responding to the common tendency within world music scholarship to undertheorize the extent to which spatial politics inflect cultural globalization processes, I conceptualize the relationship between musical production and spatial formation as dynamic and interactive, rather than linear or causal. To think together the dynamic entanglement of spatial and sonic work, I argue, enables a fruitful interrogation of precisely how—through material structures and landscapes, disciplinary frameworks, and/or aesthetic regimes—the value of worlded music is "placed": that is, how capitalist value both accumulates in and is contested through ideological assessments and/or abstracted processes of alienation; and, correspondingly, how both monetary and extramonetary forms of value are produced by and reproduced through spatial(ized) relations of musicking.

As a case study, the AMI serves as a useful point of departure through which to engage two, interrelated theoretical questions concerning the spatiality of contemporary cultural industries and their critical discontents. First, how are geographies of world musicking both produced by and reconfigured through "emplaced musical relations"? By "emplaced musical relations," I mean the dynamic interaction through which modes of sonic production are enabled or constrained by access to particular material sites—the professional recording studio, the commercial record store—or particular physical locations—be it the "Band Aid" festival or Carnegie Hall. To be sure, it is most often the case that dominant world music emplacements such as these enact the spatial logics of racial capitalist exploitation, territorializing institutional ideologies and structures that inhibit the economic success and aesthetic innovations of, and regulate the political visions expressed by, global Southern musicians. As my account of the AMI will demonstrate, however, nonconventional performance geographies of world musicking can effectively activate new modes of cultural and economic (re)production and political solidarity.

Second, how do world music formations both compose and orchestrate "relational musical emplacements"? Here I refer to the ways in which aesthetic variations—instrumentation, rhythm, technological production values—are heard to sound the ostensibly authentic and essential differences between relational places, such as global North/South, rural/urban, or nation/diaspora. Again, nonconventional geographies of world musicking such as the AMI not only call into question the disturbingly colonial-capitalist underpinnings of such geographic binarisms, but equally importantly, they exert critical pressure upon the dominant geopolitical frameworks within which world music relations are often discussed.

To address these and other related questions, what follows chronicles the hemispheric formation of contemporary Andean fusion and Andean pop across multiple, noncontiguous stages of cultural and economic production and exchange. I suggest that this nonconventional performance geography of world musicking occasions a critical discussion of the specifically spatialized tensions of world music's "dangerous crossroads": fissures and friction points between the (inter)national and the popular, the constraints of commercial markets, and the oppositional potential of newly accessible, although extensively policed, public spheres.[12] With the aim of contributing to emergent trends within popular music studies and critical geography, I make a case for an approach that conceptualizes world and other modes of transnational musical production as materially and ideologically *situated* as well as abstracted, and as historically and geographically *dynamic* as well as contextual. I argue that by highlighting the role of music as a technology through which contested expressions and manifestations of place and time are made sense of, consolidated, and/or reordered, such an approach productively troubles common theoretical slippages between "popular" or "traditional" cultural forms and ethnic or nationalist essences.[13]

INTERNATIONAL WORLDINGS

As I discussed in chapter 1, the transnational and transregional circulation of Andean musical traditions dates back at least a century; though understudied, these musical migrations have undoubtedly influenced popular styles and genres throughout (and perhaps even beyond) the Americas.[14] Yet the arrival of Andean music to the global stage in the late 1960s signaled a momentous aesthetic and technological shift in U.S.-based folk-rock production, and consequently, a significant moment in the history of Andean music's diffusion. Paul Simon's release in 1969 of "El Condor Pasa (If I Could)" not only topped international charts and earned him a Grammy Award; it irrevocably transformed the folk scene of the era by cultivating a constituency of international listeners for an emergent genre of sonic fusion: world music. In the decades that followed, the commodification of "world music" as a commercial category was cemented by a series of international musical collaborations-cum-humanitarian relief projects sponsored by equally famous international recording stars from the global North.[15] By the 1990s, it was this "demand" for world music in the global North that led Putumayo's Dan Storper to found one of the most monetarily successful world music compilation businesses in the world.[16]

While Simon's release of "El Condor Pasa," the organization of international benefit concerts, and the advent of world music labels may appear at first glance to be three entirely different projects, all shed light on the discursive technologies and material relations of neocolonial development that have often underpinned the production, distribution, and consumption of "world music" since its commercial incarnation. In accordance with the tenets of Western developmentalism, U.S. and European artists have been celebrated in the international media for their interventionist role in "collaborative" world music projects. Such unequal partnerships between global North and global South have been realized under the guise of material support for the preservation of the "vanishing cultures" that postcolonial nation-states have ostensibly been either economically unable or ideologically unwilling to support.[17] As a result, the cementing of the world music industry and its concomitant expropriation of global Southern cultural resources have been legitimated through at least three spurious raced and gendered presumptions about the so-called third world, its residents, and its diverse forms of cultural production: first, that these musical cultures can or should be *valued* only when circulated (thereby accumulating *value*) in the global North; second, that such international circulation necessitates the mediation and/or curation of white male artists in the global North (e.g., Paul Simon or Dan Storper); and finally, that the world music industry should be celebrated for its role in financing and supporting music—and people—of the "developing world."

The entrenchment of the world music industry as what Stuart Hall aptly referred to as a "cultural bureaucracy" has prompted an ever-growing body of interdisciplinary scholarship concerned with the uneven relations of race, gender, and capital that structure transnational relations of cultural and, specifically, musical production.[18] However, few critical analyses of and responses to the world music industry have attended to this phenomenon as a spatial problematic—that is, as a vexed assemblage of relations and practices both constituted by and constitutive of distinct and contested sites and scales of dynamic geographic interaction.[19] To do so requires careful consideration of the relational aspects of musical emplacements that enable particular sounds to be heard at once as familiar and foreign, national and international, immediate and worldly. At the same time, it requires an interrogation of how and why particular cultural mores and geographic norms ostensibly cohere or misalign as well as the political projects at stake in such harmonious or dissonant spatiosonic renderings.

Take, for example, "music of the Andes"—the moniker most often used to describe the recordings that circulate within the AMI. While it might be tempting to assume that it would be more precise to describe Andean musical forms in nationalist terms such as "Peruvian" *huayno* or "Bolivian" *saya*, these geocultural renderings can enact their own forms of effacement. As I argued in the previous chapter, statist claims to worlded regional musics are often bound up in the twin colonial strategies of cultural and bodily expropriation and erasure.[20] It is true that, as cultural critic Néstor García Canclini has persuasively argued, culture industry marketers often deploy general regional markers to "decontextualize" and thus homogenize safe and standard products for consumption in the global North.[21] However, artists in and of the global South also engage in their own forms of geographic contest. In the case of the AMI, the mobilization of a regional affiliation—"the Andes"—has served as a means of troubling nationalist patrimonial claims, of highlighting ongoing histories of colonial-racial-capitalist displacement, and of emphasizing alternative modes of belonging.

To expand upon my interest in the spatial work of world musicking, I now turn to an instance of globalized musical production that, when read through a geographic lens, complicates both uncritical celebrations of the world music industry and essentialist critiques of contemporary globalized culture. The AMI provides one among many provocative examples of how Latin American immigrant artists have negotiated the sociospatial politics of global economic restructuring in creative and unexpected ways. Attention to its performance geographies in urban San Francisco, I argue, reveals how practices of musical transposition such as the creation of informal networks of transnational cultural and commercial exchange can potentially disrupt the logic and coherence of naturalized geographies of containment (such as the proper raced and gendered body, the state-sanctioned workplace, the white-supremacist patriarchal nation), thereby reterritorializing alternative expressive individual and collective subjectivities as they are imagined across scales.[22]

WORLD MUSIC AND ITS CRITICAL DISCONTENTS

Both an expression and a force of late capitalist globalization, the world music industry was born of and at a moment of international economic restructuring that signaled a devastating shift in U.S. / Latin American relations. While the cross-continental implementation of structural adjustment policies, hyperinflation, and the privatization of public works dramatically restricted the capacity of the working and nonworking poor to survive economically, the consequent mass migration of Latina/o immigrants to the global North satisfied the United States' demand for cheap immigrant labor to staff a burgeoning service sector.[23] It was in this context of economic neoliberalization that a handful of musical groups hailing from the Andean nations of Perú, Bolivia, and Ecuador—including Raíces, Markahuasi, and Picaflor—embarked on northbound journeys to pursue artistic and economic avocations.[24] Over the next several years, these and other indigenous immigrant musicians together forged provisional transnational performance and migration networks (e.g., where to play without police or merchant interference, and in some cases, how to get there while evading the risk of deportation) that connected urban centers in the Andean region to cities throughout Central America, Mexico, and, later, the United States. Within a decade, in parallel with the exploding world music industry, these provisional transnational circuits were transformed by Andean artists and their audiences into a thriving U.S.-based informal economy of performance, distribution, and migration networks that spanned South, Central, and North America and Europe.

While the birth of the Andean music industry coincided with (and as I will soon demonstrate, strategically exploited) world music's mass popularization, the international and intraregional circulation of Andean music is itself a much older tale. At least two moments within the longer and broader history of Andean sonic production were central to the AMI's late twentieth-century contingent institutionalization: the transnational circulation of *música latinoamericana*, in the 1960s and 1970s, and the transregional migration and subsequent popularization of pan-Andean music in the national capitals of La Paz and Lima in the 1970s and 1980s.[25] In the case of the former, Nueva Canción artists predominantly hailing from the Southern Cone popularized a range of regional Andean rhythmic traditions, positing these as national resources for the fomentation of anti-imperialist struggle. This musical tradition was then transported to Europe in the 1970s, when, in the wake of military coups in Argentina and Chile, a number of New Song performers were exiled to Europe. The international success of these pan–Latin American folklore ensembles cultivated an international public of listeners, and in turn inspired and sustained indigenous Andean music industry migrants' northbound journeys in the 1980s.[26]

The popularization of pan-Andean music in Lima and La Paz circa 1970s–80s also marked a critical antecedent to the AMI's late twentieth-century organization.[27] In the case of Lima, the "Andeanization" of the coastal, criollo-identified city, coupled with the transregional circulation of Afro-Colombian *cumbia* through national urban radio networks, birthed a new genre of popular dance music that heavily influenced U.S.-based *música andina: cumbia andina*, or as it is more commonly referred to, *chi-cha*.[28] For Andean migrants and their children, this new musical formation sounded the multilocatedness and displacement of indigenous migrant life in Lima's urban *pueblos jóvenes*: for example, chicha lyrics often move between Quechua and Spanish, and incorporate distinct patterns of speech and song. Rhythmic and singing patterns within the genre enact intermittently awkward and seamless shifts between coastal and highland styles, locations, and temporalities, while also articulating distinctly pan-Andean musicking practices.

For the musicians who would later migrate to the United States to form the Andean music industry, chicha was often the music of their childhood, and its grassroots popularization in many ways served as a model for U.S.-based Andean street performance. First, other than public radio, many of the venues crucial to chicha's diffusion were spontaneously configured and emphemeral: *chichadromos*, or parties organized in makeshift public places including parks and soccer stadiums, and *asados* and *polladas*—"house parties in which each attendee contributes to a cause with the amount of money that they can afford to contribute."[29] Often, these instances required a collaborative reoccupation of government or public property, and were occasions when leisure time and work time (making music and making money) were strategically combined. Next, in contradistinction to regionalized traditions such as *huanyo huancaino* that sound provincial pride and belonging via highly localized rhythmic, instrumental, and lyrical expressions, chicha is an unapologetically hybrid cultural form. Rather than appeal to regional sentimentalities, chicha's musicality and lyrics embody pan-Andean aesthetic expressions of and affective responses to racial-colonial modes of displacement and devaluation.

Carlos Lara Yupanqui, a founding member of Markahuasi, was among this generation of indigenous Andean youth born in the highlands and raised in Lima's *pueblos jovenes*. His parents migrated to the capitol when he was a toddler, joining fellow *huancaino* migrants in a squatter's camp located in the city's ever-extending outskirts. It was there, amid the soundwaves that foretold the transformation of highland song into urban chicha, and migrant settlements into permanent neighborhoods, that Lara Yupanqui's love of music was born. "My parents always listened to folklore on the radio, and I began to like it," he recalls.[30] Lara Yupanqui was particularly taken with *los vientos*—the woodwinds—that sounded the melodic narrative of Andean song. At the age of six or seven, he fashioned his first *quena* from that which was available in his emergent coastal *barrio*—salvaged PVC piping.

Lara Yupanqui became active in the youth pan-Andean folklore scene of greater Lima in the late 1970s. By the age of twelve, he had mastered the *quena* and *zampoña*, and began performing at grassroots venues throughout the capital. "We were invited to play in different places . . . *polladas* . . . schools . . . to play for the laboring class, supporting the workers. We played at the leftist party's protests, union events. That's why our group was called Liberation."[31] Following the rise of political repression in the wake of the Sendero Luminoso (the Shining Path), Lara Yupanqui migrated to Ecuador at the urging of his parents, who feared that the association between Andean folklore, leftist politics, and unionism put Lara at risk. There he would spend several years honing his craft before traveling to Colombia, where he would meet fellow Markahuasi member Freddy Franco.

Franco, an Afro-mestizo university student in Cali, Colombia, was active in leftist politics and the Nueva Canción movement. His musical repertoire included South American folklore as well as Cuban Nueva Trova, música tropical, and other African diasporic musics. Franco's instrumental expertise included Andean guitar, *charango*, and *tiple* as well as vocals.[32] The two paired up to become migrant minstrels, busking in public squares, parks, and other urban centers as they wended their way northward through Central America. On arriving in Antigua, Guatemala, they met Peruvian brothers Carlos and José Hilario, the former also an expert in *vientos*, and the later a charanguista.[33] It was there, in 1987, that Grupo Markahuasi was founded. Like most Andean music groups that would come to perform in the United States, Markahuasi was established in transit, at the geohistorical crossroads of grassroots musical activism, hemispheric aesthetic exploration, and regional economic necessity.

From the aesthetic innovations of Andean fusion, to the political sensibilities of Nueva Canción, to the economic success of world music, the longer history of transnational and transregional musical circulation and indigenous migration both literally and figuratively sets the stage for the creation and entrenchment of the U.S.-based Andean music industry. I now turn from a discussion of the socioeconomic forces that shaped its creation to a reading of the sociosonic work that it performed, giving particular attention to how this world music formation both responded to and at times challenged overlapping processes of colonial and capitalist violence and displacement in the indigenous Andes.

THE ANDEAN MUSIC INDUSTRY AND THE URBAN CITYSCAPE

A geohistorical reading of the Andean music industry as a unique spatio-sonic formation that straddles aesthetic inspiration and political commit-ment, geographic situatedness and multiscalarity, creative innovation and economic success, calls forth important questions regarding contemporary relations of world musicking. At a moment of U.S. crisis in capital accu-mulation and a concomitant surge in legal and extralegal anti-immigrant revanchism, how might we read the political significance of this perfor-mance geography of cultural and economic (re)production? How does the circuitous development of the Andean music industry trouble linear narra-tives of musical globalization and the decline of "authentic" sonic cultures? And finally, what kind of model does the Andean music industry offer for thinking through Latina/o cultural politics in the United States as a "mi-nor transnational" response to the significant economic, legal, and ideo-logical violence of globalization at the scale of the global Southern nation *and* the urban northern metropole?[34] To explore this set of related ques-tions, this section focuses on the nexus of sociospatial relations that over-determined a single vital site on the Andean musical circuit: San Francisco's Union Square. Local skirmishes over the appropriation of this public venue illustrate both the immediate and broader contexts of state-sponsored nativ-ism, capitalist exploitation, and cultural contest that have shaped the AMI's formation.

Located less than a city block from the Powell Street cable car turn-around—a must-see for any tourist—Union Square marks the intersection of San Francisco's hotel, shopping, and financial districts, and is easily acces-sible both by Bay Area public transport and, with the advent of a new super-sized underground parking lot, by car. The expansive plaza setting of stone terraces and manicured promenades, coupled with the year-round tourist traffic that the square attracts, makes it an ideal spot for street perform-ers to busk for tips and sell recordings. Consequently, in the early to mid-1990s, Union Square became "the place to play" for dozens of Andean music bands. On Wednesday through Sunday, during the summer and Christmas

2.1 The band Markahuasi. Photo by Alejandro Stuart.

seasons, more than a half-dozen bands appropriated the designated public space of the historic square to serve as a site of cultural (re)production that encompassed both making music and making money.

Markahuasi (figure 2.1) was among the first of roughly twenty Andean folk bands to exploit the plaza as a key performance venue. Inspired by the increased international popularity of "world" music, its members—boasting artistic backgrounds ranging from Andean chicha to *música latinoamericana* to Caribbean cumbia to modern rock—had migrated from their respective countries to the global North to pursue a professional musical career. On coming together in Guatemala, the band's four founding members collectively set their sights on establishing themselves in the United States. Following their arrival in 1988—following several perilous border crossings— they teamed up with other freelance musicians with whom they had crossed paths at various points in Central America and the U.S. Southwest: Peruvian guitarist Argurio Buendía, and U.S.-born musician Andrew Taher who was raised in Chile. After a brief stint in Colorado the band took up residence in San Francisco, California. The city's robust, perennial tourist industry and

2.2 Markahuasi vending table. Photo by the author.

mild climate made it an ideal location for Markahuasi to launch their career as street performers.[35]

Similar to the culture of performance that popularized Andean chicha in urban Lima, the AMI's stages were most often improvisational, made possible by temporary, strategic appropriations of public space. Venues were constructed day by day on street corners in San Francisco's commercial districts, and consisted of elements that could easily be stored in a cargo van—a small table (figure 2.2), a transportable generator-fed amplification system, and instruments. Able to be erected or dismantled at a moment's notice, this portable commercial and artistic outfit allowed bands the mobility and flexibility necessary to accommodate fluctuations in weather conditions and the instability of foot traffic, while granting them access to diverse consumer crowds. More important, this improvisational method of staging enabled the industry's many undocumented workers to maneuver potential incursions by police or immigration officials.

Although street busking eked out enough money to support musicians' bare necessities, commercial success for groups like Markahuasi only began with the retail sale of sound recordings to audience members and passers-by during public performances. In keeping with the "do-it-yourself" logic of the industry, these albums were self-produced and self-published, purchased on an as-needed basis from small-scale recording reproducers. The remarkable ascendancy of recording sales posed a new dilemma for AMI artists: should industry musicians pursue the corporate sponsorship of the world music labels that sought to recruit them, or should they retain control over the production process? Like most of the bands that comprised the Andean music industry, Markahuasi chose the latter option. Maintaining artistic control over recording production and distribution arguably benefited the industry both financially and artistically: not only did the musicians retain the rights and profits from their recordings, but their independence enabled them to contract informally with experienced studio technicians worldwide who specialized in producing and mixing Andean instruments such as the *siku, kena,* and *charango.*

Interestingly, the rise of self-produced album sales signaled yet another moment in which the Andean music industries experienced a form of worlding that operated counter to and in conjunction with that of the world music industry. In order to retain both independence and specialization, the AMI necessarily came to function across geographic scales: while musical production and performance sites remained locally based, the recording and sales through which groups and group members reproduced themselves depended on decentralized processes of production and transnational economic and cultural relationships. It was not uncommon for a recording session taking place in Bolivia, featuring invitational musicians from across the globe, to provide the raw materials for a recording that would be produced and sold in the United States. These finished recordings were then distributed through highly localized nascent informal economic circuits such as Union Square. These worlded musical commodities wend their way back to South America as well: more than once, I have spotted bootleg recordings of popular AMI bands in Lima's downtown pirate markets, and I suspect that these are readily available in other urban centers throughout the region.

With the advent of independent recordings, informal public performances became more, rather than less, crucial to the industry's success. The street corner, subway station, and public square that were once interim busking venues were reestablished as permanent staging grounds for the advertisement and sale of compact discs and cassettes (see figure 2.2). Key to AMI tactics was this practice of sonic transposition—specifically, the leveraging of "public" space as beyond the domains of private and commercial control. For example, the intervention of industry musicians into the historic and commercial landscape of Union Square strategically leveraged the city plaza's intended purpose as a liminally public zone through which to funnel the throngs of commercial traffic visiting the highly concentrated commercial properties of San Francisco's downtown. Unlike the surrounding sidewalks and street corners—where individual businesses in adjacent

2.3 Carlos Lara. Photo by the author.

storefronts can (and do) exert the authority of property to evict panhandlers, the homeless, or busking musicians—the square's delineation as a "public" space allowed Andean bands access to a socioeconomic constituency that the combined effects of racism, urban segregation, and increased gentrification had previously made entirely inaccessible.

At the same time, the appropriation of Union Square by indigenous immigrants from the global South signaled a strategic subversion of the nationalist-capitalist project in which plaza is embedded, and of which it is a product. The ideological function of this historic downtown plaza is to provide a central vantage point from which the pedestrian onlooker—tourist and resident alike—can admire the ostensible grandeur of San Francisco's downtown—a display of the concentrated wealth and power of this increasingly white and upper-middle-class city. By converting the plaza into a makeshift stage, Andean bands subverted this icon of the urban cityscape by threatening its stringent racial and class orders; while poor people of color constitute a crucial segment of the downtown San Francisco workforce, those who carry out the city's reproductive labor are intended to remain invisible. This unmediated display of embodied and sonic "otherness" threatened the coherence of the square's representational function by converting it into a spectacle of work and play for a population upon whose concealed labor the economic foundations of California's wealth largely depend: undocumented migrant workers from the global South.

"URBAN CLEANSING" IN UNION SQUARE

The social vulnerabilities and political stakes that shaped the AMI's ongoing improvisational staging tactics are best understood in the context of the particular public discourses and socioeconomic trends that structured California politics during the 1990s. As Ruth Wilson Gilmore has persuasively argued, the California "racial state" has managed ongoing crises in capital accumulation over the last several decades through the deployment of state- and war-making tactics that have contained, isolated, and abandoned poor communities of color.[36] The militarization of the U.S./Mexican border, the passage of California Propositions 187 and 227, and the burgeoning carceral industry are among the numerous state projects that dramatically constrained the sociospatial mobility of California's immigrant populations by designating the state's classrooms, hospitals, workplaces, and social service offices as serving English-speaking, middle-class white citizens only.[37] The implementation of these California-based policies in turn generated a new national paradigm for the racialized resolution of a perceived crisis: the unprecedented waves of Latin American immigration to the United States that resulted from the aforementioned global-economic restructuring at national and international scales and its attendant military and political violence.

Articulated through foreign, national, and state policy and through public discourse, these interconnected racial projects operated in tandem with socioeconomic restructuring strategies implemented on local scales.[38] At the same time public policy and the private market conspired against the working and nonworking poor of urban city environments in a campaign of "unabashed revanchism" scripted by "a race/class/gender terror felt by middle and ruling class whites."[39] Such projects of raced and classed urban management can be readily observed in the political skirmishes between state authorities and immigrant artists that took place throughout San Francisco in the 1990s. Faced with the increased visibility of merchant communities of color within its commercial and representational core, the city sought to revamp its urban center, calling upon the coercive capacities of its local and state police units to forcibly eject the casualties of California's racialized economic warfare.

In Union Square, this process of "urban cleansing" gained particular traction in the wake of the Silicon Valley boom, as business owners and policymakers conspired with local police to prevent Andean bands and other "unlicensed" musician-merchants from playing music or selling re-cordings in the downtown area. The battle to evict the city's street musi-cians first began with the local San Francisco Police Department issuing buskers citations for selling CDs and cassettes without a permit. Penalties for this infraction not only included a hefty fine, but also the confiscation of recordings and sound equipment, and occasionally even arrest. Andean music industry musicians responded to this clampdown by petitioning the city for vendors' licenses in order to semiformalize their cultural-economic endeavor. While these permits did provide industry musicians with nomi-nal property and commercial protections, they did not extend permission to conduct commercial transactions in the Union Square venue. Thus, in order to remain in the square, Markahuasi and other AMI players developed less conspicuous modes of promoting their cassettes and CDs, such as em-ploying crowd-roving vendors and concealing merchandise in nondescript cardboard boxes.

When the "unlawful business" citations failed to effectively impede An-dean musicians' performance in Union Square, local business owners and city officials resorted to other means of hindering the musical project. On several occasions, immigration officials were called to investigate the "legal status" of the AMI musicians. While these spontaneous immigration raids threatened the socioeconomic viability of the Andean music industry's San Francisco base—not to mention the individual welfare of its participants—regular performances in Union Square persisted, with a band often installed at each of the square's four corners. The Andean music industry continued to thrive in San Francisco for at least six summer and holiday seasons.

Local efforts to dismantle this project, however, were unremitting. In 1994 the city launched a new and more effective plan of attack: the intro-duction of a decibel ordinance that prohibited amplified sound in Union Square. Although efforts to leverage municipal business codes as a means of ousting the musicians from the public square had previously failed, the decibel ordinance provided a targeted institutional means to silence AMI performance. Without amplification, the surrounding cacophony of crowds, city traffic, and public transport completely overwhelmed the acoustic string and wind instruments. This effectively disabled the musicians' ability to communicate with the public and, consequently, to successfully promote their recordings. Although bands initially ignored the decibel restrictions, perpetual confrontations with the local San Francisco Police Department became increasingly difficult to withstand: while unlawful business citations were possible to circumvent, twin 2.5 foot Bose speakers, dozens of yards of electrical cable, and a fifty-pound generator were difficult to conceal and impossible to quickly transport, thus making the Andean bands a conspicuous police target and, eventually, driving them out of the square altogether.

The loss of Union Square as a performance venue had a severe impact on the ability of Andean music groups to survive the ever-increasing cost of living in San Francisco between festival seasons.[40] As the industry's stronghold in the Bay Area region suffered decline, the majority of locally based bands relocated to urban centers in the neighboring Southwest region. Through the early 2000s, migrant Andean musicians continued to engage in similar localized struggles over the strategic appropriation of public places in commercial sites such as San Antonio's Riverwalk, Old Town Albuquerque, and the Santa Fe Plaza.

VIRTUAL NETWORKS

By the late 1990s, the commercial success of AMI street performance began to wane, thus requiring musicians to adopt new strategies for album promotion and sales. Consequently, the Internet has become an increasingly crucial site for the continued construction and reproduction of AMI networks. Websites such as the Asociación Internacional de Músicos Andinos (AIMA) generated virtual public locales that link industry musicians throughout the Andean diaspora—both within urban centers such as Lima and La Paz and throughout the United States, Europe, and Asia. The AIMA featured a free bulletin board for freelance musicians to connect with operating bands or other musicians interested in founding a musical group. Additionally, the site contained multiple links and forums dedicated to the discussion of aesthetic trends, musical technology, and popular performance venues throughout the United States and Europe.

An interesting commercial twist that emerged within AMI virtual networks was the mass-produced "Music of the Andes" CD—a prerecorded album available for order at wholesale prices with uniquely tailored album jackets by any individual or band.[41] In some ways, the manufacture and distribution of these recordings replicate dominant world music industry structures in that they emplace segmented relations between recording artists, sound brokers, and consuming audiences. Designed to compete with world music compilations produced by corporate enterprises such as Putumayo, these aesthetically abstract and materially abstracted musical commodities have enabled AMI musicians who have yet to record to launch their performance-based careers. However, these commercially driven compilations most often feature pirated tracks lifted from other artists, or contracted recording sessions endeavored by global Southern wholesalers who pay poor musicians a flat fee to record popular Andean folk songs. Paradoxically, then, the "music of the Andes" CD expands employment opportunities for Andean migrant musicians in the global North, but at the expense of further entrenching the exploitation of poor indigenous artists in the global South. Moreover, while the successful promotion of these albums via AMI performance networks hinges heavily upon the musician's ability to perform for audiences an ostensibly (and not unproblematic) "unmediated," or "authentic" interaction with Andean music and culture, these encounters ironically depend upon the inability of U.S. audiences to capture the heterogeneity of indigenous Andean instrumentation, genre, and aesthetics.

Like the advent of world music then, contemporary Andean fusion is both an expression of and force within overlapping histories of transnational and transregional musical conflict and conversation; however, its globalization has not occurred via conventional world music industry's circuits. Rather, Andean fusion has been popularized on quotidian, improvisational stages and commercialized through nonconventional musician-based networks. Thus, as a performance geography, the AMI offers both an example of and model for modes of world musicking that confront, exploit, and even resist the constraints of dominant cultural bureaucracies.

The AMI's capacity to survive throughout dispersed physical and virtual locales has in no small part depended upon the political and economic relationships that emerged from the industry's struggle to reproduce itself in urban centers such as the San Francisco Bay Area. Despite the stiff competition among San Francisco's Andean bands, the industry's overall survival relied upon collaboration: exchanging festival contacts, sharing stylistic and technological innovations, and providing legal and practical information and updates vital to the security of undocumented performers. In the process of collectively converting public spaces of capital into contingently oppositional performance venues, the resulting network of relations established through the industry's entrenchment also enabled the emergence of a new spatiocultural formation: a diasporic pan-Andean community. Defined by its linguistic and aesthetic heterogeneity as well as by its grassroots economic logic, this pan-Andean community was structured through the invocation of a displaced homeland—the Andes—reimagined in the global North as a site of collective political affiliation.

RACE, GENDER, AND PLACE MAKING

I am in no way suggesting that the U.S.-based Andean musical community is idyllic or utopian. This grassroots industry was not immune to conflict and contradiction, and like all forms of collectivity, its construction has been accompanied by troubling forms of exclusion. It is to a brief discussion of the relations of power and difference replicated by the industry's institutional and aesthetic structures that I now turn.

The employment structure within the U.S.-based AMI is generally organized according to a gendered division of labor in which men perform the creative/aesthetic labor (public performance, set development, musical composition, etc.), while women perform reproductive and wage labor (technical and administrative tasks such as booking and maintaining a performance schedule, setting up and tearing down sets, driving, and managing recording sales). Interestingly, Andean music industry bands have primarily collaborated with U.S.-born, Spanish-speaking Latina and white women. Within industry circles, these women have come to be known as Las Malinches, a reference to the eponymous Mexican historical figure archived for her apocryphal role in facilitating Spanish imperial expansion in the New World.[42] The raced, gendered, and sexualized discourses that constitute Malinche as the symbolic sexual traitor exploited in the service of colonial expansion offer a lexicon for rationalizing the exploitation of women—particularly women of color, by the contemporary Andean music industry. Moreover, in situating the relationship between Andean male musicians and female employees within a discourse of empire, Las Malinches are invoked as a point of counterposition for the decolonizing male subject's masculinist assertion of his right to be "here because you were there," eliding the complex and uneven gendered modalities through which racial and colonial violence are enacted and experienced.

The racial politics of the Andean music scene are equally messy and complex. Appealing to the emergent global music constituency has often required, or at least included, the strategic exploitation of racialized stereotypes of "Indian-ness" that do not necessarily reflect the ethnic or regional identification of musical performers and/or the songs that they perform. Moreover, the promotion of Andean music as "Indian" music serves to flatten the cultural and linguistic heterogeneity of Andean-descended communities while effectively obfuscating the Afro-Andean origins of many of the industry's most popular songs.[43] Thus, while the creation of a pan-indigenous community contests many of the national ethnic divides within Peruvian, Bolivian, and Ecuadorian indigenous politics, it likewise risks the resurrection of the monolithic notions of race and culture through which Black and indigenous cultural production in Latin America have most often been understood. Pan-Indian claims of authenticity signified through long hair and colorful woven vests invoke a commercial notion of indigeneity that may provide for a strategic erosion of the codified lines between *mestizo*, *cholo*, and *indio*; nonetheless such claims fail to acknowledge the shifting, complex racial and cultural history within Andean geographies, thus affirming the disconcerting ahistorical binary between what constitutes "Black" or "Indian." As I argue elsewhere, these racist and sexist nationalist stagings of Andean music as equivalent to "Peruvian music" or "Bolivian music" are far from monolithic—indeed, as I discuss in the subsequent chapter, they have been troubled by contemporary Afroperuanismo and the internationalization of Afroperuanidad.

WENDY SULCA: "LA ESTRELLITA DE YOUTUBE"

Since the early 2000s, U.S.-based geographies of Andean street performance have all but disappeared, owed to factors ranging from the increased policing of unlicensed street performance and sales, to the physical strain of perpetual pageantry, to the perils of undocumented travel, to a global decline in physical storage formats such as cassettes and CDs.[44] With the advent of the digital revolution, the Andean music industry, like other recording industry regimes, has experienced nothing short of a revolution in relations of sonic production, distribution, and consumption. New media technologies such as digital storage formats, global file sharing platforms, and social networking sites have prompted a transformation in the AMI's gendered structures of sonic labor, the proliferation of new aesthetic trends, the emergence of reverse modes of sonic appropriation, and the establishment of virtual performance geographies. In Peru—a continental center of digital piracy distribution in the Americas—access to recording hardware and software has become increasingly widespread, enabling unsigned artists to launch their careers via self-produced *clips*: audiovisual recordings that can be uploaded to multimedia websites such as YouTube and Instagram.[45] These grassroots methods of staging and self-promotion within regional and international virtual spheres have enabled the catapulting of musical careers among classes of artists conventionally constrained by raced and gendered conventions of physical and social mobility. The decade-long career of indigenous Andean artist Wendy Sulca Quispe (figure 2.4) represents a noteworthy example of these shifts; an international phenomenon, Sulca's rise to fame was enabled by the AMI's emergent, South American–based online networks, which are now sustained virtually through the itinerant transfer of files via email, blogs, social media, search engines, and video-sharing platforms.

In 2005, eight-year-old singer Wendy Sulca Quispe made her Internet debut on YouTube—a website that at that time neither she nor her mother, Lidia Quispe, had ever visited. The idea to promote Sulca via virtual networks was born several months earlier, when the child artist participated in a youth talent contest sponsored by renowned Andean chanteuse Sonia Morales, "La Reina del Huayno con Arpa" (The Queen of Huayno with Harp).[46] Sulca's parents, also musicians, were extremely supportive of their daughter's love of singing, and hoped that the competition would earn her some professional exposure and seasoning if not the grand prize of a studio recording contract. It was at that event that Wendy's mother, Lidia Quispe, was first approached by a producer of *videos caseros*—self-produced amateur videos that are sold by media hawkers in marketplaces throughout greater Lima. The music producer affirmed Sulca's raw talent and proposed creating a promotional video to showcase her work.

Quispe was intrigued by the proposition, but as a recently widowed single mother employed at a stuffed toy factory, the funding of such a project

2.4 Wendy Sulca.
Photo by Juan Ignacio Iglesias.

presented a serious financial challenge. With the help of friends and family, Quispe set out to raise money for Wendy's musical pursuits by organizing a series of *polladas*. With the funds earned from the first event, she purchased fabric, boning, and notions and spent her spare hours hand-sewing Wendy a *pollera*—a knee-length skirt layered over multiple petticoats worn by indigenous women throughout the Andes. She then composed original lyrics for her daughter's promotional single based on a topic that some have dubbed controversial: Wendy's love of breastfeeding as a toddler. Following a second successful fundraiser, the filming date was arranged. With the musical accompaniment of her teenage cousins on electric harp, bass, and drums, Wendy's inaugural *clip* (music video), "La tetita" (The little breast) was filmed in a single afternoon in her parents' home department of Ayacucho.[47]

Wholesale video reproduction—widely available throughout Lima for twenty-five to thirty cents on the dollar—is a common promotional tool used by aspiring Peruvian musicians because units can be produced in small batches to be sold on consignment in public markets. The music producer that worked with Quispe, however, convinced her to pay an additional 260 soles (around seventy-five dollars or two months' full-time salary for a sixty-hour work week) to upload the clip to YouTube. Denizens of the *cerros* of San Juan de Miraflores, a *pueblo joven* in the outskirts of Lima, the Quispe Sulca family did not have a computer in their modest three-room home.[48] Thus, though the video was an immediate virtual sensation, it was not until several weeks later that Wendy learned of her rising YouTube popularity from her classmates. Inspired by this newfound fan base, Sulca released two more original clips shortly thereafter, "Papito por qué me dejaste" and "Cerveza, cerveza."[49] Within a year, Wendy Sulca's clips received more than ten million hits on YouTube, rivaling the popularity of crossover artists such as Shakira.[50]

Though "La tetita" received noteworthy international attention, its reception was decidedly mixed; while her fans were quick to declare Sulca a child prodigy, her critics mocked the clip's visual content, lyrics, and her piercing vocal register.[51] The latter of these responses, which have largely been concentrated outside of South America, is not surprising. The campy aesthetics, vocal acrobatics, and synthesized sound of contemporary Andean fusion no doubt departs from the nostalgic imperial fantasies of those who crave the consumption of what they envision "traditional" Andean music to be: unplugged, instrumental, "ethereal," and so on. These imaginaries have no doubt been shaped by the sounds that have circulated through AMI networks throughout the United States, Europe, and Canada since the late 1960s; as I have previously argued, these musical currents arose at the intersection of folkloric revival movements within South American urban centers embraced by both displaced Andeans and working- and middle-class mestizos engaged in labor, socialist, and anti-imperialist activism. Sulca's early work departs from these AMI aesthetic trends in several ways: it eschews revival politics in favor of experimentation with local diasporic trends; it engages in communal rather than individual modes of storytelling; it embraces the arduous, ugly, and controversial aspects of quotidian indigenous life in Lima over idyllic depictions of life in *la sierra*; and it employs carnivalesque forms of visual and textual humor to subvert audience expectations and, in some cases, to contest social ideals.[52] As Peruvian anthropologist and DJ Alfredo Villar notes, "sus códigos parecen peruanos, pero están atravesados por elementos occidentales que son pervertidos constantemente con una irreverencia y un sentido de humor" (her codes seem Peruvian, but they are crossed with Western elements that are constantly perverted with irreverence and a sense of humor).[53] Analyzed through a lens attentive to Villar's insights and the above-mentioned innovations, Quispe's lyrics and Sulca's performance of "La tetita" can be read as an intergenerational feminist critique of the (inter)national pathologization of indigenous maternity and reproductivity.[54]

"La tetita," described by one journalist as "[un] homenaj[e] al seno materno" (an homage to the maternal breast), opens with a pan of a boutique toyshop, where Wendy sits surrounded by plush animals. Perhaps these stuffed creatures represent the fruits of Lidia Quispe's low-wage labor in the toy factory or, more generally, the perilous, undercompensated work performed by hundreds of thousands of indigenous women in factories throughout Lima. Or possibly it depicts the absurdity of Western notions of an idyllic childhood rooted in practices of capitalist consumption. It is here, in the starkly white marble toy salon that we are introduced via a radioesque emcee to "la pequeña Wendy," the singer and protagonist of the clip. As the music begins, the video alternates between shots of Wendy whimsically dancing amid pastoral landscapes, and indigenous babies and children suckling at their mother's breasts. Commencing with the spoken dedication, "Con mucho cariño para todos los niños del Perú" (With much love, to all of the children of Peru), Wendy begins to sing in the upper register soprano conventional among Andean female vocalists:

De día, de noche
quisiera tomar mi tetita
de día, de noche
quisiera tomar mi tetita

Cada vez que la veo a mi mamita
me está provocando con su tetita
Cada vez que la veo a mi mamita
me está provocando con su tetita

Ricoricoricorico, que rico es mi tetita
mmm! rico!! que rico es mi tetita . . .

From day to night
I would like to suckle my *tetita*
From day to night
I would like to suckle my *tetita*

Each time I see my *mamita*
I crave her little breast
Each time I see my *mamita*
I crave her little breast

Delicious! How delicious my *tetita is* mmm!

Delicious! How delicious is my *tetita*

A song about breastfeeding may seem an odd debut choice for an aspiring child musician, but the polemics that inform this catchy if kitschy tune are significant and complex. "La tetita" was inspired by Wendy's resistance to give up breastfeeding as a four-year-old child. In an interview with *Rolling Stone Argentina*, Sulca relayed: "Yo era una niña [de cuatro años] y la perseguía a mi mamá para que me la dé" (I was a [four-year-old] child and I pestered my mom so that she would give me the breast).[55] Here "La tetita," stages and sounds a carnivalesque audiovisual narrative about public breastfeeding that both invokes and inverts dominant symbols of indigenous maternity and, concomitantly, condemns attendant practices of state-sanctioned raced and gendered violence against Andean communities.

The "Andeanization" of Lima that peaked in the 1980s fueled a conservative backlash among middle- and upper-class criollos that viewed *campesino* migrants (indigenous peasants) such as Sulca's parents as uncivilized and undesirable. State actors and policy pundits responded to this population influx with draconian measures, including the widespread implementation of oral and surgical sterilization campaigns; these targeted low-income indigenous and Black women, whose reproductive bodies were designated a threat to national development and international mobility. Between 1996 and 2000 alone, anthropologist Kimberly Theidon estimates that an estimated 270,000 women were subject to enforced sterilizations, enacted under the guise of "family planning."[56] These punitive state practices were publically legitimated by and promoted through the tropic representation of indigenous maternity as deviant and indigenous kinship structures as pathological. Specifically, mainstream popular cultural and media outlets commonly depicted indigenous women as "bad mothers" whose "out of control" reproduction fueled intergenerational cycles of poverty and ultimately, national "underdevelopment." The quintessential image of this aberrant maternal figure is the impoverished migrant *campesina*; bucking gendered codes of public modesty and decorum, she is most often depicted as a street beggar who breastfeeds her brood well beyond an "appropriate" age because she cannot afford to buy food or milk. At once a bad mother, a failed consumer, and an unassimilable migrant, this figure of the deviant *madre campesina* sutures multiscalar tensions around national belonging, urban development, and racial hegemony.

If we are to situate Sulca's text within the geohistorical context of its elaboration, "La tetita" can be alternatively read as an indictment of the state-sanctioned annihilation of indigenous kinship structures and cultural practices of mothering. While in the popular press the public breastfeeding of toddlers and children is depicted as a mode of depraved mothering, "La tetita" reorients the practice as an intentional and desirable mode of childrearing. In an interview from 2010 with *Rolling Stone Argentina*, Sulca, then fourteen, spoke eloquently of her commitment to portraying controversial social issues from an indigenous perspective: "I don't only sing about my life, I sing about the lives of other people, for the young and old, for children who love their mothers, for children who have no father, either because he has passed, or their parents have divorced, or he has abandoned the family, or in 'Cerveza, Cerveza,' the story of someone who works in a dark place like a mine, who lost their love or their baby and to forget what they are suffering through, or have suffered, they drink beer. Really, I want people to take my music seriously."[57] Sulca, now twenty, continues to prioritize realist portrayals of Peru's indigenous *cerranos* in her work. But she has also begun to explore new modes of sonic expression—in particular, through appropriations of U.S. pop. Over the past two years, Sulca has released unlicensed bilingual covers of Madonna's "Like a Virgin" and Miley Cyrus's "Wrecking Ball" on YouTube. Both have received hundreds of thousands of views, and are arguably consumed in no small part owed to the pleasure that the consuming texts that invert typical relations of musical appropriation brings to her loyal fan base. And both Wendy and Lidia are now very active on social media, the latter providing daily updates on Facebook, Instagram, Twitter, and YouTube.

As Wendy Sulca's career dramatically illustrates, the advent of new media platforms and the subsequent digitalization of Andean music industry networks have engendered important shifts in the raced, gendered, and economic relations that constitute contemporary South American musical transits. On the one hand, nonconventional methods of staging and self-promotion within web-based domains has enabled classes of artists whose social and spatial mobility has historically been constrained to access new listening publics and, in some cases, establish professional musical careers. On the other hand, the work of curation, publicity, and distribution has been relocated to quotidian sites of encounter and exchange; in a dramatic departure from the U.S. world music industry standards that have enriched Dan Storper and global Northern entrepreneurs of his ilk, the sale of video clips and CDs by artists such as Wendy Sulca occurs within the piracy markets and vendor stalls staffed and patronized by Lima's working and non-working poor. These sites of musical encounter serve to publicize emergent artists and cultivate fan bases which, in turn, fuel commercial success on virtual platforms such as YouTube channels. In short, the contemporary Andean music industry represents a model of musical circulation that continues to eschew individualistic notions of authorship, property, and value in favor of pirated production, open file sharing, and other extralegal networked practices of sonic popularization

CODA

A pan-indigenous immigrant collectivity sustained through informal economic networks, nonconventional staging practices, and self-directed cultural production, the AMI is a world music performance geography that both exploits and exceeds dominant global music industry relations. Its unique relations of culture and capital both index and confront socioeconomic constraints experienced by indigenous immigrant musicians within regional and international contexts and at multiple scales. In the realm of quotidian cultural and economic reproduction, U.S.-based AMI networks have generated steady employment within a largely undocumented, non-English-speaking community constrained by California's nativist social policies. Contemporary virtual AMI networks have further democratized gendered access to listening publics, while likewise enabling (inter)national platforms for political dialogue and artistic exchange. In doing so, the AMI can be read as a dynamic performance geography that consistently defies the enforced homogeneity and neocolonial mediation of the global music industry regimes via the emplacement of novel modes of popularization. Moreover, by offering a diasporic regional affiliation rather than a national identification, this musical project responds to the problematic tendency within Andean nations such as Peru to assert a nationalist claim over regional folkloric traditions while failing to address state complicity in the production and sedimentation of racialized violence and death enacted upon indigenous communities.

In my discussion of the Andean music industry, I have argued for modes of cultural analysis that attend to the intersubjective politics of social and spatial emplacement. I have proposed a framework that conceptualizes globalized sonic production as historically and geographically situated as well as transient, dynamic, and contextual. In the case of this performance geography, such an approach reveals contradictions within dominant patterns of cultural globalization while highlighting how indigenous artists from the global South have seized upon such openings. In the midst of making music and making a living, whether on the streets of San Francisco or in the *cerros* of Ayacucho, AMI musicians have managed to create a delocalized place of their own—a networked community of political affiliation and economic franchise structured to promote rather than constrain the production and reproduction of everyday indigenous life at local, national, and international scales.

3

(INTER)NATIONAL STAGES, *MUJERES BRAVAS*, AND THE SPATIAL POLITICS OF DIASPORA

In the early 1980s, Afro-Peruvian artist Susana Baca sustained her faltering singing career by performing in the community soup kitchens of Lima's impoverished *pueblos jóvenes*.[1] In tribute to the devalued and undercompensated labors of her largely Black female audience, Baca's staple repertoire included a musical arrangement of "María Landó," a short poem coauthored by her lifelong friend and mentor Chabuca Granda and artist César Calvo.[2] With its stretched vocals, antiphonal lyrics, and suspended syncopation, the haunting ballad appropriately narrates the rhythmic drudgery of low and unwaged gendered work. Both homage to and a departure from the conventions of Peru's Black urban musical traditions, Baca's innovative "María Landó" earned her intermittent public accolades, particularly among her working-class women listeners, who "felt it was their anthem, their song."[3] Its popularity, however, failed to generate a recording contract, and the middle-aged crooner hardly anticipated that her quotidian battle song would one day enjoy international circulation.[4] Yet in 1996, following a chance encounter with pop star David Byrne, "María Landó" became the breakout hit of world music label Luaka Bop's award-winning compilation *The Soul of Black Peru*, reaching consumer audiences throughout Europe and North America.

Apart from Baca's headlined track, *The Soul of Black Peru* features a fairly predictable cross-generational, cross-genre collection of mid- to late twentieth-century Afro-Peruvian standards.[5] Nonetheless, the album earned considerable critical acclaim in the United States owed to its oft-proclaimed status as one of the first international releases of Black Peruvian music. For example, its self-congratulatory liner notes exclaim, "This is a secret music—a collection of beautiful songs and infectious grooves that's been hidden for years in the coastal towns and barrios of Peru . . . Black Peruvians? Yes, Peru was involved in the slave trade too—and this wonderful music is part of that legacy."[6] In this sense, the making of *Black Peru*, its promotion, subsequent success, and the resultant catapulting of Baca's career clearly rehearse the familiar raced and gendered tropes of world music origin stories: auspicious "discovery," careful "curation," and paternalistic "rescue." Perhaps less apparent, however—though equally troubling—is the extent to which this multiculturist project likewise recounts and emplaces dominant world music geographies. *Black Peru*, we are told, sounds a cartographic anomaly within chattel slavery's pan-American history, introducing to global Northern audiences the music of South America's Spanish-speaking Black Pacific.[7] Formerly absented from world music stages and "hidden" from international view, previously confined to the paltry venues of the urban "barrio," Afro-Peru's purported invisibility and improbability are the products of its own geographic provincialism, to be auspiciously remedied by world music's cosmopolitanism.

I open this chapter with a discussion of Susana Baca and *The Soul of Black Peru* as an entry point into the work that follows for two reasons. First, Luaka Bop's album illustrates the extent to which conventional world music narratives and culture industry structures consistently parochialize Afro-Peru and its soundscapes. Here and elsewhere, Black Peru is conjured and cast as a peripheral story and remote location in contrast to the presumably familiar, more cosmopolitan musical cultures of the Black Atlantic. These deceptive tropes offer a point of contrast against which an alternative geohistorical trajectory of Afro-Peru's contemporary cultural formation—the thematic subject of this essay—might be framed. For despite its claims, *The Soul of Black Peru*'s featured artists—such as Susana Baca, Cumanana, and Perú Negro—are not alienated cultural producers laboring in provincial isolation, but are in fact the progenitors of a popular musical movement born of and actualized at the global crossroads of Black internationalism, Pan-American anti-imperialism, and diasporic Black feminism.

Second, the historical and geographic erasures that *Black Peru*'s promotional materials enact also indicate broader trends often replicated in the very academic disciplines that are most poised to critique such omissions: Latin American cultural/sound studies and U.S.-based Black diaspora studies. Despite a proliferation of scholarship on Afro-diasporic cultures within both fields over the last several decades, academic attention to the African-descended populations concentrated throughout Latin America's Pacific coastline has been remarkably scant, particularly within the fields of ethnic, gender, and cultural studies.[8] In Peru, national scholarship on race, blackness, and Afroperuanidad has received little international circulation, and within the United States and Europe only a handful of books and articles on these subjects have been published.[9] So rare are transnational engagements with Afro-Peru, in fact, that renowned U.S. scholar of Black literary and cultural studies Henry Louis Gates Jr. recently revealed that his first encounter with "Black Peru" was in fact via *The Soul of Black Peru*. In *Black In Latin America*, the Harvard professor describes happening upon the album in a "world music" display at a Cambridge bookstore, recalling, "I'd never heard of Baca, but what surprised me more was that I'd never heard of 'Black Peru.'"[10] Gates's ironic yet revealing anecdote directs us toward a primary theoretical concern: the ongoing *provincialization* of Afro-Peru within both domestic and international sites of cultural encounter, social mobility, and academic knowledge production. Here and throughout, I employ the term "provincialization" to reference both the technologies and effects of the sociogeographic structures, discourses, and practices that have colluded to marginalize, contain, and disavow Afroperuanismo as a locally situated, yet transnationally oriented, diasporic cultural formation.

Against this tendency to treat Afro-Peruvian cultural production in general, and the work of Afroperuana artists such as Baca in particular, as anomalous, provincial, or inconsequential, this chapter charts a vibrant geohistory of Black women's cultural activism in Lima, Peru from the mid-twentieth century to the present. Combining the analytics and vocabularies of sound studies, critical race and gender studies, and feminist geography, it examines convergences within the transnational, cross-generational work of five Black women artists—U.S. dancer, choreographer, and anthropologist Katherine Dunham; Afro-Peruvian poet, folklorist and choreographer Victoria Santa Cruz; Afro-Peruvian singer and songwriter Susana Baca; and Afro-Peruvian percussionists Peta and Kata Robles. I argue that despite differences in content and form, and at times even approach and aspiration, their collective work as political activists and cultural producers can be understood as both formed by and formative of *performance geographies of Black feminist diasporicity*. Deploying a geocultural reading of their performance texts and pedagogical practices, I detail how artist-activists have mobilized spatialized expressive practices such as siting and staging, and spatial imaginaries such as "the coastal," "the Pacific," and "the Afro-diasporic" to advance deprovincialized manifestations of the historical continuities, transnational ties, and internationalist impulses that connect otherwise localized and specific stories of diasporic cultural formation in the Black Americas.

The geographies of political colloquy and communion imagined and activated by the above-mentioned Afroperuana artists are instructive for several reasons. First, they articulate powerful, nuanced critiques of and responses to the commonsense geographies of race, gender, and place that have physically and ideologically contained Black cultural production and political struggle in postcolonial, postmanumission América del Sur. By working across and against commonsense spatial divides such as "public" and "private," and scalar typologies such as the "*mestizo* nation" or the "Black Atlantic," these artists not only index and challenge the geographic technologies that enact their erasure, but also shift the relations of power and difference that inhere in their making. In this sense, their work can be seen to constitute a Black feminist performance geography of diasporicity. Next, they highlight important convergences among three sociocultural movements that are rarely coexamined: Peru's mid-century Black Arts Revival, Black liberation struggles in the U.S. and continental Africa, and internationalized forms of Latin American musical production such as Nueva Canción. In doing so, they not only amplify transatlantic mappings of the African diaspora; they also reveal a vital if neglected history of Afro-Latino participation in the region's pan-Americanist social movements of the 1960s–1970s. Finally, the contours of these Black feminist performance geographies effectively challenge and recalibrate the dominant racial-regional designs that most often inform popular and academic discourse on blackness and indigeneity in the Southern Americas, impelling novel forms of what Caribbean feminist VéVé Clark has dubbed "diaspora literacy"—that is, hermeneutics attentive to the palimpsestic meanings layered within popular cultural forms and practices that "supersede those of . . . Western or westernized signification."[11]

READING AND WRITING BLACK PERU

Afro-Peruvian artist Nicomedes Santa Cruz's poem *Ritmos Negros del Perú* registers a particular geopolitical moment within contemporary race relations in urban Peru. Beginning in the 1950s, African-descended artists and cultural workers responded to the ongoing provincialization of blackness within nationalist cultural imaginaries through the establishment of an artistic movement aimed at historicizing Peru's imbrication in the African slave trade, the expropriation of Black labor, and the endurance of oppositional expressive practices among the nation's coastal Black communities. The poem concludes with these lines:

Murieron los negros viejos
pero entre la caña seca
se escucha su zamacueca
y el panalivio muy lejos.
Y se escuchan los festejos
que cantó en su juventud.
De Cañete a Tombuctú,
De Chancay a Mozambique
llevan sus claros repiques
ritmos negros del Perú.

The old *negros* have died
But in between the dried-up cane
You can hear their *zamacueca*[12]
And from afar, their *panalivio*.[13]
And you can hear celebrations
That they sang in their youth
From Cañete to Timbuktu
From Chancay to Mozambique
You clearly hear their resonances
Black rhythms of Peru.

Over the past decade, a small cadre of U.S.-based scholars have published rich ethnographies detailing the lives and work of Afro-Peruvian artists and performers such as Santa Cruz. Two salient examples of this growing body of scholarship include the work of ethnomusicologists Javier León Quirós and Heidi Feldman.[14] In the much-acclaimed *Black Rhythms of Peru: Reviving African Musical Heritage in the Black Pacific*, Feldman charts how Afro-Peruvian artists "have *rescued* their own traditions from obscurity" by deploying what she calls "memory projects": social agendas that guide individuals or collectives to remember and/or memorialize particular aesthetic elements and cultural practices.[15] Each of the book's chapters examines how enmeshed interactions between Black artists and intellectuals, white *criollo* curators, and recording industry producers resulted in the creation of the competing memory projects that have together informed the "re-invent[ion of] Afro-Peruvian music and dance" in "rural and urban contexts in Peru as well as the international sphere."[16] While Feldman's carefully researched monograph offers a comprehensive, chronological survey of prominent "Afro-Peruvian revival" cultural workers active between the 1950s and 2000s, León Quirós's body of publications are more narrowly focused on recent (1990s–present) generations of Afro-Peruvian cultural producers.[17] Much of his published research addresses how contemporary professional musicians strategically negotiate their overlapping (and at times, contradictory) roles as "artists, academics, and cultural bearers" in order to "best maintain the musical legacy that they inherited from an earlier generation of individuals invested in the *rescue* of traditions, many of which were on the verge of being forgotten."[18] For León Quirós, this formidable endeavor has required Afro-Peruvian cultural workers to contend with the dialectics of tradition and innovation, marginalization and institutionalization, popularization, and cultural commodification.

This chapter builds upon this important body of work, yet diverges from its premises and conclusions in several significant ways. My field research in Peru, conducted over a period of eleven years (2003–14), led me to interview many of the same artists, attend many of the same peñas,[19] and pore over many of the same archives. Yet my interest in the mutually animating relationships between heteropatriarchal racial capitalist formation, spatial politics, and performance practices has occasioned the positing of different questions and the adoption and application of distinctive methods and frames. Drawing upon ethnomusicological literatures and vocabularies, the above-mentioned scholarship narrates twentieth-century Afro-Peruvian cultural institutionalization through the tropes of "obscurity," "loss," and "rescue," thereby privileging attention to continuity over dynamism and stasis over circulation.[20] Such an approach to the study of Black expressive cultures in the Americas is not uncommon, yet has garnered considerable criticism within the field of Black studies. As Cedric Robinson, among others, has persuasively argued, Western scripts concerning the political cultures and cultural politics of New World Africans most often emphasize the severing and dissolution of historical and cultural ties with the "Old World" continent.[21] In doing so, they instantiate a dissimulative tautology that at best elides and at worst disavows genealogies of Black radicalism in the Americas: if the African descended are a people without a history, they are a people without culture; and conversely, if they are a people without culture, they are foreclosed subjects of history.

Robinson's insights underscore the importance of deploying lenses of cultural inquiry that rather than presuming that the political history of Latin America's African descended is one of loss, capitulation, and assimilation are instead attentive to shifting conditions, strategies, and terrains of struggle. For if particular histories of Black resistance and radicalism have not or cannot be articulated within extant Western theoretical or disciplinary frames, this does not amount to their absence or failure, but rather, a need to rehone existing analytical toolboxes and geopolitical frames. As cultural historian Robin Kelley has argued, such a rehoning demands that we redefine "the political" by questioning "common ideas about what are 'authentic' movements and strategies of resistance" and by attending to those "hidden transcripts"—repertoires of political dissidence expressed in and through everyday cultural practices such as music, dance, and storytelling that are often invisible by design.[22]

Following this call for a turning toward "the margins" within Black studies research, contemporary theorizations of diaspora have offered a delocalized hemispheric analytic that, against statist attempts to fix the cultural within racial, national, or ethnic essences, emphasizes the salience of international and interregional networks of political dialogue, cultural exchange, and solidarity work among the African descended in the New World.[23] Of course, applications of diaspora within U.S.- and European-based Black studies scholarship in the Americas have been uneven, and in consequence have produced their own elisions or margins. Salient critiques of these omissions cohere around the prevailing circumscriptions that have commonly informed contemplations of Africa's diasporic cultures in the Americas: geographical circumscriptions, in that Black diaspora studies research has disproportionately focused on Atlantic-based circuits and urban centers in the global North; thematic circumscriptions, in terms of its tendency to focus on popular texts and expressive practices found in these locations; and conceptual circumscriptions, in terms of a disproportionate focus on educationally and or economically privileged English- or French-speaking male subjects in cosmopolitan urban centers.[24] In contrast, a diasporic approach to the study of Afro-Peru remains enabling, as it proffers an antiprovincial model of inquiry attentive to the dynamic, relational interplay of cultural flows, racial politics, and spatial formation that have taken place in both the margins of the Peruvian nation-state *and* the margins of Latina/o American and Black diaspora cultural studies scholarship.

As numerous historians of the postcolonial, postmanumission republic have demonstrated, ongoing structures of surveillance, containment, and unfreedom served to provincialize Afro-Peruvian cultural practices, such that prior to the 1950s these remained largely relegated to *marginalized spaces* such as the private or domestic sphere, and *marginalized modes of memorialization* such as oral tradition and intergenerational transmission.[25] Given this, this chapter eschews the narration of Peru's Black Arts Revival through the linear tropes of loss, rescue, and reinvention that commonly orient world(ed) musical inquiry. In lieu of offering an ethnomusicological assessment of what remains empirically "intact" or historically "endangered" within Afro-Peruvian cultural repertoires, it instead turns to these margins as crucial sites of political struggle, exploring how Revival artists and their epigones have engaged in protean, protracted battles over the emplacement of Black bodies and culture within dominant circuits of intellectual and aesthetic exchange. Specifically, it adopts a geographic lens to chart how, in distinctive historical moments and geographic contexts, Afro-Peruvian cultural workers have confronted gendered and classed forms of anti-Black racism through creative practices of sonic transposition.

GENDER, GEOGRAPHY, AND BLACK FEMINISM

It is nearly impossible to think the history of Black Peru without think-ing geographically. In the plain yet profound words of Black feminist geog-rapher Katherine McKittrick, "Black matters are spatial matters."[26] This is particularly true, she argues, of political geographies in the diaspora, which have been indelibly shaped by "racist paradigms of the past and their on-going hierarchical patterns."[27] Indeed, the making of the African diaspora in the Spanish colonies is a geographic story. Displacement from a ravaged homeland. Coerced migrations across sea and land. Ongoing captivity. Physical containment. Social immobilization. And the innumerable bru-tal, intimate violations made possible by divesting racialized bodies of legal or social personhood . . .[28] For centuries, Peru's African descended were subjected to these spatialized tactics of social differentiation and physical immobilization that materially instantiated and morally legitimated chat-tel slavery as part of Spanish colonial rule in the New World.[29] To this day, these "paradigms of the past" have successively accentuated the "ongoing hierarchical patterns" that have structured geographies of blackness in the postcolonial and postmanumission republic.[30] From discourses of embod-ied biocultural pathology, to state and extralegal practices of segregation within residential and labor markets, to outright debarment from physi-cal and social access to public resources and space, the sociogeographic management of Peru's African-descended has—as Afro-Peruvian artists, activists, and scholars have persistently argued—been a central feature of Peruvian national formation.[31] In return, domestic struggles against anti-Black racism have been animated by the strategic politicization and contest of inherent linkages between social immobility and spatial immobilization.

A central premise subtending this chapter, then, is that the geographic is a productive analytic for apprehending the dialectics of oppression and opposition that have shaped both the Black Americas generally, and Black Peru specifically. Its engagement with the spatial is informed by at least three related principles that commonly orient feminist, antiracist geographic in-quiry. The first of these principles stems from a central axiom of geographic theory: that space is constructed and dynamic rather than natural or fixed. From this, these geographers of difference have extrapolated that the logics and practices that undergird social processes of spatial organization—most particularly those that demarcate seemingly distinct places (from the body, to the home, to the nation) and/or that dichotomize different kinds of places (such as public and private, labor and leisure, or straight and queer) are inherently political, plural, and contested.[32] Ongoing struggles over *the place* (and *dis-placement*) of Black Peru within both domestic and international spatial imaginaries and geographic orders have figured as a defining preoccupation of Afro-Peruvian cultural labors and collective repertoires. As such, teasing out the geohistorical specificities of these constraints and responses to them is central to understanding a vital if neglected ethos of Afro-Peruvian cultural politics.

The second of these principles builds off the first, positing that relations of space and relations of difference are coanimating. As Katherine McKittrick and Linda Peake, among others, have persuasively argued, we must theorize racial, gender, sexual, and class difference "through socially produced markers *and* their attendant geographies" because "the relationship between these markers and their geographies is a dialectical one: one constitutes the other with neither being understood outside the context of the other."[33] In other words, discourses of racial/gender/sexual/economic alterity are made meaningful through their material instantiation—be it through techniques of bodily inscription, codes of socioeconomic delineation, processes of boundary demarcation, or other means. As such, my interest in tracking Black feminist performance geographies in Peru is necessarily contextualized by attention to the dynamic geographic arrangements of racial capitalist, heteropatriarchal regimes within and against which Afro-Peruvian cultural practices are staged.

The third of these principles concerns the geographic scope of sociocultural inquiry. Political geographers ranging from Neil Smith to David Harvey to Doreen Massey have illustrated the myriad ways in which the places within a particular spatial order are *relationally* constituted.[34] That is, the (re)production of racial capitalist space entails the coordination of, and contradictions among, cross-cutting interrelations across and between various sites, scales, and landscapes. Building from this premise, geographers of difference have persuasively evinced the importance of utilizing a multiscalar approach to the theorization of seemingly "small places" (like the South American Black Pacific) and "marginal people" (like Peru's African descended).[35] Such an approach refuses the presumption that provincialized places and/or populations are uniquely localized, aberrant, or inconsequential, or that their geopolitical marginality is natural or inevitable. Instead, multiscalar frames of inquiry reveal how even the smallest social units are bound up in networked interrelations that traverse local, regional, and national boundaries.

Integrating these methods and frames, what follows offers a feminist, geocultural reading of two multiscalar methods of sonic transposition— "respatialization" and "rescaling"—enacted by four generations of Afroperuana cultural workers. Here, I use the term "respatialization" to describe the negotiation and/or remapping of dominant sociospatial orders in a manner that imagines or/and activates distinctive relations of race, gender, economy, and place—from relations of embodiment and emplacement, to those of mobility and boundary transgression. The term "rescaling," in turn, is a kind of respatialization. It references the reconfiguration of sociogeographic categories of analysis and engagement in a manner that challenges the foreclosure of particular sites, subjects, and schema of inquiry. In this case, I am particularly interested in the ways in which the artists examined herein have literally and metaphorically put Afroperuana musical production on the map—in regional, national, and international contexts. It bears reiteration that as a feminist, antiracist geographer, I understand the relationship between cultural production and spatial formation as mutually animating, such that practices of Afro-Peruvian music and dance do not merely occur in these contexts, but in fact, actively produce and/or irrevocably transform them.

That I describe the texts and practices discussed with the modifier "Black feminist" is not meant to suggest that the artists themselves *self-identified* as Black feminists, or that they possess an uncomplicated relationship with local, regional, or other feminist formations. Rather, it is to mark the ways in which their collective political and aesthetic work can be *read* as critical contributions to the project of Black feminism in the Americas. Here, I understand Black feminism as Sara Clarke Kaplan has defined it, that is, as "less a uniform ideology or institutionalized political structure than an ethical and analytical stance, and a political praxis."[36] This integration of oppositional thought and practice is inherently spatial, as it involves, as feminist geographer Linda McDowell has noted, "nothing less than the dismantling of the basis of everyday social relations, most institutions and structures of power and the theoretical foundations on which current gender divisions stand."[37] Thus, my reading of Afroperuana performance is less concerned with categorizing performers according to a codified notion of feminist identity, and more attentive to the ways in which such performances and performers challenge gendered structures of oppression and containment, whether they are identified or described as such. This includes challenging or transgressing divisions between public and private, the domestic and the political, the local and the global, or, shirking dominant codes of gendered emplacement by engaging in regional or international travel, performing in male-dominated spaces, taking up masculinized instruments, and so forth.

To emphasize the important feminist work of disobeying normative raced and classed conventions of femininity, domesticity, and docility, I introduce the term *brava* to both mark and reclaim its typically pejorative connotations. Loosely translated as "dauntless, spirited, rough, wild, or unrefined," the term is often used by Peruvians and other Spanish speakers to describe the Black women performers chronicled herein, at times in keeping with, and at times regardless of, their public lives and personalities. Rather, here *brava* describes the raced and gendered stakes of occupying public spaces designated for the participation, politicking, and pleasure of light-skinned men. Moreover, it recognizes the suspicion and hostility directed toward women artists who, by choosing to perform in clubs, travel and tour, and/or refrain from marrying or having children, disrespect the heteropatriarchal expectations enacted upon them. Despite this, few scholars of gender and culture in the global North have engaged the work of artists such as Santa Cruz, Baca, or the Robles sisters in these terms. Thus, my aim is to locate histories of Afroperuana cultural activism within broader genealogies of Black feminism in the Americas, which to date have rarely engaged the cultural texts and politics of the African-descended in South America.

GEOGRAPHIES OF RACIAL AND NATIONAL FORMATION IN LIMA, PERU: 1854–1961

On May 13, 1961, Lima, Peru's preeminent newspaper *La Prensa* published an article in which the headline declared, "On the census race will not be questioned: there is no racial problem in Peru."[38] The report publicized the historic decision of census technical advisor Pedro Gutiérrez to eliminate racial demographics from Peru's national census survey—a move celebrated by civic leaders and government officials as a "symbolic national victory." At the time of Gutiérrez's adjudication, however, and in contradistinction to the national government's public contention that race was of "miniscule significance . . . in defining the cultural, social and economic status" of the Peruvian citizen, Afro-Peruvian artists and intellectuals remained engaged in a decade-long decolonization struggle that, mirroring those of other antiracist, anticolonial intellectuals throughout the globe, placed race at the center of its political agenda.[39]

The Peruvian state's public declaration of the ostensible insignificance of race—and specifically, blackness[40]—in mediating relations of culture and capital was just the final discursive step in a 120-year-long racial recategorization of Peru's civil population via processes of postcolonial nation building in the wake of national independence and the statewide manumission of African slaves.[41] Strikingly, while on the eve of Peru's postcolonial sovereignty, state census records categorized over half of the viceroyalty's "independent"—albeit unfree—urban population as "Black," the passage of fifty years saw the official population of free Black Peruvians decrease to less than 10 percent.[42] At the time of *La Prensa*'s celebratory announcement, that number had dropped to only one half of 1 percent.[43] This dramatic shift in national demographics has received little scholarly attention. And, if referenced, it is most often dismissed as the inevitable result of decades of "intermarriage" between the African and indigenous descended.[44] A reading of these statistics via a racial analytic, however, raises a number of provocative questions. Bearing in mind that the collection of census data was a state-mediated project, we might alternately conclude that this statistical quantification of blackness via a calculus of "dilution" reveals the depth of the state's investment in expunging it from the postcolonial national body. Scholars of race in the United States might note the stark contrast between U.S. laws of hypodescent that aimed to preserve "Black" as a legal status within "mixed race" populations, and Peruvian state practices of racialization, which sought to eradicate "Black" as a mode of racial identification through the proliferation of alternative demographic categories such as *sambo* and *castizo*. Here, again one can observe a provincializing logic at work: taken together, these postcolonial discourses and practices effectively render blackness that which must be contained, marginalized, and ultimately disavowed—an ever-disappearing marker of the remote and static past that will inevitably be overcome by an ever-evolving *mestizo* present.

This postcolonial state project of racial reordering via demographic and other bureaucratic practices found its aesthetic twin in the discourse of *criollismo*. If the former mobilized biological *mestizaje* as a strategy of national formation, the latter provided a companion imaginary of cultural *mestizaje*. Steeped in the logics of Western modernity, criollismo aimed to interweave Peru's dissonant and fragmented regional and ethnic histories into a coherent narrative of national hybridity articulated through racialized notions of cultural development and progress. In a multilingual nation where o/aural and visual traditions have historically afforded the most extensive audiences, the development of criollismo in the nineteenth century was particularly dependent on the appropriation and resignification of popular sonic and visual texts for the purposes of nationalist propaganda. As ethnomusicologist Javier León Quirós has observed, the contemporary artistic genres popularly known as *música* and *baile criollo* have been indelibly shaped by Afro-Peruvian lyrical, rhythmic, and melodic traditions.[45] Yet these influences have consistently been minimized or disavowed, as *lo Africano* within these genres is typically represented as the embryonic vestiges of a "primitive" cultural past.[46] This past, in turn, ostensibly has been triumphed over by the order and reason of European and mestizo contributions.[47]

Deployed in strategic alignment with emergent rhetorics of colorblindness circulating throughout the hemisphere, the long-standing idealization of criollismo within Peru served the efforts of national elites to consolidate their political interests in the face of the international threat posed by the multiscalar global crisis in post–World War II racial politics.[48] However, the criollo state met its counterhegemonic opposition in the late 1950s. The proliferation of decolonization movements throughout French and British colonies in Africa and Asia, the entrenchment of civil rights activism in the southern United States, the advent of postcolonial intellectualism throughout the Caribbean, and the rise of socialism in Latin America together produced an unprecedented international visibility for antiracist movements throughout the globe. Moreover, these struggles were both informed by and formative of Black internationalist struggles motored by a radical convergence of aesthetics, politics, and knowledge production throughout the Black diaspora.[49] It was in this context of contact and exchange between decolonization movements, internationalist struggles in the global South, and antiracist activism in the global North that the Katherine Dunham Company found its way to the public stages of Lima, anticipating the birth of Peru's own Black Arts Revival.[50]

STAGING AFROPERUANIDAD: PERFORMANCE GEOGRAPHIES
OF FEMINIST DIASPORICITY, 1950–1967

In the fall of 1950, African American anthropologist, choreographer, and dancer Katherine Dunham traveled with her New York–based dance company to Buenos Aires in preparation for their South American tour. It was while abroad, in response to news of the failure of the Eighty-First U.S. Congress to approve antilynching legislation, that Dunham researched, composed, and choreographed what became known as the most controversial piece in her oeuvre: *Southland*. Since its 1951 debut in Santiago de Chile, Dunham's *Southland* has received due scholarly attention, both for its content, which proffered an explicit condemnation of racial violence in the United States, and its reception, which included a withdrawal of funding by the U.S. State Department and public and state pressures to permanently omit the ballet from the company's repertoire. Yet few of these studies have considered this creative work as part of a repertoire choreographed and performed for the Dunham Company's historic tour of South America. Attention to Dunham's South American project as a whole reveals important connections between the cultural and spatial politics of expressive practice in the Black diaspora—specifically, how diasporic feminists such as Dunham have choreographed and leveraged performance geographies as means of interrogating and reimagining dominant raced and gendered boundaries of social existence in general, and blackness in particular.

As I have argued thus far, "performance geography" connotes the range of situated and imagined places at and through which the collective cultural task of materialization—including embodiment, mobility, attachment, and imagination—collides with the physical and ideological constraints of context. A conceptual frame for apprehending the ever-evolving conjuncture of sonic and spatial intra-action, performance geography is a theoretic attentive to practices of musicking as at once *in situ*, or emplaced in particular materiodiscursive relations, and *in flux*, or perpetually (re)shaping the very function and meaning of such contexts of elaboration. In this sense, performance geography signals an analytical departure from ethnomusicological approaches to the study of Afro-Peruvian traditions described above. As I posited above, such approaches tend to rely upon anthropological constructions of a static, bounded "field" that desires localized modes and forms of cultural production. Such uncritical celebrations of "music in place"—that is, the extolment of sonic practices that are viewed as, and thus valued for, their ostensible aesthetic invariability and geographic endogeny—invariably provincialize global Southern aural forms by emphasizing rootedness and continuity over movement and dynamism.

To conceptualize the Dunham Company's South American tour as a performance geography is to conceptualize the complex relationship between geographically situated and relational performance events produced in and through the dynamic interaction of not only artist and audience, but also text and context. In other words, it is to engage in a cultural reading practice that examines not only the content and form of a particular cultural text, but how said text is emplaced within particular geopolitical landscapes. For example, the Dunham Company's appearance on the stage of Lima's Teatro Municipal—the nation's "premier concert hall and playhouse"—enacted a historic desegregation of the institution's featured artists.[51] At the time of Dunham's performance, the political and cultural locus of Black expressive culture in Peru remained legally and discursively relegated to the "private" spheres of the home, neighborhood associations, religious fraternities, and isolated coastal villages. As feminist and critical race theorists have demonstrated exhaustively, such mutually reinforcing material and metaphorical divisions between "public" and "private" have served to naturalize the raced and gendered differentiation of labor, knowledge production, and political subjectivity. In this case, fortified by long-standing criollo discourses that deemed Black cultural practices vestigial remains of an unsophisticated culture, such geopolitical divisions between "public" and "private" literally and figuratively *placed* Peruvians of African descent outside of the material and ideological boundaries of nation. The Dunham Company's literal introduction of blackness to Peru's national stage, then, was simultaneously a symbolic reconfiguration of the national public sphere, given that cultural and political subjectivity are inextricably intertwined.[52]

While the mere occurrence of Dunham's performance was in itself a controversial matter for Lima's upper stratum, the content of "Rite of Passage"—a choreographed ethnographic sketch of Black women's lives as laborers, lovers, and mothers—spurred particularly hostile reactions among Peruvian audiences and critics. "I remember it as if it were yesterday," recalled Nicomedes Santa Cruz in an interview from 1973 with *Caretas* magazine, "how during the spectacle, the aristocratic ladies of our hypocritical society abandoned the Municipal [Theater's] rows and balconies because they could not bear the scandalous scene: a 'rite of passage' in which a *yao* [played by Lucille Ellis] received instructions about the conjugal life from a *babalao* [played by Lenwod Morris] through a choreography that mimicked copular acts. . . . Of course, for the women of our society at that moment, such an act was a 'Black thing.'"[53] What can be inferred from Santa Cruz's astute observation about dominant conceptions of culture and place is that the perceived threat of Dunham's controversial performance inhered in the dramatic spatial reorderings that it posited: a disruption of the boundaries between "high" and "low" culture; a remapping of hegemonic material and ideological "placements" of Black expressive culture; and an interrogation of the sociospatial politics of nation building as they relate to the making and unmaking of raced and gendered bodies.

Given the history of appropriation, denigration, and effacement of Black expressive culture upon which the postcolonial Peruvian national popular was constructed, these first two political processes of "respatialization" enacted through the performance of "Rite of Passage" should be evident. However, to fully comprehend the spatiopolitical intervention that the Dunham Company's performance made into the imbricated raced and gendered processes of nation making and subject making in mid-century Peru, and thus understand its symbolic significance to Lima's incipient Black cultural revival, requires that we situate the event within a broader historical trajectory of the raced and gendered logics of nation building in postcolonial Peru at the scale of the body. As historian of Afro–Latin America Patricia Fox has noted, for preeminent postcolonial intellectuals such as José Carlos Mariátegui, blackness emblematized the nation's imbrication in histories of colonialism and chattel slavery, and was thereby coded as the racial signifier both of African primitiveness and of Peninsular imperialism: "Colonial society, which made the Black a domestic—very rarely an artisan or a worker—absorbed and assimilated the Black race to the extent of intoxicating itself with their hot tropical blood. The Black was as detestable and tamed as the Indian was inscrutable and distant. . . . The mulatto, colonial even in his tastes, unconsciously favors things Hispanic, rather than autochthony. He naturally feels closer to Spain than the Incan world."[54] As imagined by Mariátegui and his compatriots, blackness was antithetical to the emergent nation, a "contagion" to be harnessed and contained lest it threaten the postcolonial social order. Within this raced and gendered national narrative, the male "mulatto" body indexed the contamination of the sovereign national body via his ostensible disposition toward servility and nostalgia for European imperialism. As the biological and cultural carrier of the "contagion" of blackness, the Black female reproductive body was envisaged as the geographic nexus of a particularly violent conjunction of the scales of the individual, home, and nation: a magnified threat to national security and justifiable object of state violence.

In contradistinction to these long-standing national discourses, Dunham's performance of agential Black female sexuality on Peru's national stage deployed a cartographic strategy that both literally and figuratively territorialized Black women's sexual and reproductive labor not as a centuries-old expropriable resource for criollo nation building, nor as pathological threat to be contained within the boundaries of the nation-state. Rather, by representing the Black female body as the material manifestation of an anticolonial global Black cultural presence, Dunham produced an embodied opposition to the multiscalar processes of bodily violence that render "self-possession and other forms of spatial ownership virtually unavailable" to Black female subjects.[55] Arguably, Dunham's counternarrative of agential embodiment was made possible, in part, by what Latin American performance theorist Diana Taylor has described as the potential of such performative acts to "[call] into question the very contours of the body" itself.[56] A spatially interested reading of Taylor's provocative contention suggests that performance is a critical mechanism through which the body as a political geography can be materially and discursively remapped. Viewed through this lens, one can interpret the Dunham Company's performance as dramatizing on Peru's national stage a critical, multiscalar respatialization of the Black female body.

By bringing her dance company to the stage of Peru's national theater to perform African-influenced work in front of a largely criollo-identified audience, Dunham underscored the continuity in the Americas of "an international Black cultural presence."[57] Simultaneously she critiqued the epistemological mechanisms through which knowledge production about such histories and peoples had been distorted and or disavowed. Indeed, Dunham's "Rite of Passage" was only one of the many projects developed at her New York school, where collaborative research and exchange between artists, students, and intellectuals hailing from national and regional locations throughout the United States, Latin America, the Caribbean, and the African continent were fostered through an interdisciplinary choreographic method that combined oral history, ethnography, and performance. By juxtaposing Latin American and Caribbean dance with plantation songs, African American spirituals, and Afro-syncretic religious practices, the dance company effectively engaged in a project of diasporic history-making that underscored the cultural and political interconnectedness of seemingly disparate parts of the Americas and Caribbean, challenging the nationalist frameworks of knowledge production about peoples of African descent within which Black expressive culture had traditionally been either disparaged or effaced.

Among those in attendance at Dunham's controversial performance was a brother and sister duo that would soon become pivotal players in Peru's Black Arts Revival: Victoria and Nicomedes Santa Cruz. The Katherine Dunham Company's arrival to Lima marked a momentous turning point for the Santa Cruz family: Victoria would later study Dunham's work on ethnographic dance and was profoundly influenced as a choreographer and instructor by Dunham's methods. Nicomedes's encounter with Dunham would be the first of critical future connections that the artist would establish with an international cadre of Black intellectuals and Latin American artist-activists. As a critical rupture in the racialized and gendered geographies that had historically buttressed the subjugation and erasure of Peru's population of African descent through the containment of the Black female body and codification of binary spatial logics such as public and private, political and aesthetic, national and diasporic, Dunham's performance foreshadowed the strategies of sonic transposition mobilized during Peru's Black Arts Revival.

BLACK OR PERUVIAN, BLACK AND PERUVIAN?
THE CULTURAL POLITICS OF AFROPERUANIDAD

Eight years after the Katherine Dunham Company's Lima debut, Victoria Santa Cruz teamed up with her brother Nicomedes to codirect Cumanana, the first and most renowned performance collective of Peru's Black Arts Revival. Attentive to connections between the processes of cultural appropriation and historical erasure that characterized the construction of national(ist) genres such as *música criolla*, Cumanana's primary mission was to systematize the research, production, and performance of Afro-Peruvian expressive culture.[58] Toward this end, the collective enlisted a number of creative spatial strategies that extended the geopolitical challenges posed by the Dunham Company's notorious Teatro Municipal performance a decade earlier. Employing Dunham-esque methodologies, Cumanana exploited popular archival technologies including theater and dance, musical recordings, and printed media to put pressure on the gaps and erasures of dominant historical narratives, thus "making space"—both materially and ideologically—for new sites and forms of knowledge production by and about Peru's people of African descent.

Over the next two decades, a number of performance collectives emerged to follow in the path laid by Cumanana. While these subsequent enterprises each cohered around distinct artistic visions and political goals, three ideological undercurrents united the loosely connected artistic networks that constituted Peru's Black Arts performance geographies. Profoundly influenced by the ethnographically informed dramatic and choreographic methods of Victoria Santa Cruz, Black Arts performance groups developed research agendas that unapologetically privileged collective memory and vernacular practice over mainstream historical archives; demonstrated an explicit commitment to drawing on these alternative sources to complicate progressive narratives of national history by exposing previously negated connections between past and present modes of racial subjugation; and, finally, strategically exploited local, national, and international media circuits—recording companies, public theater stages, the popular press, and university workshops—to popularize the Black Arts Revival's antiracist struggle.[59] The creative use of these nonconventional research methods allowed Revival practitioners to spatialize what scholar of Caribbean literature and culture VéVé Clark has called "memory of difference."[60]

In her discussion of the "research-to-performance" methods that defined Dunham's creative and pedagogical work, Clark posits "memory of difference" as an analytical framework within which to theorize the dialogic relationship between research and performance, and correspondingly, history and memory.[61] Using examples from Dunham's repertoire, Clark reconfigures French historian Pierre Nora's formative historiographic narrative of modernity's shift from *milieux de mémoire*—environments or cultural settings of memory—to *lieux de mémoire*—places or sites of memory. Clark calls into question Nora's linear model of spatial and temporal progression away from "true memor[ies]" expressed through the often embodied "ritual repetition of a timeless practice in a primordial identification of act and meaning."[62] Clark instead characterizes these different forms of historical knowledge as dynamic, dialogically constituted means of producing individual and collective memory. Indeed, Clark argues, Dunham staged milieux de mémoire in order to create lieux de mémoire—that is, through her study, reimagination, and performance of expressive cultures that resided outside of official archives, she inscribed in the public sphere competing, counter, or disavowed forms of memory. It is out of this conjunction of popular performance, diasporic countermemory, and expressive cultures, Clark argues, that Dunham's "memory of difference" was produced. By staging this ostensibly private or localized memory of difference in public venues, Dunham put pressure upon dominant geographies of knowledge production, thereby *making space* in both the public sphere and the hegemonic archive for new ways of understanding the past and its relationship to the present.

Clark's "memory of difference" offers a useful approach for understanding the ethnochoreographic techniques that shaped Peru's Black Arts Revival performance geographies in general, and the work of Victoria Santa Cruz in particular. During her tenure as director of the performance company, Teatro y Danzas Negras del Perú (Black Theater and Dances of Peru; 1966–72), and later as the head of Peru's Conjunto Nacional de Folklore (National School of Folklore; 1973–82), Santa Cruz popularized her own research-to-performance methods, which combined practical and theoretical elements of ethnography, music, and dance.[63] For Santa Cruz, musical traditions of the Black diaspora afforded a particularly critical milieux de mémoire; her pedagogical writings emphasized rhythm as an enduring practice of countermemory.[64] A central focus of her life work was the research and reconstruction of popular Afro-Peruvian rhythms and their corresponding dances. Both on stage and in the classroom, Santa Cruz repositioned these traditions as "memories of difference"—that is, not as the vestigial raw materials of creolized national music, but as narrative fragments of a cultural past marked by the terrors of slavery and subsequent forms of subjugation.

It is critical to note the daunting intellectual and artistic task endeavored by Santa Cruz and her cohort. The songs and dances that these cultural workers aimed to document or reconstruct seldom appeared in the official historical record; their rare mention was most often limited to declarations of prohibition, punishment, or disparagement. Secondary research on Peru's African descended likewise remained scant in the mid-century. Thus, to address these gaps, Santa Cruz honed a unique ethnographic method that integrated community knowledges, oral tradition, and artistic speculation. Eschewing traditional research designs and modes of inquiry, the artist-intellectual instead turned to rhythm as an orienting principle for her studies. For Santa Cruz, *ritmo* provided a rich, untapped "repertoire" of countermemory.[65] Rhythmic technologies and practices harbor stories of enslaved labor and racial violence, as well as community ingenuity and survivance—all of which were muffled by mainstream archives and nationalist discourses. For example, the *cajón*—a six sided wooden box played by slapping the hands on its top or rear faces—was created by plantation workhands who converted discarded packing crates into percussive instruments.[66] Reconstructed choreographies such as *festejo* and *alcatraz* encoded ongoing, quotidian practices of slave opposition. From these we learn of how Peru's African descended shirked the stringent codes that forbade collective assembly and musical production to dance the night away, sharing in stolen moments of conviviality while reclaiming their laboring bodies, sexual freedom, and creative expression. In collaboration with her brother, Nicomedes, Santa Cruz (figure 3.1) worked tirelessly to assemble fragments of gesture, rhythm, and song into a rich artistic canon that, to date, still offers the most comprehensive account of Black Peru's cultural traditions.

For Santa Cruz, community-based instruction in Peru's Black Arts traditions served as a critical "means of self-discovery" for practitioners, and a pathway toward the development of a gendered Black political consciousness rooted in embodied connections to Afro-diasporic history and memory.[67] As an instructor, a cornerstone of her pedagogical approach involved a choreographic technique that Santa Cruz dubbed *ritmo interior*, interior rhythm.[68] In her 1971 publication entitled *Discovery and Development of a Sense of Rhythm*, Santa Cruz described rhythm as the "great organizing principle" of "nature and lived experience."[69] Her teachings thus emphasized the development of a "rhythmic consciousness"—a process in which performers "listen with the body" rather than with their "intellect" in order to succumb to, and ultimately become one with, rhythm's Afro-diasporic logics.[70] Through these exercises of rhythm-driven self-expression, practitioners become "a part . . . of the work," and by extension, members and keepers of the historical record.[71] Arguably, Santa Cruz's pedagogical meth-

3.1 Victoria Santa Cruz

ods both anticipate and activate what French spatial theorist Henri Lefebvre dubbed a half-century later "rhythmanalysis"—that is, the bodily practice of "listen[ing] to the world, and above all to what are disdainfully called noises, which are said without meaning, and to murmurs [rumeurs], full of meaning—and finally . . . to silences."[72]

A geographically inflected reading of Santa Cruz's artistic and pedagogical pursuits allows for attention to the creative and critical potential enabled by her ethnochoreographic praxis and the theoretical orientations that guided it: a critical, creative engagement with the spatial politics of embodiment and, correspondingly, an emphasis on the imbrication of politicized performance practice and the interested production of historical counter-memory. A powerful example of Santa Cruz's engagement with the geographic in her creative work can be found in the seminal performance piece "Me gritaron negra."[73] Integrating poetic storytelling and choreographed gesture with rhythmic accompaniment and choral antiphony, "Me gritaron negra" relates a semiautobiographical account of Santa Cruz's process of coming into political consciousness as an Afro-Peruvian woman. As its narrative unfolds, the performance uses shifts in vocality, tempo, and gesture that range from subtle and delicate to dramatic and forceful to demonstrate how dominant tropes of raced and gendered embodiment can be respatialized to instead signal political empowerment, cultural citizenship, and diasporic solidarity.

Dressed in a wide-collared knit shirt and dark pants, sporting chunky gold hoops and a full afro, Victoria Santa Cruz stands stage right, slightly anterior to her five-member Afro-Peruvian chorus. Still and silent, the artists gaze into a westward distance as the cajón enters with a moderate, rhythmic progression. Such an opening is befitting. The cajón conjures a powerful retelling of the provincialized history of Peru's Black Pacific; it sounds the enduring ingenuity and resistance of Peru's enslaved African descended, who transformed the wooden crates used to transport the fruits of their coerced agricultural labor into instruments that could animate stolen moments of collective performance and pleasure.[74] Moreover, this percussive opening affirms Santa Cruz's insistence that rhythm is the galvanic pulse of Afro-Peruvian culture.

As the third rhythmic cycle nears its close, Santa Cruz begins to speak, layering her rich low voice with notes of urgency and anger:

Tenía siete años apenas,
apenas siete años,

¡Qué siete años!
¡No llegaba a cinco siquiera!

De pronto unas voces en la calle
me gritaron ¡Negra!

I was barely seven years old
barely seven

Not even seven years old—
I hadn't even turned five

When suddenly voices in the street
Shouted at me: *Negra!*

Abruptly, the chorus enters, echoing in fiery unison: "*¡Negra! ¡Negra! ¡Negra! ¡Negra! ¡Negra! ¡Negra! ¡Negra!*"

These introductory stanzas of "Me gritaron negra!" poignantly narrate Santa Cruz's earliest encounter with gendered racialization. In an interview featured on the documentary television series *Retratos de TV Perú*, Santa Cruz recounted the childhood events that inspired this performance piece.[75] Raised in Lima's impoverished urban neighborhood of La Victoria—a district historically known as a hub of urban Afro-Peruvian life and culture—the young Santa Cruz cherished the friendships she had fostered with similar-aged children on her block, all of who were indigenous-descended *mestizas*. But it was that very *barrio*, only paces from her front door, that Santa Cruz first experienced the visceral effects of gendered racism, when a light-skinned girl new to the neighborhood referred to her by the racist epithet *negra* rather than by name. Leveraging her light-skinned privilege, the new girl compelled the other children to ignore Santa Cruz, admonishing them that it is inappropriate to socialize across racial-ethnic lines. During the television interview, Santa Cruz recalls asking her childhood self: "¿Acaso las calles tienen reglas?" (Do the streets even have rules?).[76] As Katherine McKittrick astutely observes, "Existing geographic rules unjustly organize human hierarchies in place and reify uneven geographies in familiar, seemingly natural ways. And yet, these rules are alterable and there exists a terrain through which different geographies' stories can be and are told."[77] Here, in response to the violent words and actions of her peers, the young Santa Cruz contemplates the geographic logics of raced and gendered exclusion. Both her prose and her subsequent commentary interrogate the seemingly natural racial-spatial orders that govern the occupation of and interactions within the most immediate and familiar of public spaces, marking these as sites of ongoing political contest. Reflections upon what McKittrick dubs "the interplay of geographies of domination (such as transatlantic geography and racial-sexual displacement) and black women's geographies (such as their knowledges, negotiations and experiences)" animate the narrative arc of the poem, which knits together various anecdotes reflecting Santa Cruz's shifting experiences of gendered racialization at the scale of the body, the home, and the city.[78]

The next segment of the poem unfolds with an antiphonal exchange between artist and chorus, symbolizing interanimating articulations of subjectivity and processes of subjectification. Again, Santa Cruz illustrates the ways in which processes of becoming are always-already geographic, her prose vivifying how bodily inscriptions of difference enact mutually animating modes of psychic violence and spatial containment:

Santa Cruz: ¿Soy acaso negra?—me dije
Coro: ¡Sí!
Santa Cruz: ¿Qué cosa es ser negra?"
Coro: ¡Negra!
Santa Cruz: Y yo no sabía la triste verdad que aquello escondía.
Coro: ¡Negra!
Santa Cruz: Y me sentí negra,
Coro: ¡Negra!
Santa Cruz: Como ellos decían
Coro: ¡Negra!
Santa Cruz: Y retrocedí
Coro: ¡Negra!
Santa Cruz: Como ellos querían
Coro: ¡Negra!
Santa Cruz: Y odié mis cabellos y mis labios gruesos
Y miré apenada mi carne tostada
Y retrocedí
Coro: ¡Negra!
Santa Cruz: Y retrocedí . . .

Santa Cruz: Am I *negra*, I asked myself?
Chorus: Yes!
Santa Cruz: What is this *thing*, to be *negra*?
Chorus: *Negra!*
Santa Cruz: And I didn't know the sad truth that such a thing hid.
Chorus: *Negra!*
Santa Cruz: And I felt *negra*,
Chorus: *Negra!*
Santa Cruz: Just as they said
Chorus: *Negra!*
Santa Cruz: And I stepped back
Chorus: *Negra!*
Santa Cruz: Just like they wanted

Chorus: *Negra!*
Santa Cruz: And I began to hate my hair and my thick lips
And saddened, I looked at my toasted skin
And I stood down
Chorus: *Negra!*
Santa Cruz: And I stepped back . . .

Santa Cruz describes the affective experience of racist and sexist objectification, asking "¿Soy acaso negra? . . . ¿Qué cosa es ser negra?" (Am I *negra*? What is this *thing*, to be *negra*?) For Santa Cruz, the psychic experience of gendered racialization entails not only the ideological violence of denigration; it likewise involves the negotiation of an imposed and naturalized sociospatial order. The physical contours of her body—her lips and skin and hair—become a geography inscribed with social meaning, an ideological imposition intended to enact and legitimate her ongoing displacement. "Y me sentí negra . . . Como ellos decían . . . Y retrocedí . . . Como ellos querían" (And I felt *negra* . . . Just as they said . . . And I stepped back . . . Just like they wanted). Here, Santa Cruz demonstrates the ways in which socially produced markers of difference both imply and impose attendant geographies of containment.[79] To be interpellated as a gendered Black subject is to be simultaneously disparaged and displaced; the above stanzas mark how gendered racialization constrains both physical mobility (within the streets of La Victoria) and social mobility (within a national-racial order that privileges phenotypical and cultural constructions of whiteness).

The following segment of the poem describes the ongoing experience of gendered racialization as an ever-accumulating "burden" born by Black women. This *carga* is dramatized as physical and vocal constraint. Santa Cruz's posture becomes rigid, her fists clenched, and her wrists crossed as if bound. Her tone becomes increasingly desperate and pained, lingering in its break:

. . .

Y pasaba el tiempo,
Y siempre amargada
Seguía llevando a mi espalda
mi pesada carga
¡Y como pesaba! . . .

Me alacié el cabello,
me polveé la cara,
y entre mis entrañas siempre resonaba la misma palabra

¡Negra! ¡Negra! ¡Negra! ¡Negra!
¡Negra! ¡Negra! ¡Negra!
Hasta que un día que retrocedía, retrocedía y que iba a caer . . .

. . .

And time passed,
And always bitter
I continued to carry on my back
my heavy burden
Oh! And how much it weighed! . . .

I straightened my hair,
I powdered my face,
And within my entrails the same word repeatedly resounded

Negra! Negra! Negra! Negra!
Negra! Negra! Negra!
Until I stepped back and I stood down to the point that I was about to
give up . . .

Here, the embodied burden of negotiating ever-encroaching boundaries
of physical and ideological constraint is encumbering to the point of total immobilization: "Hasta que un día que retrocedía, retrocedía y que iba
a caer . . ." (Until I stepped back and I stood down to the point that I was
about to give up . . .) It is at the point of imminent capitulation, of near
surrender, that the poem takes a dramatic turn. This moment of transition,
of transformation, is sudden, dramatized through an increasingly clipped,
measured prose that mirrors the progressively frenetic rhythm of the cajón.
Thrusting her elegant hands into the air as if casting away manacles, Santa
Cruz elevates her chin, turns her eyes toward the audience, and pronounces:

. . .

Coro: ¡Negra!
Santa Cruz: Sí
Coro: ¡Negra!

Santa Cruz: Soy

Coro: ¡Negra!

. . .

Santa Cruz: Negra soy

. . .

Santa Cruz: ¿Y de qué color?

Coro: Negro!

Santa Cruz: ¡Y que lindo suena!

Coro: ¡Negro!

Santa Cruz: ¡Y que ritmo tiene!

Coro: ¡Negro! ¡Negro! ¡Negro! ¡Negro!

. . .

Santa Cruz: Al fin comprendí

Coro: ¡Al fin!

Santa Cruz: Ya no retrocedo

Coro: ¡Al fin!

Santa Cruz: Y avanzo segura

Coro: ¡Al fin!

Santa Cruz: Avanzo y espero

Coro: ¡Al fin!

Santa Cruz: Y bendigo al cielo porque quiso Dios
que negro azabache fuese mi color
Y ya comprendí

Coro: ¡Al fin!

Santa Cruz: Ya tengo la llave

Santa Cruz con coro: Negro, Negro, Negro, Negro . . .

Santa Cruz: ¡Negra soy!

. . .

Chorus: *Negra!*

Santa Cruz: Yes

Chorus: *Negra!*

Santa Cruz: I am

Chorus: *Negra!*

. . .

Santa Cruz: I am *negra*

. . .

Santa Cruz: What color?
Chorus: *Negro!*
Santa Cruz: And how beautiful it sounds!
Chorus: *Negro!*
Santa Cruz: And what rhythm it has!
Chorus: *Negro! Negro! Negro! Negro!*

. . .

Santa Cruz: I finally understood
Chorus: Finally!
Santa Cruz: I no longer stand down
Chorus: Finally!
Santa Cruz: I proceed with confidence
Chorus: Finally!
Santa Cruz: I proceed and hope
Chorus: Finally!
Santa Cruz: And I praise the skies because God wanted
Me to be jet black
I finally understand
Chorus: Finally!
Santa Cruz: I now have the key
Santa Cruz with Chorus: *Negro, Negro, Negro, Negro* . . .
Santa Cruz: I am *negra!*

Once a technique of domination enacted upon her body, gendered blackness is respatialized here as a source of personal and collective political empowerment. Upon pronouncing "¡*Negra soy!*" (I am a Black woman), the chorus moves from shouting "¡*Negra!*" to chanting "¡*Negro!*," signaling a shift from acts of individual interpellation to the practice of collective coalitional identification. Now artist and composer, Santa Cruz turns her gaze to the audience, and with her hands gracefully emulating the gestures of a conductor, proclaims "¡Y que lindo suena! . . . ¡Y que ritmo tiene!" (And how beautiful [*negro*] sounds . . . and what rhythm it has . . .) Here, blackness is no longer a static thing, but a dynamic relation between people rooted in a shared history of bodily displacement and expropriation, as well as concerted cultural responses to these violent processes. It is at this moment that Santa Cruz and her troupe erupt into dance; with equal parts grace and force, their pelvises thrust forth, and with backs arched, shoulders rolled, and heads held high they continue to chant in chorus: "¡Negro! ¡Negro! ¡Negro! ¡Negro!" Self-possessed and resplendent, Santa Cruz closes her performance with a reflection upon the transformative power of articulating alternative imaginaries of Black female corporality, proclaiming "Ya no retrocedo . . . Y avanzo segura . . . Avanzo y espero . . . Y ya comprendí . . . ¡Al fin! . . . Ya tengo la llave . . . *Negro, Negro, Negro, Negro* . . . ¡Negra soy!" (I no longer stand down . . . I proceed with confidence . . . I proceed and hope . . . I finally understand . . . I now have the key . . . *Negro, Negro, Negro, Negro* . . . I am a Black woman!).

If, as feminist geographer and literary critic Mary Pat Brady has argued, "categories of social difference such as race, gender, and sexuality are spatially enacted and inhabited," then Victoria Santa Cruz's "Me gritaron negra" demonstrates how performance can offer a powerful vehicle through which the body—and by extension, broader, mutually relational geographies of scale—can be materially and discursively remapped.[80] Like Katherine Dunham, Santa Cruz's teaching methods stressed an embodied intra-action with processes of knowledge production, anticipating vital connections between performance, subject constitution, and bodily instantiation. In both her teaching and her creative work, Santa Cruz promoted a feminist politics of embodied performance that exploded a number of ostensible sociospatial binaries: divisions between mind and body; between high and low culture; between public and private spheres of performance; between rural and urban expressive cultural forms and practices; between the local and the international. She achieved these respatializations, in part, through the content and form of her work, which combined poetry, theater, and dance to dramatize the physical and sexual exploitation of enslaved Black women, and conversely, how Black women in Peru have "taken possession" of their bodies through engagements with Afro-syncretic religious and cultural traditions.

In addition to engaging the spatial politics of embodiment in her creative work, Santa Cruz accomplished the disruption of dominant spatial orderings through her techniques of staging—that is, her use of embodied performance to challenge and/or reconstitute extant sites and processes of spatial differentiation.[81] For example, her dance troupe, Teatro y Danzas Negras del Perú, was selected to represent the nation at the Summer Olympic Games in 1968—the first occasion in which Afro-Peruvian cultural production was staged in this venue as representative of Peru's national cultural. Equally significant was Santa Cruz's appointment as director of the Centro de Arte Folclórico. This public acknowledgment of her achievements and the valuable work of Revival artists more generally marked an unprecedented material and symbolic characterization of Afro-Peruvian expressive practices as a constitutive element of the historical and contemporary national popular. In short, as a feminist cultural worker, Santa Cruz reconstituted public theaters, educational, and cultural institutions as sites where embodied "memories of difference" could be staged, thereby transforming existing spatial prescriptions concerning the "proper" places for the production and storing of knowledge. Moreover, Santa Cruz's geopolitical revalorization of oft-disparaged and disremembered techniques and forms of embodied practice territorialized a trenchant critique of the privileging within Western academic traditions of what Taylor has described as the "*archive* of supposedly enduring materials (i.e. texts, documents, buildings, bones)" over the *repertoire* of embodied practice/knowledge (i.e., spoken language, dance, sports, ritual).[82]

The archival accounts and elisions of Peru's "official" past—particularly those employed to establish a numeric and representational hegemony over the racialized bodies of the nation—have functioned as key mechanisms for the (re)production of this postcolonial racial state.[83] As the creative and pedagogical work of Victoria Santa Cruz indicates, Black Arts Revival performance geographies disrupted the ascendancy of such material and narrative state capacities in two ways. On the one hand, Revival texts and practices territorialized a sonic and visual reconfiguration of Peru's exclusionary and intensely segregated local, urban, and national landscapes, calling into question schisms within the lived geographies of what Gramsci has called the national and the popular.[84] On the other hand, these performance geographies radically contested the hegemonic purchase of criollismo and mestizaje—each celebrations of national hybridity that foregrounded a linear narrative of cultural development to obscure raced and gendered forms of physical, sexual, and epistemic violence.

SUSANA BACA, PERU'S "GLOBAL DIVA"

Since the advent of Peru's mid-century Black Arts Revival, the study and practice of Afro-Peruvian expressive cultural forms has become increasingly institutionalized; as a result, the contemporary sonic and choreographic interpretations of Afroperuanismo taught at dance academies and cultural institutions most often reflect a canonical commitment to the pedagogical conventions of the Santa Cruz siblings and their epigones. The twin processes of institutionalization and canonization have consequently produced ethnic nationalist discourses concerning the authentic content and form of Black Peruvian performance. Bearing in mind U.S. Black feminist critiques of the nationalist cultural canons of the Black Arts Movement of the 1960s and 1970s, it is perhaps unsurprising that institutionalized Afro-Peruvian forms often rehearse familiar nationalist tropes of heteromasculinized empowerment: the positioning of women as sexual objects rather than artistic subjects, the casting of women as homebound nurturers of cultural survival, and the articulation of desire and its fulfillment as unequivocally heterosexual. As feminist scholars of race, gender, and nation have exhaustively argued, the concept of nation and conceptions of national belonging cannot wholly be divorced from the historical discourses from which they emerge: Eurocentric projects of nation building that defined their ideal citizen-subject as the white propertied male who effectively governed his own domestic domain—the heteronuclear household.[85] These practices of racial-colonial nation making entrenched particular gendered scripts of belonging that prevailed through their adaptation by ethnic nationalist architects.

As a singer-songwriter and a scholar of Afro-Peruvian popular culture, Susana Baca emerged from this history of the Black Arts Revival and its institutionalization. Baca was born into a prominent immediate and extended family of Afro-Peruvian musicians, including famed artists Ronaldo Campos, member of Cumanana and Teatro y Danzas Negras and founder of the renowned Perú Negro, and renowned folklorist, singer-songwriter, and *cajonero* Caitro Soto. Baca's introduction to sonic expression was thus defined by her immersion in Revival traditions and practices of transmission. When I interviewed Baca in her Chorrillos home in 2012, the artist recalled, "I believe that I first felt the urge to express myself through Afro-Peruvian music because it is something that I lived since I was a girl. I lived it at home and at the houses of relatives. . . . When we went to a relative's house, there was always music. . . . If I was at home, I sang for my mother . . . and she taught us to dance. . . . Thus, I grew up expressing myself in that manner."[86] These early influences would continue to shape Baca's musical formation. As a young woman, the artist went on to hold a musical assistantship with famed singer and composer of Afro-Peruvian music, Chabuca Granda, with

3.2 Susana Baca. Photo by João Canziani.

whom she would nurture a lifelong friendship.[87] In both her creative work and public life, Baca (figure 3.2) has forever acknowledged her indebtedness to this first generation of Revival practitioners, whose aural echoes can be heard in the rhythmic arrangements and instrumentation commonly featured in her recordings.

At the same time, Baca's body of work has challenged the boundaries of canonical Afro-Peruvian rhythmic, sonic, and textual traditions in critical ways. Having grown up listening to international artists ranging from Afro-Cuban *son* musician Beny Moré to African American jazz vocalist Billie Holiday to South African singer Miriam Makeba on the radio, Baca was also deeply inspired by diasporic sonic forms:

> One grows . . . upon listening to other musics and becoming aware that throughout the world there are other African-descended children . . . that make distinctive music. . . . I listened to everything. . . . and within myself I began to feel the seeds of an awareness that just as there was a community of African-descended peoples here (in Peru), there were

African-descended peoples in other parts of the world as well. And we shared commonalities: antiphony, rhythm, cadences mixed with different elements from different countries. . . . That is [the essence] of music, it marks you and causes you to be reborn.[88]

These processes of listening and learning irrevocably transformed Baca as an artist, who became disenchanted with the rigidity of Revival canons. Her first musical group, Tiahuanaco 2000, which combined spoken word poetry with melodies and beats produced through the use of found objects, foreshadowed the diasporic bricolage that would become central to Baca's aesthetic. Although her later work would return to her Revival roots, her music consistently embraces what one might call an aesthetics of transit: a commitment to building on the familiar but breaking with the static, and to honoring the transformative power of ongoing travel, dialogue, and encounter: "Here the trend was to only copy [Revival songs and aesthetics]. . . . But it is possible to make new music out of Afro-Peruvian song."[89] Her recordings as a solo artist have actuated this logic of intertextual fusion, combining Afro-Peruvian melodic and rhythmic traditions with borrowed or experimental arrangements and instrumentation, and often original poetry.

In this sense, Baca's contemporary work performs traditional Afro-Peruvian melodies, lyrics, and rhythms while simultaneously troubling their canonization. For example, her signature song "María Landó" puts lyrics written by Peruvian poet César Calvo to a melody that combines rhythmic samplings of the *criollo* rhythm *vals* with the Afro-Peruvian *festejo* and *landó*. Moreover, the narrative structure of the song departs from that of Black Arts Revival–era *landós*, instead echoing the structure of verse-*montuno* characteristic Afro-Cuban son.[90] Baca's incorporation of non-Afro-Peruvian elements into her music has made her simultaneously recognizably and unrecognizably Afro-Peruvian to a national audience: at the same time that her bodily and artistic "blackness" positions her within the sociocultural margins to which Afroperuanidad has traditionally been relegated, her refusal to faithfully reproduce "pure" Afro-Peruvian musical forms has led listeners and cultural critics within Peru to read Baca's work as a corrupted or impoverished imitation of "authentic" Afro-Peruvian expressive traditions. However, an alternative reading of Baca's creative strategies that attends to the political and creative possibilities produced through the interrogation of seemingly naturalized notions of cultural, racial, or national continuity, however, might read in Baca's music a disruption of foundational categorical binaries of ontology and invention, past and present, nation and diaspora that enables the production of new spatialized configurations for raced and gendered meaning.

This hybrid and destabilizing approach to "musicking" has made Baca's work unpopular among Peruvian audiences, and for years Baca struggled to secure a recording contract to no avail. Baca's languishing career, however, took an unexpected international turn following her collaboration with musical artist and world beat producer, David Byrne. Under Byrne's corporate sponsorship and artistic direction, *The Soul of Black Peru* was introduced to global audiences in 1995. As is often the case with such projects, Byrne's interest in Afro-Peruvian song originated in a chance encounter: an assignment in a New York–based Spanish class that required him to translate the lyrics to Susana Baca's "María Landó." After watching a video-recording of Baca's performance, Byrne was so impressed that he learned the song to perform it on the South American leg of his *Rei Momo* tour.[91] Baca's rendition of "María Landó" would later become a featured track on *The Soul of Black Peru* alongside a compilation of digitally reproduced popular songs from the Black Arts Revival, the rights to which Byrne secured through negotiations between his world music label Luaka Bop and local recording companies in Lima. *Black Peru* was simply the most recent of Byrne's music curatorial projects: during Luaka Bop's eight-year existence, he had already sponsored successful world beat compilations of artists from Japan, Brazil, and Cuba.[92] When asked in an interview about the artistic concept of his world music company, Byrne replied: "Sometimes it takes a naïve foreigner to appreciate what people who live in a country don't realize they have."[93]

However unintentionally, Byrne's flippant response serves as an index of the complexities of globalized cultural industries. At the same time that his defense of transnational recording projects such as *The Soul of Black Peru* uncritically rearticulates the uneven relations of capital and representation undergirding musical collaborations between social actors of the global North and South as benign boosterism, it also appropriately locates the politics of cultural travel as one nexus of the imbricated, if partitioned, geographies of production and exchange. In this sense, Byrne's world beat project calls into question the assumption that popular, regionalized, or rarified forms of cultural practice are best—or even feasibly—addressed within a static or essentialized framework of "nation." Ironically, despite the title of Byrne's compilation, the extent to which Peru's Black coastal traditions are currently recognized or celebrated as a "national" music remains a matter of debate, and the arrival of Afro-Peruvian music to the national public sphere was the product not only of local cultural politics but of transnational relationships and international events. Moreover, in centering "María Landó" and Baca in his compilation, Byrne effectively re-presents Baca; his claim in introducing her as a renowned world music artist on the global stage relied upon his interpellation of her as an authentic exemplar of Afroperuanidad. Indeed, her ostensibly emblematic status, as well as her talent, was crucial to her emergence as the international face of Afro-Peruvian music.

To offer a critique of Byrne's "naïve" and profoundly limited description of world music relationships is not to suggest that Baca's arrival to the global stage is reducible to a cautionary tale either of international appropriation or of hybridized assimilation; certainly, Susana Baca's own complex personhood impedes such a critical move. Significantly, Baca has leveraged her international fame as a "global diva" and the resources that her renown has garnered to revitalize the Instituto Negrocontinuo, a public archive and research center founded by Baca and Ricardo Periera dedicated to the study of Black expressive culture in the Americas. Housed in Baca's home in Chorrillos, a historically working-class, interracial urban neighborhood of Lima, the center has institutionalized Baca's efforts to revitalize and transform local and national Afro-Peruvian cultural networks by initiating recording and publication projects that resonate closely with the work of Baca's mentors and predecessors of the Black Arts Revival. Deeply influenced by the performance and research methodologies of Victoria Santa Cruz and Peru Negro, Baca has worked with scholars, particularly ethnomusicologists, to collect, perform, and record Afro-Peruvian sonic culture; she has also initiated an experimental musical oral history project throughout the Black Pacific, painstakingly piecing together undocumented melodies, choreographies, and lyrics from fragments that she and other practitioners recall collaboratively. And like Victoria Santa Cruz, Baca's music and poetry have drawn upon raced, gendered, and sexual tropes of enslavement and sexual exploitation, creating a thematic emphasis on the expropriated bodies and labor of Afrolatinas.

Yet neither Baca's continued recording career, nor her work with Instituto Negrocontinuo, can be seen as an uncomplicated continuation or extension of the work of Victoria Santa Cruz, or the Black Arts Revival as a whole. For while Baca builds on the theoretical and ideological premises upon which the mid-century Revival movement was constructed, both her approach and intent depart from that of her predecessors. Rather than seeking to reconstruct an Afro-Peruvian countermemory to challenge the national erasure of blackness in the name of postcolonial unity, Baca's artistic and scholarly work places Afro-Peruvian expressive culture in dialogue and collaboration with multiply located Black diasporic expressive forms in order to produce what Periera has dubbed "a new negritude"—that is, a Black diasporic consciousness that is both situated within and extends beyond the territorial boundaries of Peru.[94]

For example, in collaboration with the Puerto Rican urban hip-hop band, Calle 13, Afro-indigenous Colombian singer, Totó la Momposina, and Brazilian Jazz vocalist María Rita, Baca recorded the Grammy Award–winning song, "Latinoamérica," in 2010. In keeping with Baca's aesthetic signatures of rupture and fusion, as well as her political commitment to hemispheric dialogue and coalition across and among communities of color, "Latinoamérica" breaks with the bounds and binds of race, nation, and genre. While music critics have largely focused on the compelling lyrics of the ballad, which proffer a trenchant critique of U.S. militarism, Western imperialism, and neoliberalism, few have addressed the unique coalitional politics likewise enacted through its aural transgressions. If we instead address "Latinoamérica" as a layered multimedia text, "listening in detail" for the socioaesthetic logics that animate it, we can read it as a sonic critique of and response to the limits of both nationalist musical canonicity and international culture industry structures.[95]

"Latinoamérica"'s musicality is forged through the integration of instruments ranging from the *cuatro venezolano*, to the *quijada* and *cajón peruano*, to the guitar, synthesizer, and violin, and stylistic fusions of Caribbean hip-hop and Argentinian *chacarera* as well as other elements of African and indigenous South American popular forms.[96] It features a creative layering of distinctive vocal styles and lyrics, incorporating spoken word, nonlexical vocables, and scat singing with melodic and harmonic crooning, interpreted in both Spanish and Portuguese. This sonic mash-up is reflective of the diversity of collaborating artists, whose collective work is informed by genres as variant as jazz, *son*, *rumba*, and *bossa nova* to *reggaeton* and hip-hop, to *festejo*, *landó*, and *zamacueca* to *cumbia*, *bullerenge*, and *chalupa*.

Yet, this commingling of numerous musical forms and styles and the geopolitical histories that they connote is not intended to stage the kinds of crude multiculturalist "partnerships" that characterize typical "world music" collaborations. Nor is it adherent to the patriotic (and by extension, patriarchal) nationalist canons that position aural expression as a bounded state resource and hybrid musical forms as a measure of progress or symbol of unity. Rather, in its embrace of regional musical variation as representative of geocultural specific histories of racial-ethnic formation informed by hemispheric processes of colonialism, chattel slavery, war, resource extraction, and labor exploitation, "Latinoamérica" posits sonic difference as a critical point of departure, rather than fissure, in the formation of pan-Americanist coalitions. In doing so, it troubles "Latin" as a monolithic commercial category of musical promotion, as well as the tendency within earlier incarnations of pan-Americanism to privilege artists of "universal" appeal (read urban, mestizo men) over those representative of particularistic traditions (indigenous and African-descended women of poor and/or peasant backgrounds). In short, "Latinoamérica" can be read as a collective articulation of a uniquely Afro-Latino diasporicity that acknowledges the aesthetic influences of New World indigenous communities in shaping expressive cultures of América's African descended.

In a case, then, of what Paul Gilroy or Amiri Baraka might describe as "the changing same" of Black Atlantic culture, Baca's Black Pacific–based projects proffer a "repetition and revision" of the signifying work of the Black Arts Revival, producing Baca's own memory of difference of Victoria Santa Cruz's memory of difference.[97] At the same time, Baca's resignification of Afroperuanidad and Black diasporicity proffers multiple, overlapping feminist interventions. Within Afro-nationalist circles, her work enacts a reconceptualization of Black female body as a vehicle for agential creative reinvention rather than passive authentic reproduction, thus staging a critical sonic challenge to conventional forms of knowledge production. At the same time, her work can also be read as a sonic response to popular and academic diasporic canons that privilege the lives and work of urban lettered intellectuals in and of the cosmopolitan Black Atlantic over the geohistories and cultural forms that emanate from the provincialized Black Pacific.

CAJÓN ROBLES

In the predawn hours of her childhood, Carmen Petralina "Peta" Robles Izquierdo would often lie awake in the bedroom she shared with her sister, Maria Katalina (Kata), listening for the stirrings of *una jarana*.[98] In the late 1970s, Peta and Kata's family home in Barrios Altos, Lima was often host to these boisterous sonic events, in which adults gathered to commune through singing, music, dance, and drink. Peta recalls, "My uncles were musicians and they would always arrive . . . at night . . . with folks from the peñas and would wind down their evenings at my house."[99] Though the young Robles sisters were prohibited from attending these "fiestas de adultos" (adult parties), *la jarana* played a crucial pedagogical function in their artistic formation. Kata recounts: "We learned to play by ear. . . . The window in my room was right across from the living room, which was where [the adults] would gather to play music, sing, and dance. So, we would clamber up to the window and stay awake for the entire night, and when my papa was not paying attention we would begin to play."[100] Here Kata relates the moment when the Robles sisters first learned to play the cajón. She notes that their introduction to its percussive methods was wholly aural; though they longed for formal instruction, their father forbade his daughters to learn the instrument owed to its popular equation with the performance of Black masculinity. "My father would say, 'No! I do not want [you to play *el cajón*] because only men play [that instrument],'" Peta recalls. Even so, captivated by the cajón's textured sounds and rhythmic cadences, the Robles sisters exploited the distractions of *la jarana* to secretly nurture their musical pursuits. The two passed countless sleepless nights in the dark of their bedroom, mounting an overturned wooden chair while listening to and emulating the rhythmic slaps of famed *cajoneros* performing in the adjacent room.

Women percussionists in 1970s urban Lima were extremely rare; indeed, Peta recalls knowing of only two *cajoneras* who were part of professional music circles: Marta Panchano, and Peta and Kata's maternal aunt, Vicky Izquierdo.[101] With her trailblazing career as an artist and choreographer, her refusal to observe gendered codes of public respectability, and her status as an unmarried woman reputedly partnered with other women, Izquierdo herself was widely known as "brava." An established vocalist and dancer in Victoria Santa Cruz's Teatro y Danzas Negras del Perú in the 1960s, Izquierdo's true passion was the cajón.[102] However, professional opportunities for *cajoneras* were scarce, as most Revival artists viewed percussive performance as exclusively suited to the physicality of the "male" body and sociality among men. Thus, at a moment when Revival musical groups were almost exclusively directed and staffed by men, she founded and led her own performance collective: *El Poder Negro de Vicky Izquierdo* (The Black Power of Vicky Izquierdo).[103]

As I noted in the previous section, Revival institutions and canons have more often reified than reconfigured the heteropatriarchal organization of public performance scenarios. This is evidenced in Afro-Peruvian artistic circles, where heteronormative codes of bodily comportment maintained a gendered division of musical labor in which the "masterful" labors of creative direction and instrumental performance were perceived as inextricable from heteromasculinity. In founding El Poder Negro, Izquierdo both disrupted and challenged the dominant geocultural imaginaries and arrangements that (re)produced these gendered divides. At that time, Revival troupes typically emerged from "musical families" that traced their roots through patriarchal genealogies of instrumentalists; within the "musical family" configuration, women were trained as dancers and vocalists, but musical production remained a masculinized domain. By naming the performance collective after herself, and by situating it within internationalist Black freedom struggles, Izquierdo effectively respatialized the provincialism of the national sphere and the parochialism of the national family. Within the coanimating terrains of the national and the familial, El Poder Negro opened up material and subjective space for aspiring Black women musicians, and in doing so, paved the way for a subsequent generation of female performers—most notably, her nieces.

By the time they entered their teens, Peta and Kata had become formidable percussionists proficient in the Revival repertoires of their elders. Izquierdo, who was living with their family at the time, tasked herself with providing the sisters with formal training and mentorship, which culminated in an invitation to perform professionally with El Poder Negro. Despite their artistic connections and undeniable talent, however, the Robles sisters encountered social barriers and familial constraints commonly faced by female musicians that aspire to access masculinized landscapes within the aural public sphere. Although their mother was herself a performer from a well-known musical family, their father staunchly opposed his daughters' musical ambitions, which he equated with venues and behaviors that transgressed dominant social mores of femininity and respectability. Peta recounts: "My father would say, 'You are a woman! What are you going to do in the predawn hours in the peñas? Huh?' . . . He never wanted . . . me to play or sing, or anything like that. He did not want me performing in peñas, because generally one has to spend late nights, you know, amidst alcohol, cigarettes, etc."[104]

Throughout the twentieth century, las peñas were regarded as sites of masculinized politicking and pleasure; women who entered these spaces as performers or patrons risked having derogatory and dangerous assumptions made about their sexual promiscuity, lack of refinement, and questionable femininity. Nonetheless, las peñas were hubs of Afro-Peruvian performance, and as such, crucial venues for both the cultivation of listening publics and the expression of feminist cultural citizenship. By the ages of fourteen and fifteen the Robles sisters were regularly performing with El Poder Negro at peñas throughout greater Lima.[105] And, while their very presence as young Black women marked them as "out of place" within the cultural setting of la peña, their performing bodies as *cajoneras* emplaced what Deborah R. Vargas has dubbed a "dissonant sonic scene"—that is, a *scene* that, when *seen*, registers a different kind of sound owed to its disruption of the anticipated alignments of the visual and aural.

In her discussion of the accordion as a symbol of heteromasculinity within the Tex-Mex *conjunto*, Vargas astutely observes that "certain instruments have come to represent etiologies of musical genres, cultures, and subjects."[106] Vargas's assertion is useful for apprehending the symbolic power of *el cajón* within Revivalist discourse, particularly as it relates to gendered genealogies of apprenticeship and geographies of instrumentalism that prevail within cultural nationalist circles. As Kata and Peta are quick to note, *el cajón's* emblematic status has oft been mobilized to tether the heteromasculinist investments of *afroperuanismo* to gendered and sexualized cultural labors and bodily practices. Within Revival repertoires, el cajón provides the percussive foundation of the sonic event, orienting and ordering musician and dancer, performer and audience, in space. This rhythmic hailing and the somatic postures and positions that it prescribes are both gendered and sexualized. *El cajón* stages an entry point into the sonic text, as *el ritmo* registers its tone and plotline. To play requires physical strength and broad reach—characteristics identified with masculine strength and endurance. And it requires the percussionist to mount the instrument in an open-legged straddle—a posture associated with heterosexual erotics and male domination. For these and other reasons, Revival practitioners and canons of the era dubbed el cajón an intrinsically masculine art form: on the one hand, a woman publically performing astride the wooden box was viewed by many as an obscene gesture of sexual availability; on the other hand, such displays were often likened to acts of sexual penetration, thus rendering performances by *cajoneras* inherently queer acts. Kata relates, "It has always been difficult to play music. When you are a woman, the first thing that people say to you if you play the cajón is '*marimacha*' [a pejorative term for lesbians]. Because the cajón is a masculine instrument, people would say that a woman who plays cajón is, as they say here in Peru, '*machona*' (butch) or '*marimacha*.' Always."[107]

Feminist geographer Linda McDowell has aptly argued that "spatial divisions . . . are also affected by and reflected in embodied practices."[108] In other words, geographic relations are inherently political, and operate on the scale of the body through ideologically determined and often materially enforced codes of emplacement and embodiment. As Kata's comments suggest, within Afro-Peruvian musical circles, *la cajonera* disrupts the coherence of Revival narratives that prescribe gendered divisions of musical labor as her performing body is marked as "out of place" within the hetero-masculinist relations that constitute a "proper sonic scene." If, as Revival artists of the 1960s asserted, a central imperative of Afro-Peruvian cultural activism was to reimagine and reclaim the racialized body and its myriad dis-placements within the spheres of the national and the urban, then we might understand Afro-Peruvian *cajoneras* as extending that project by performing embodied and aural contests to the gendered and sexual constraints that have endured within it.

Nearly thirty years have passed since *las hermanas* Robles first took to the stage as *cajoneras*. Since then, Peta and Kata have established themselves as prominent feminist cultural workers within Lima's Afro-Peruvian community. In 2007, they joined Ambiente Criollo, "a group exclusively of women that have come together with a particular vision" of the "preservation and cultivation" of *criollo* music." Here, *criollo* is invoked as an umbrella term for musical traditions that have emerged along the Peruvian coastline, which, in addition to Afro-Peruvian rhythms, include the *marinera*, *polca*, *tondero*, and *vals*. The group's name is a play on words: while "*ambiente criollo*" roughly translates as "criollo ambience," its inversion, "*criollos de ambiente*," denotes the slang term for queer criollos. Ambiente Criollo was the brainchild of a group of Black and mestiza women musicians that, in lieu of seeking inclusion into extant male-dominated musical circles, aspired to forge "a special place" for the performance of "rhythms for women, by women!"[109] This explicitly women-centered, and implicitly queer, orientation expands and extends the feminist cultural activism initiated by El Poder Negro a generation prior.

While Ambiente Criollo embraces the performance of conventional ethnic and nationalist musical repertoires, their creative re-interpretation of the aural and visual orders and alignments that structure these canons enacts a queer feminist intervention into heteromasculinist articulations of racial and national belonging. Within Ambiente Criollo's sonic scenes, the body of the male instrumentalist is re-placed with those of women musicians who, clad in the black pants and white dress shirts typically donned by male artists, perform both sound and gender in variant ways. Popular love songs that customarily convey heterosexual longing and prompt homosocial bonding around a feminine object of male desire are recast as expressions of feminist erotics and queer female desire. Ambient Criollo's appropriation—and queering—of criollo sonic scripts thus opens up "a special place" of contest within dominant material and aural performance geographies of belonging, making space for the differential expressions of gender, sociality and desire.

Over the past decade, the Robles sisters have shifted their professional focus, now splitting their time as (inter)national performers and instructors. In 2014, Peta relocated to the San Francisco Bay Area to join the De Rompe y Raja Cultural Association. There, in addition to performing as a percussionist, vocalist, and dancer, she teaches cajón to children. When we chatted about this new project in the summer of 2015, Peta spoke eloquently about her pedagogical approach to rhythmic instruction, which integrates bodily movement (jumping, stomping, and slapping), percussive practices (clapping, shaking, and striking), and political education about Afro-Peruvian culture and performance. Kata, a member of the Lima-based performance collective Teatro del Milenio, describes a similar didactical method, which emphasizes the art of transforming everyday objects—chairs, broomsticks, or wooden spoons—into percussive instruments. Strikingly, when I asked Kata about her experiences as a teacher at Milenio during an interview in 2014, her response was uncannily similar to Victoria Santa Cruz's reflections on coming into political consciousness nearly a half century earlier: "That is what I have learned [as a performer and teacher] at Milenio. The love of blackness. . . . I learned what it means to feel like a proud, African-descended woman, no? I learned to love myself as an African-descended woman, no? But the most important thing I learned was to accept myself. Because here the first thing that you experience are insults, and you grow up bearing the weight of those insults."[110]

While Revival institutions and canons have popularized decisive critiques of and responses to anti-Black racism within both regional and international spheres, they have simultaneously emplaced their own heteropatriarchal divisions and exclusions. Against these constraints, the Izquierdo-Robles line of *mujeres bravas* has territorialized an alternative performance geography of Afro-Peruvian feminist cultural production. Their collective musical activism has effectively respatialized myriad raced and gendered technologies of containment and constraint as they operate on and within the intimate scales of the body and the home. First, Izquierdo's El Poder Negro made space for the reconfiguration of the musical family among Afro-Peruvian Revival artists. In doing so, what was once a site of heteropatriarchal division and exclusion was reterritorialized as a place where feminist genealogies of musicianship could be established. Next, from their presence, physicality, and dexterity to their technique, creativity, and charisma, *las cajoneras* Robles rewrote dominant scripts about the performing body itself, challenging dominant scripts concerning "natural" and "appropriate" modes of public embodiment. Finally, by performing in the public sphere—particularly in las peñas—Izquierdo and *las hermanas* Robles have effectively challenged the raced and gendered codes of comportment that render the Black female body as "naturally" or "appropriately" in or out of place—within the immediate family, the racialized community, and the national imaginary.

CONCLUSIONS

I have intentionally bookended my account of Peru's mid-century Black Arts Revival by recounting four pivotal moments in its internationally situated national development. By opening with the historic desegregation of Lima's municipal theater, historicizing the birth and development of Peru's Black Arts Revival, and then concluding with contemporary disruptions of Revival repertoires and canons, I have drawn attention to critical convergences in the projects of Black women artists-cum-activists who were otherwise separated by their respective temporal and geographic contexts. Arguably, Dunham, Santa Cruz, Baca, and the Robles sisters cross paths not only as social actors in Peru's Black cultural renaissance, but also as feminist diasporic intellectuals who have sustained a transgenerational dialogue regarding the interplay of race, culture, and subject formation in the Americas.

While the creative and pedagogical endeavors of these "mujeres bravas" vary according to the temporalities and geographies of their distinct contexts and the contingencies of their distinct struggles, one can trace three theoretical/methodological convergences that inhere in their respective projects. First, each scholar-artist strategically rejects positivist conventions of conducting and presenting research, eschewing "authentic" or documentarian-style portrayals of culture in their creative work. From Dunham's and Santa Cruz's innovative stagings of "memories of difference" to Baca's inventive use of "repetition and renovation," to the Robles sisters' queering of Revival practices and institutions each of these cultural workers deploys research methods that challenge dominant conceptions of ontology and objectivity. Second, in each of these cases, a departure from dominant musical and stylistic canons has been central to the political project of each artist. Strategic intertextual engagements with aesthetic, rhythmic, melodic, and choreographic methods within and among different places of diaspora enabled each of these cultural workers to critique and disrupt the dominant historical narrative and spatial orderings of their respective contexts. Finally, each of these artists employs innovative interdisciplinary approaches to knowledge production, blurring the theoretical, disciplinary, and practical boundaries between "archive" and "repertoire," social text and spatial context.

The transgenerational performance geographies of political colloquy and communion imagined and actualized by these Black feminist cultural workers are instructive for several reasons. First, they reflect important convergences among three sociocultural movements that are rarely coexamined: Peru's mid-century Black Arts Revival, Black liberation struggles in the United States and continental Africa, and internationalized (and often internationalist) formations of Latin American musical production. Next, they expand transatlantic mappings of the African diaspora by drawing attention to regional, national, and global cultural work and political contributions of the formerly enslaved communities concentrated on the American Pacific (1970s). Finally, by working across and against commonsense spatial divides such as "public" and "private," and scalar typologies such as the "mestizo nation" or the "Black Atlantic," these artists not only index and challenge the geographic technologies that enact their containment, provincialization, or erasure; they also effectively shift the relations of power and difference that inhere in their making. In other words, their stories powerfully demonstrate how geographic emplacement has served as both a primary technology of discipline and erasure and, when paired with cultural production, a creative strategy of political organizing and empowerment.

Taken together, the cultural histories of respatialization and rescaling heretofore examined proffer meaningful contributions toward the development of a spatialized feminist diasporic praxis. However, the performance geographies that constitute this transnational, transgenerational conversation are most often conceptually foreclosed within current transnational feminist and African diasporic frameworks. If the national import of Peru's Black Arts Revival has remained largely underestimated or ignored, this elision has been replicated at the international scale, as the significance of the movement's diasporic strands remains equally uninterrogated. In part, this elision is owed to regional, thematic, and linguistic divides within current regimes of academic knowledge production. For like many histories of transnational cultural production, that of Peru's Black Arts Revival is unruly and circuitous. It is a story that penetrates regional, national, and continental borders; that is remembered in fragments of Spanish and/or English; and is recorded and retold through rhythm and sound. To address this multiscalar history of Black diasporic intellectualism, then, would require a blurring of the institutionalized geographic foci, linguistic orientations and disciplinary boundaries that currently delineate the fields Black Atlantic studies and Latina/o studies.

If the fundamental critique of Peru's Black Arts Revival concerns the historical impossibility of a Black *and* Peruvian subject, then this erasure has all too often been replicated in current academic literatures. And the study of Afroperuanismo is not the only scene in which this epistemological dilemma is staged. Within the fields of both U.S. Latina/o and Latin American studies, the political interplay of race, nation, and Afro-Latinidad remains remarkably understudied. Even the most useful and politically progressive paradigms for the study of postcolonial relations within the Americas fail to fully grapple with the implications of slavery in the context of Latin American nation building.[111] Within the fields of U.S. Latina/o and Latin American studies, crucial to this consistent foreclosure has been the continued salience of a concept of colonialism that emphasizes the invasion and seizure of land-based territories. Such a delimited understanding of the violence of colonialism necessarily elides the concomitant processes of expropriation on the scale of the *body* through which the Black slave—particularly the reproductive body of the Black female slave—became an integral element in the production of the colony, and by extension, the postcolony.[112] The continuing trend within U.S. Latina/o and Latin American studies to reiterate a historical narrative that centers the indigenous and/or mestizo subject frequently, however unintentionally, serves to replicate the original social death and civil exclusion that defined African chattel slavery.

Conversely, within the field of Black studies, slavery and subjection have been most often explored through a diasporic framework that emphasizes the United States, Europe, the French- and English-speaking Caribbean, and, to a lesser extent, continental Africa. In no small part due to the remarkable influence of "Black Atlantic" models of diasporic travel, displacement, and exchange, Black studies has, by and large, continued to neglect the many Pacific and continental locations of Black diasporicity in Latin America and much of the Spanish-speaking Caribbean.[113] As Brent Edwards reminds us, "the discourse of diaspora is . . . both enabling to black studies . . . and inherently at risk, in that it can fall back into either racial essentialism or American vanguardism."[114] Following Edwards's admonitions, I would suggest that the continuing intellectual hegemony of English-speaking scholars within Black diaspora studies has (re)produced— albeit inadvertently—its own form of U.S. exceptionalism; that is, a model of Black studies in which the political and cultural specificities of blackness in the United States are abstracted to serve as the theoretical point of origin from which to understand blackness in the Americas.

What then, does the journey of Afro-Peruvian expressive culture through local and global performance circuits proffer to scholars committed to rethinking the thematic, linguistic, and disciplinary boundaries within Inter-American studies? I would suggest that the Black Arts Revival's long-standing, multiscalar struggle over autonomous political and aesthetic representation, in both popular and academic spheres, reveals important methodological and theoretical insights for rethinking the dominant geotemporal frames through which particular sites and subjects of history are commonly (re)-presented. Consequently, it suggests several possible new directions for the study of race, place, and culture in the Americas.

First, the Black Arts Revival's sonic, textual, and embodied reconfiguration of space points to the necessity of continuing to rethink the geographic conventions through which both disciplines and interdisciplinary fields have traditionally conceived of themselves. In particular, the delocalized sociospatial epistemology underlying Afroperuanismo, which expresses a diasporic performative rearticulation of the historical and geographic processes of national formation, introduces an inventive model of theorizing the temporal and spatial contingencies of the national and the popular. Second, the unconventional methodologies employed by Afro-Peruvian activists, artists, and intellectuals—in particular, the comparative analysis and intertextual exchange of sonic, linguistic, and rhythmic technologies throughout the Latin American and Caribbean Black diaspora—represent innovative modes of exposing the contradictions of dominant historical paradigms, nationalist discourses, and exclusionary narratives.

I want to conclude by suggesting the importance of such interdisciplinary theoretical and methodological engagements in the development of new directions in Afro-Latino studies. In recent years, scholars of Afro-Latinidad have argued for increased attention to the historical and contemporary function of the coastal-based cultures of Latin America. A significant strand of this work emphasizes the Peruvian viceroyalty's centuries-long role as the center of African chattel slavery in the Spanish New World, during which hundreds of thousands of captive Africans traveled a vast distance of sea and land from the island slave societies of the Spanish Caribbean to the Peruvian seaport of Callao.[115] For many, "Black Pacific" has served as an emergent framework of African diasporicity that critiques the failure of models such as the Black Atlantic to address the "ambiguous relationship [of blackness] with local creole and indigenous cultures and with the black Atlantic itself" at play in the so-called Black Pacific.[116] Conversely, the Black Pacific gives name to those sites and subjects positioned at the physical and ideological limits of both the postcolonial nation-state and the Black Atlantic, drawing critical attention to the dispersed and diverse sites that make up the Black Americas more broadly.[117]

My own thinking on a globalized Black Peru takes as its starting point the validity and critical importance of such interventions: the mass trade in human chattel from Africa certainly had long-standing effects on the racial demographics of both the colonial territory and the Spanish Americas and has profoundly influenced the historical trajectory of nation building in postcolonial Peru and the emergence of a Pacific-based diasporic consciousness in Latin America. As a vehicle through which to explore the political and theoretical stakes of a feminist spatial politics of diaspora, however, my interest in Afro-Peruvian expressive culture lies in its indexical relationship to multiple constitutive foreclosures—that is, not only that of Afro-Latinidad from models of Black diasporicity, but of the political geographies of blackness from formulations of the postcolonial Latin American nation-state, of the so-called private scales of human interaction and ideological production from (always raced and gendered) conceptions of the political, and of localized renegotiations of race, gender, and place from current paradigms of globalized cultural exchange. In short, if the disavowal of Afro-Latinidad has filled a necessary function in the production of the spatiopolitical categories both of "diaspora" and "nation" in the context of the Americas, then the work of artists such as Katherine Dunham, Victoria Santa Cruz, Susana Baca, and the Robles sisters carries the potential to radically intervene in the cartographic structures and meaning making practices that (re)produce these effacements. To hear the interventions of these *mujeres bravas*, scholars in the global North are compelled to listen both across and against multiple and often divergent epistemological boundaries, not only between theoretical trajectories and thematic foci, but also across Spanish and English, between rhythm and sound, and across ever-shifting conceptions of the local and the global.

4

"YOU CAN'T HAVE A REVOLUTION WITHOUT SONGS"

Neighborhood Soundscapes and Multiscalar
Activism in La Misión

On a chilly June evening in the summer of 1992, an extended network of San Francisco–based artists and their friends gathered on the outdoor patio of queer Chilean poet and photographer Alejandro Stuart's basement apartment (figure 4.1) for a night of musical revelry. This seemingly provincial event—hosted in an aging Victorian rental in the residential heart of San Francisco's largest Latina/o neighborhood, the Mission—was much more than a weekend house party.[1] It marked the inauguration of a collaborative undertaking many months in the making: the establishment of a grassroots neighborhood venue where artists, activists, and audiences could convene to produce sonic, visual, and performed art; trade relevant news and resources; and mobilize around local and international political issues. With founders representing at least three generations and four regions of Latin American and Latina/o artists and intellectuals, this lofty endeavor was hatched from lengthy imaginative and logistical community synergies; the former produced a vision for a cultural center capable of operating beyond the juridical and economic purview of local authorities, while the latter actualized it through practices that included the collective recovery and purchase of secondhand chairs, the construction of a makeshift stage, and the word-of-mouth recruitment of patrons. The institution born of these

4.1 Alejandro Stuart's residence. Photo by the author.

coactive efforts would endure for a near decade, representing a remarkable convergence of overlapping political aspirations, hemispheric histories, and practices of musicking: San Francisco's first permanent *peña*, La Peña del Sur.[2]

Politically oriented niteries where artists gather to perform or display their work for local audiences, peñas were first popularized in Latin America during the anti-imperialist struggles of the 1960s. In response to the industrialization of Western mass media, these neighborhood cultural centers were heralded as alternative, grassroots forums for the instruction, development, and showcasing of regional Latin American musical genres. Venue programming typically featured artists and instructors of the Nueva Canción (New Song) tradition—a hemispheric musical movement that linked regional sonic cultures through a shared critique of U.S. imperialism and racial capitalism.[3] Although the character and function of these organizations differed across regional contexts, the peña was arguably the emblematic institution through which the Nueva Canción movement sought to attain its musical goals: to foment political dialogue and solidarity across racial, regional, national, and class divides, and ultimately, to create a broad-based anti-imperial, anticapitalist movement in the Americas. La Peña del Sur was born of this mid-century hemispheric history, yet realized according to the contemporary sociospatial contingencies of immigrant of color activism in San Francisco. Its founders and participants effectively transposed the typically nationalist framework of the mid-century peña into a translocal context with the explicit aim of bringing together the heterogeneous immigrant classes of urban San Francisco.

This chapter draws together the analytics and vocabularies of critical geography, sound, and performance studies, and of feminist and queer of color theory to offer a geosonic reading of La Peña del Sur's rich cultural history. In chronicling this organization's story as the making of a performance geography, the chapter likewise takes interest in how the staging conversations within and across these fields might exact critical pressure upon conventional (inter)disciplinary methods and frames. Toward the development of fresh modes and novel lenses of analysis, it asks: What is enabled by an interpretative framework that attends to the dynamic interplay of the sonic and the spatial within formations of social contest? How might such an analytic engender and/or require new approaches to the study of cultural politics—approaches that emphasize the performative logics and improvisational strategies of quotidian political organizing? And in our current political moment, what might we learn from previous community struggles that have leveraged a spatialized politics of musicking as a creative means of organizing against multiscalar socioeconomic abandonment, relishing moments of leisure and pleasure, and envisioning and territorializing new modes of transnational, multiracial community formation?

To address these questions, this chapter emphasizes three vital elements of La Peña del Sur as a performance geography. First, it offers a queer geographic reading of the peña's unconventional organizational structure, which, I argue, productively troubled commonsense geotemporal boundaries between public and private spheres, aesthetic and political practice, and labor and leisure time. Next, it surveys the multiscalar political work performed through La Peña's conceptual imaginary of "Southernness," which positioned the organization as both locally situated and transnationally oriented. Finally, it reflects upon La Peña's ongoing confrontation with debates concerning competing conceptions of sustainability as they relate to the limits and possibilities of institutionalization. It concludes with the argument that, taken together, these defining features of La Peña del Sur—and the ongoing sociosonic negotiations that produced them—enrooted a vital venue for otherwise unlikely encounters among Mission-area residents, which in turn enabled creative coalitional responses to issues ranging from California Proposition 187 to the Zapatista revolution in Mexico, to the gentrification of San Francisco's neighborhoods of color.

PART ONE: MAKING MUSIC, MAKING PLACE

In this section, I offer a queer geocultural reading of La Peña del Sur's anti-institutional organizational structure and the imperatives that shaped it, giving emphasis to how these enabled productive modes of congregation, conversation, and collaboration. To address these and other related thematics, I engage in a reading method that integrates the grammars of critical geography with what Rod Ferguson and Grace Hong have described as the necessarily "comparative" and "relational" approaches of women of color feminism and queer of color critique.[4] I begin with a brief description of this hermeneutic, reflecting on how queer geography and critical race, gender, and sexuality studies might be productively brought into conversation. I argue that the concatenation of these approaches provides a useful framework for interrogating how coalitional politics and spatial praxis were equally central to La Peña's creative mission. Subsequently, I detail the creative strategies and practices that territorialized La Peña as a venue. It is my contention that these productively defied and disrupted many of the institutionalized temporal norms and geographic arrangements that constrain contemporary immigrant of color sociality and organizing in San Francisco.

Sustained engagements with the sexual politics of space and place represent a relatively recent turn within the field of geography.[5] A significant contribution emerging from this work has been attention to and accounts of how normative heterosexuality is concomitantly inscribed in and maintained through material arrangements of space and dominant topographical imaginaries.[6] However, as feminist geographer Natalie Oswin cogently argues, approaches to these important questions have largely assumed or relied upon binary conceptions of straight and queer space, the latter defined as concrete locations fashioned or occupied by sexual dissidents.[7] The result has been an overarching emphasis within the discipline on "queer space," lauded as "a reterritorialization of heterosexual space" that "purportedly enables the visibility of sexual subcultures that resist and rupture the hegemonic heterosexuality that is the source of their marginality and exclusion."[8]

The social relations and material designs that constituted La Peña del Sur as a place arguably reflected the common quantitative markers of "queer space" presupposed by much of geography's work on sexuality. Indeed, the center's location, leadership, and patrons meet the identitarian criterion of the "queer space" calculus: formerly located at the crossroads of San Francisco's largest (white) gay neighborhoods—Valencia Street and the Castro—La Peña's leadership and patronage counted a number of queer folk among its ranks. And, in addition to its occasional inclusion of sexuality-oriented programming, it was even known for by many and exploited by some as a spot for queer cruising. However, in my view, geographic approaches to sexual politics are only enabling to the extent that they effectively grapple with how relations of power and difference are territorialized in and through the social production of space. In other words, the critical traction of queer as a geographic theoretical maneuver inheres in its ability to unsettle how normative categories of emplacement and embodiment are sedimented through the (re)production of dominant sites and landscapes. Here, the "queer space" approach falls short for several reasons.

Conceptions of place or location that presuppose a fixed or absolute divide between straight and queer disavow the internal contradictions and external erasures inherent to these unstable categories. By failing to address how sexual relations, identities, and practices are crosscut by ideologies and structures of gender, racial, and class difference, the "queer space" approach risks the uncritical celebration of "heterosexual space"'s reterritorialization—a process of geographic resignification that is oft accomplished through material and rhetorical strategies of occupation and settlement. It is not surprising that, within such accounts, poor neighborhoods of color come to represent the areas in need of homonormative occupation, and the violent forms of socioeconomic conflict that enable this production of "queer space" is at best neglected, at worst alibied.[9] As Jasbir Puar has aptly argued, "While it is predictable that the claiming of queer space is lauded as the disruption of heterosexual space, rarely is that disruption interrogated also as a disruption of racialized, gendered, and classed spaces."[10] In the case of La Peña del Sur, this distinction is particularly important. The ever-encroaching gentrification of its northern and western parameters via the expansion of the city's wealthy Eureka Valley "gayborhoods" has been celebrated by those communities as the diversification and development of "queer space" rather than the targeted displacement of queer and straight working-class Latina/os.[11]

Despite the conceptual shortcomings of the "queer space" model, however, a geographic analytic can provide valuable investigative tools for scholars of critical race, gender, and sexuality studies and cultural criticism. Yet, such a framework can only be useful to the extent that it engages these literatures. Eschewing geography's conventional thematic emphasis on "queer space" in favor of what Natalie Oswin has called a "queer approach to space" is one example of what such an interdisciplinary spatial analytic might look like.[12] For Oswin, a queer approach to space utilizes queer theory "to deconstruct the hetero-homo binary and examine sexuality's deployments in concert with racialized, classed, and gendered processes."[13] Following Oswin, it is clear that spatial engagements with the politics of difference—that is, with the logics and structures through which differential emplacements and displacements are realized—can productively refocus the queer geographic lens to address more pressing political questions. For example, to understand the interanimating politics of anti-immigrant revanchism and white gay gentrification in 1990s San Francisco, it is crucial to examine how media outlets and public discourse inscribed in the city's working-class ethnic neighborhoods racialized and classed notions of pathology, deviance, and backwardness. The Mission District, for instance, was often represented as a crossroads of economic lawlessness, masculinized violence, and reprosexual excess. Nonnormative arrangements of economy (informal exchange and undocumented labor), tenancy (multigenerational or occupancy rentals), and civil status (migrants, refugees, and the undocumented) were heralded as markers of a blighted community that threatened public safety and drained local and state resources. These images of a neighborhood in decline stood in stark contrast with popular portrayals of neighboring white middle-class "gayborhoods." In the case of the latter, as San Francisco rebranded itself in the early 1990s as the West Coast hub of gay tourism and urban hipster culture, the adjacent Castro, Dolores Heights, and Valencia Street areas were promoted as the epicenter of the city's boutique retail markets, trendy nightlife, and foodie culture.

Although rarely described as such, an interrogation of how normative geographic imaginaries and arrangements of social space function to construct, regulate, exploit, and otherwise devalue particular bodies and communities has figured as a central point of inquiry within women of color feminism and queer of color critique. Among the many points of convergence within these interanimating projects is the ongoing exploration of how imposed ideals of embodiment and emplacement enact death-dealing delineations between the normative and the pathological, the sanctioned and the criminalized, the protected and the vulnerable, the civically empowered and the socially disenfranchised inhere in geographic imaginaries and material geographic arrangements. Yet, a few notable exceptions notwithstanding, conversations between critical race, gender, and sexuality studies and the discipline of geography remain remarkably rare.[14] This scholarly trend is unfortunate, as women of color feminism and queer of color critique have much to offer modes of spatial inquiry. Take, for example, Grace Kyungwon Hong and Roderick A. Ferguson's contention that a political project common to women of color feminism and queer of color critique is a profound "question[ing] of nationalist and identitarian modes of political organization."[15] Such interrogations of seemingly fixed or discrete political identities productively destabilize static or absolute models of territorialization such as "queer space" by interrogating how socially and historically constructed identities such as "gay" or "lesbian" "have often worked to establish and police the lines between the "normal" and the "abnormal.""[16] Moreover, by foregrounding "alternative understandings of subjectivity, collectivity, and power," women of color feminist and queer approaches both invite and potentially offer critical geographic attention not only to the logics and machinations of dominant spatial imaginaries, but more important, their aberrations and oppositions.[17] In short, by emphasizing the dynamic and relational textures of structural formation and subject constitution, women of color feminism and queer of color critique potentially offer both a model and a method of geographic inquiry—one that conceptualizes geographies of difference as inextricably imbricated, dynamically processual, and necessarily contested.

An experimental organization–cum–neighborhood musical stage–cum–activist resource center, La Peña del Sur is a quintessential example of how the synchronization of coalitional politics, expressive cultures, and spatial practices can carve out new political and aesthetic terrains. Here, the critical import of this project lies not in its territorialization of an authentic or idealized "queer migrant space." Rather, of interest is its "queering" of the normative geotemporal boundaries that constrain migrant sociality, labor, and political organizing. As such, it is a project that requires analyses of culture, politics, and space not as autonomous agential spheres, but as mutually calibrating social forces.[18] Read through such a framework, La Peña del Sur can be understood as a performance geography that offers provocative examples of how practices of musical transposition can productively trouble commonsense divisions between public and private spheres, aesthetic and political practice, and labor and leisure time. It is to my reading of La Peña del Sur's anti-institutional structure that I now turn.

PART TWO: SETTING THE IMPROVISATIONAL STAGE

As a political project La Peña del Sur was envisioned and inaugurated in the shadow of various Latina/o and Latin American cultural centers that had thrived in the San Francisco Bay Area since the late 1970s. Perhaps the most influential of these was Berkeley's La Peña, a self-described "non-profit multi-cultural organization" that "promotes and supports Bay Area, California, nationally and internationally recognized music, dance, theater, film, inter-disciplinary and visual artists."[19] Berkeley's La Peña was incorporated on September 11, 1974—exactly one year following Augusto Pinochet's military coup in Chile, and opened its doors in the summer of 1975. In keeping with the tenets of the Nueva Canción movement, its pronounced mission was "to make the necessary connections between art and politics."[20] Alejandro Stuart (figure 4.2) was among the handful of exiled Chilean activists who founded the center.[21] It operated in a small rented commercial storefront on South Berkeley's Shattuck Avenue.[22] While initially focused on Chilean art and politics, Berkeley's La Peña became a haven for Central American artists during the dirty wars of the 1980s, as the center's cultural workers introduced programming that linked U.S. militarism in the middle-Americas to other, overlapping histories of U.S. imperial and anticommunist intervention in the hemisphere. As the center's constituency grew, its leadership opted to expand and formalize the locale. By the early 1990s, Berkeley's La Peña was a registered nonprofit funded by numerous federal grants and private arts foundations, and its board of directors successfully purchased the performance space, opened an adjoined restaurant and pub, and booked an impressive calendar of acclaimed international artists.

Although inspired by La Peña de Berkeley's success, founders of La Peña del Sur were unsettled by how the venue's location, cost, and institutional structure limited its management and patronage to primarily documented, bilingual, middle-class Latinas/os and Anglos. For Stuart and his cohort, these limitations breached the grassroots spirit of the Latin Amer-

4.2 Alejandro Stuart

ican peña—an institution historically associated with popular assembly, affordable fare, and improvisational encounter.[23] As the Peña founders recalled in a statement published in honor of its two-year anniversary, "considering the absence of venues within existing cultural institutions for our artistic-cultural expression, we found it necessary to form our own center, which owed to its geopolitical orientation we decided to call La Peña del Sur.[24] Specifically, La Peña del Sur's founders were critical of how the multiculturalist turn in mainstream U.S. cultural politics had permeated local institutions such as La Peña (de Berkeley), which they viewed as primarily aesthetically driven and thus disconnected from the political agendas from which they emerged. Moreover, they argued that the predominantly international focus of programming at institutions such as La Peña had eclipsed local agendas that were of concern to the Mission-based cultural workers: the soaring incarceration rates of Bay Area youth of color; the gentrification of Bay Area neighborhoods of color; and a new wave of anti-immigrant xenophobia and legislation.[25] Thus, this cadre of Mission District artists and activists collectively tasked themselves with the creation of a distinctive neighborhood peña, one that might appeal to a wider range of publics, facilitate a more improvisational and interactive event structure, and foment multiscalar modes of grassroots organizing. Following a series of informal gatherings and late-night brainstorming sessions, the group concurred that these aims would best be realized through the creation of a different kind of venue: a "Latin American cultural center that [functioned] independent of [state] authorities and official recognition."[26]

The transnational history and geographic landscape of La Misión profoundly influenced the design and implementation of La Peña del Sur. Roughly twenty-five square blocks of aging Victorian flats punctuated by retail corridors and open-air arcades, the working-class borough has been San Francisco's largest Latino neighborhood since the 1940s.[27] In the wake of post–World War II suburbanization, the district was repopulated by the city's Rincon Hill and North Beach Chicana/o and Latina/o communities—the former displaced by the Bay Bridge construction project in the 1930s, and the latter pushed out by rising rents and commercial development.[28] Its relatively affordable rental market, location along transit lines, and proximity to the downtown and South of Market employment centers made the Mission a convenient home for the city's rising population of Chicana/o and Latina/o industrial and service workers. Between the 1940s and the early 1970s, immigrants from Chile, El Salvador, Mexico, Peru, and Nicaragua—many fleeing political persecution—joined a politicized Chicano population to transform the Mission into a vibrant, pan-Latina/o neighborhood noted for its community-based activism and rich community infrastructure.[29]

Through the early 1990s, the "Miracle Mile" of Mission Street, with its crosscutting tributaries of Twenty-Fourth and Sixteenth Streets, provided local residents with produce and import markets, family-owned restaurants, and small businesses that were largely run and patronized by a Spanish-speaking Latina/o constituency. But what distinguished the Mission District from other ethnic neighborhoods of its kind was its extensive, community-based infrastructure: physical and mental health clinics, legal services, the Gay Latino Alliance (GALA, 1975–1983), the Women's Building (a clearing-house for free community assistance and wellness programs), bilingual and immersion schools, culture and arts programming, annual events and street festivals, and a bilingual public library.[30] These vital resources and services, provided by a number of neighborhood nonprofit and community-funded organizations, were the hard-won fruits of decennia of local and regional struggles sustained through collaborations between ethnic nationalist, feminist, and queer social movements of various kinds. Yet, multiscalar political and economic shifts in the early to mid-1990s signaled imminent changes within the Mission community and formidable challenges to its reproduction. The comingling of various racial capitalist agendas—from austerity politics and economic recession, to state abandonment and private development, and from deindustrialization and the dot.com boom to denationalization and renewed nativism—transformed a neighborhood once designated for racialized containment into a forefront of state-sanctioned gentrification and racialized expulsion. This excess of material and ideological displacements prompted organizers to envision and establish a peña that, by addressing the dialectics of geographic emplacement and organizing capacity, could effectively link local agendas to (inter)national politics.

TERRITORIALIZING LA PEÑA DEL SUR

Throughout its near ten years of operation, La Peña functioned outside of formal relations of publicity, commerce, and regulation. Its reproduction thus required innovative strategies of emplacement and administration. During its Lower Mission tenure (1992–2002), it would remain under the directorship of its cofounder Alejandro Stuart. Yet, in the spirit of its grassroots initiation, its ongoing management and maintenance were accomplished through the collaborative efforts of La Peña artists and supporters. A programming committee tasked with the visionary and logistical labors of the center met frequently to hammer out programmatic themes, artistic lineups, and other nitty-gritty details.[31] Initially made up of Stuart and La Peña's other four founders—Puerto Rican guitarist and singer Ronaldo Rosario, Chicano musician Enrique Ramírez, Nicaraguan vocalist and guitarist Ernesto Jiménez, and Ecuadorian musician and singer Elena Alvarado—its membership would change over time.[32] Subsequent participants would include Peruvian activist Samuel Guía and Ecuadorian artist and musician Galo Paz. As I later address, these and other changes in leadership were often the result of internal committee strife, owed in no small part to ongoing debates and dissention concerning the structure, management, and future of the neighborhood nitery. Yet, an abiding avowal of at least three political imperatives—echoing key organizational strategies of the Nueva Canción movement—consistently shaped La Peña del Sur's uniquely improvisational institutional architecture: first, that musicking can function as a vital means of political dialogue and convocation; next, that extemporaneous moments of collective reflection, respite, and revelry can encourage the renewal of imaginative and organizational political energies; and finally, that a venue endeavoring the incitement of such activities must be socioeconomically, geographically, and logistically accessible to a wide range of publics.[33]

Despite its "do-it-yourself" constitution and improvisational structure, La Peña del Sur functioned nearly every Friday through Sunday of its ten-year stint in the Mission core. In contrast with other cultural centers in the area, La Peña del Sur was located in a residential sector of the district. By day, the rented basement apartment that housed it was indistinguishable from its neighboring, high-density Victorian flats; at night, its conversion into a clandestine nitery was signaled only by a small wooden sign fastened to the unit's gated entrance. Many of its musicians and audience members were undocumented and/or exiled, and it was designed to function as a nexus for *reuniones críticas*.[34] Thus, promotion for La Peña del Sur was accomplished through word-of-mouth invitations, the circulation of fliers (figure 4.3), and ads in local bilingual newspapers.[35]

Event attendees were greeted at the door by Alejandro, who, in an adorned coffee can, collected sliding scale donations (typically two to five dollars) to compensate featured artists and to offset the costs of maintaining the locale. Children were welcome and attended for free, as did those who were unable to contribute financially. Guests were shuttled through Stuart's apartment—the principal hallway of which served as a makeshift gallery for local artists—to an outdoor covered patio. Adorned with holiday lights, hanging plants, and trellised vines, the festive courtyard-cum-theater seated forty to sixty guests in a miscellany of second-hand folding chairs at handmade wooden tables grouped opposite a small wooden stage. During the evening's proceedings, peña-goers could purchase Alejandro's home-made *empanadas* and mulled Chilean wine. On some occasions, vendors of the neighborhood's thriving informal economy circled through the crowds peddling *tamales caseras* or floral bouquets. And though "bring your own beverage" was not an encouraged practice, it was also not uncommon for contraband flasks and bottles to circulate among audience members. Yet, La Peña's grassroots orientation and informal atmosphere in no way thwarted its popular appeal; within its first two years of its tenure, La Peña del Sur at-

4.3 Early La Peña del Sur flyer. In author's collection.

tracted over ten thousand participants and hosted more than twenty visiting Latin American artists.[36]

During its near decade-long tenure as an underground cultural center in La Misión, La Peña featured an impressive range of artists and events. Fridays were reserved for poetry and *canto*—literary readings that spotlighted local and visiting authors. On the late afternoon of March 13, 1994, for example, La Peña del Sur hosted "Beneficio para 'El Semillero' [Una Publicación Alternativa]: Recital de Canto y Poesía y Comida Mexicana" (Benefit for "El Semillero" [An Alternative Publication], Canto and Poetry Recital and Mexican Cuisine). Benefits such as these were not uncommon at La Peña—they made up an average of at least two evenings of its monthly calendar, affording seed money for community publications and projects while granting oranizations and their staff free publicity and networking opportunities. La Peña del Sur also provided an important fundraising venue for local and international political causes. On October 21 of that same year, La Peña hosted "Un beneficio para La Cooperativa de Mujeres Centroamericanas, C.R.E.C.E" (A Benefit for the Cooperative of Central American Women,

4.4 "Celebración de las mujeres" flyer. In author's collection.

CRECE; figure 4.4), which featured "una presentación de nuestro trabajo como cooperativa y un programa de música, poesía, y lectura sobre nuestras experiencias" (a presentation about our work as a cooperative and to an evening of music, poetry, and lectures about our experiences).

Significantly, in addition to fundraising, events such as these highlighted how relations of race, nation, and economy intersected with those of gender and sexuality. Examples of such programming are abundant; La Peña organized exhibitions ranging from reports from Latina feminists who attended the UN international women's conference in Beijing, to annual celebrations honoring El Día Internacional de la Mujer, to tributive commemorations of famed Latina feminist artists such as Amparo Ochoa and Gabriela Mistral, to concerts to raise money and supplies for single mothers in the community. Themed performances were also common. During the month-long festivities honoring La Peña del Sur's two-year anniversary in June 1994, the center featured "De la Mujers, Por las Mujers, Para los Mujers . . . y Los Hombres" (About Women, By Women, For Women . . . And Men)—a night of poetry, music, theater, and testimony exploring issues of gender and inequality in Latina/o American communities throughout the Americas. And to commemorate its seven-year anniversary, the center sponsored "Desde Afuera del Closet: Encuentro, lectura de poesía y foro con autores y activistas de la comunidad gay latinoamérica: Mercedes Romero, Justina Jimenex, Joel Pérez, Roberto Ordeñana, Marcia Ochoa, y Alejandro Stuart. Micrófono abierto" (From Out of the Closet: An encounter, poetry reading, and forum with authors and artists of the gay Latinomerican community. Open Mic; figure 4.5). This vein of programming was exceedingly important and rare, as it engendered a place of encounter and potentional connection for members of distinctive activist groups and artistic communities. Moreover, it generated a forum for feminist and queer cultural workers to critically engage with patrons in the broader Latinoamerican Mission community.

Saturday nights at La Peña del Sur—by far the most well attended of the weekend—headlined both local and international musical talent. In constrast with the logistical arrangements of other local cultural centers and concert venues, La Peña's performances were often punctuated by or followed up with improvisational collaborations among featured artists and audience members, thereby troubling spatiotemporal divisions between production and consumption, and ideological divisions between artistic virtuosity and popular appeal. A review of the archive of the center's monthly

Peña del Sur

2870 A 22 St San Francisco CA 94110
Tel-Fax 550-1101 / E-Mail: aspeza@jps.net
Director: Alejandro Stuart

Junio 1999 mes del 7 aniversario

Viernes 4 8 p.m.   "Espacios de la Memoria"

Inauguración de exposición , óleos y acrílicos por la pintora mexicana Rosario Gutiérrez de Lerdo, Durango, con 30 exhibiciones individuales y 50 colectivas en México y Europa. Nos brinda su primera muestra en EE.UU. Música con Renato Freyggang y Mauro Correa.   Entrada libre

Nuevo Horario Viernes 8 p.m. para comenzar 8.30 - Sábados 9 p.m. para comenzar 9.30.

Sábado 5 9 p.m. "DEL SON A LA TROVA Y DE LA TROVA AL SON"

Con cierto sabor a Son y con mucha sa Son y como nos cuentan los Son eros "El Son es la raíz de lo que aquí llaman Salsa". Voces caribeñas, guitarras, tres cubano, bajo y bongó con:
Germán, Gilberto, Lily, José y Johnny.   Donativo $ 5

Viernes 11 8 p.m. "POESÍA Y CUENTOS DE CHILE Y DE CUBA"

El maestro literato chileno Fernando Alegría, autor de "Lautaro", "Caballo de Copas", "La Rebelión de los Placeres", "Viva Chile M..." y docenas de libros más nos leerá sus ultimas obras en prosa y poesía, y compartirá el podium con el profesor de literatura Hector Febles de Holguín, Cuba, quien nos leerá sus cuentos y poemas como "Novela y Fútbol" "El nombre de la risa","Solveira antes del fin", "Exilio" y "Visitaciones".   Donativo $ 2

Sábado 12 9 p.m. "EL ARPA MÁGICA GUARANÍ DE RAMÓN ROMERO"

El maestro Ramón Romero ha llevado su pasión musical de Paraguay y América Latina a prestigiosos escenarios en cuatro continentes, ha ganado grandes premios, Disco de Oro en Francia, entre otros. Aquí nos trae un concierto de folklore paraguayo, latinoamericano, andino, tangos y clásico internacional. En algunos temas le acompañará el cuatro de Jaqueline Rago.   Donativo $ 5

Viernes 18 8 p.m. "DESDE AFUERA DEL CLOSET"

Encuentro, lectura de poesía y foro con autores y activistas de la comunidad gay latinoamericana. Mercedes Romero, Justina Jimenez, Joel Pérez, Roberto Ordeñana, Marcia Ochoa, Alejandro Stuart y micrófono abierto.   Donativo $ 3

Sábado 19 9 p.m. "TENTACIÓN MUSICAL CON EL GRUPO CULEBRA"

Gran descarga de folklore venezolano y latinoamericano con un toque jazzístico contemporáneo en el virtuosismo de Jaqueline Rago con cuatro, Donna Viscuso con flauta y saxofón y más músicos, contrabajo y percusiones.   Donativo $ 5

Sábado 26 9 p.m. " TROVA DEL CARIBE Y DEL CONO SUR"

Ronald Rosario de Puerto Rico con su magnifica voz y guitarra y un amplio repertorio de trova tradicional y contemporánea boricua y caribeña compartiendo escena con el maestro canta-autor, interprete y guitarrista chileno Rafael Manríquez con temas de Violeta Parra, Victor Jara, Gabriela Mistral, Pablo Neruda y sus propias composiciones.   Donativo $ 5

Para ver nuestra programación en el internet marque <http://www.adandesign.com/pena.htlm>

POR LA DIFUSIÓN DE LA CULTURA LATINOAMERICANA Y LA PROMOCIÓN DE LOS VALORES ARTÍSTICOS DE NUESTRA COMUNIDAD.
Peña del Sur esta parcialmente financiada por el California Arts Council

4.5 "Desde afuera del closet" flyer. In author's collection.

programming calendar reveals a stunning array of musical genres, including música andina, rock en español, boleros y corridos mexicanos, música tropical, son jarocho y huasteco, samba, marimba, bomba, música afroperuana, nueva canción y trova, cumbia, merengue, bachata, reggae, salsa, rumba, bossa nova, and música afrocubana. What was both rare and innovative about La Peña del Sur's approach to programming is that these musics were staged not as representations of monolithic national cultures or unified national publics, but rather, as participatory moments of dialogue, exchange, experimentation, and pleasure. Late Stanford professor and poet Fernando Alegría—an active peña attendee and participant—attested to this heterogeneity and interchange: "*La Peña del Sur* es un intenso intercambio cultural latinoamericano, un poco de creatividad y una puerta abierta a la solidaridad de las américas" (La Peña del Sur is a site of intense Latino-American cultural exchange, a bit of creativity, and an opening to trans-American solidarities).[37] As Alegría observed, la peña's staging of political and cultural *intercambio* was structured around the forging of hemispheric solidarities through collectivized practices of musicking—dialogue and dance, singing and shouting, clapping, and foot tapping.

Read through a geographic lens, the institutionalization of La Peña can be understood as the formation of a unique type of place—one that enrooted strategic challenges to governing techniques of spatial differentiation. Geographers and cultural critics alike have demonstrated that the (re)production of boundaries between places—such as the body, home or nation—and between different kinds of places—such as the foreign and domestic, the sovereign or settled—is an inherently political and highly contested process. Such distinctions serve to sediment, naturalize, and/or manage raced, gendered, sexualized, and classed divisions within and among geographies of labor, desire, knowledge, and subjectivity. By operating in the scripted space of the domestic, and by rejecting the purview of local and state authorities, La Peña's organizational architecture defiantly reoriented reigning distinctions between public and private space, residential and commercial spheres, and licensed and informal activities. Thus, the spatial politics and practices that informed the center's formation can be read as a compelling critique of, as well as a critical response to, the co-constitutive relationship between state-sanctioned emplacement and heteropatriarchal racial capitalist management.

To be sure, establishing La Peña del Sur as an informal economy within the domestic sphere was the most expedient way to launch the project. The process of securing business permits, liquor and food licenses, and a commercial venue would have been lengthy and expensive, and would have required petitioners of a particular financial and legal status. But for Stuart and his cohort, expediency was neither the sole nor even the primary imperative informing La Peña's design. Rather, as peña collaborator Galo Paz put it, the goal of the project was to create a venue for "critical assembly . . . oriented around music rather than economy."[38] For Paz and other cultural workers, this privileging of musical encounter over monetary logics and critical assembly over consumer crowds, demanded a circumvention of the territorial techniques through which state power was exercised at the municipal scale. Siting, zoning, permitting, licensing. . . . These banal bureaucratic procedures figured at the center of the Mission's gentrification wars, as wealthy developers and white middle-class professionals exerted the force of legal authority to displace Latina/o renters, eliminate small businesses, criminalize informal employment, and police local youth of color. Moreover, as California's "new nativism" coalesced around legislative attacks on access to public and bilingual education, hospital care, and social services, state agencies were legislated into sites of immigrant policing and surveillance.[39] Thus, this refusal to emplace La Peña del Sur within sanctioned geographies of encounter and exchange can be read as a trenchant critique of the ways in which racial capitalist mediations of social space serve to protect the wealth, security, and interests of heteronormative white propertied citizen-subjects.

These acts of "respatialization"—the reorganization of imposed spatial boundaries—enabled moments of convocation that would have otherwise been foreclosed for most peña participants. And in turn, such moments of convocation engendered ideological alliances and political action that would have otherwise been implausible or unattainable. In redefining the terrains of public and private, residential and commercial, La Peña del Sur became a place where attendant scripts concerning leisure, culture, commerce, politics, and desire could be "queerly" renegotiated. The nitery's location, hours of operation (between 8 and 10 PM until festivities ended, often the following morning), and "all-ages welcome" policy made it accessible to an unusual cross-section of publics. Swing-shifters, careworkers, children and youth, the elderly, the undocumented—these and other constituencies constrained by conventional divisions of social space collectively performed, listened, danced, drank, sang, slept, argued, and applauded from late in the evening until dawn. This intergenerational comingling among community and kin effectively destabilized many of the geotemporal roles and rules that produce and preserve the heteropatriarchal nuclear family: distinctions between "gay" and "straight" space, between "adult" versus "familial" activities, between "men's" and "women's" work, and between productive and reproductive labor. Through this unsettling of normative categories of emplacement and embodiment, La Peña del Sur cultivated vibrant political dialogue, artistic exchange, and in the best of moments, nascent coalitions across inter- and intracommunity divides.

Central to the staging of these conversations and interactions was La Peña del Sur's strategic reconstitution of cultural production and community reproduction not only as habits of leisure, but also, more importantly, as generative opportunities for activist work. The center's colocation of recess and rabble-rousing allowed working-class Mission residents with scarce free time to combine moments of political dialogue and organizing work with opportunities for respite and revelry. La Peña del Sur's cultural workers developed this unique programming structure with the practiced awareness that historically, similarly structured New Song events held in local peñas, regional festivals, and international *encuentros populares* were crucial to the recruitment of large and diverse crowds, the renewal of waning political energies, and the spontaneous formation of coalition. Central to the actualization of La Peña as an alternative performance geography was the mobilization of music as method: its deployment as both an organizing tool and, as Paz observed, as an organizational schema.

Scholar of race and sound Shana Redmond opens her illuminating book *Anthem: Social Movements and the Sound of Solidarity in the African Diaspora* with an astute observation: "Music is a method. Beyond its many pleasures, music allows us to do and imagine things that may otherwise be unimaginable or seem impossible."[40] Redmond goes on to argue that, among the African descended, music has figured as a critical "meaning making endeavor" that has been strategically deployed "to develop identification between people who otherwise may be culturally, ideologically, or spatially separate or distinct from one another."[41] Similarly, it can be argued that the Nueva Canción movement strategically adopted and adapted the power of song to mobilize a pan–Latin American public across regional, national, ethnic, cultural, and linguistic divides. As Jane Tumas-Serna and Fernando Reyes Matta have argued, in the face of state censorship and corporate domination of mass-media outlets, Latin American communist and anticolonial organizers identified the need to establish grassroots communication networks across universities, industries, and regional geographies.[42] Many of these cultural workers turned to sonic production as a means of actualizing these political goals. On the one hand, they mined popular musical practice for tactical strategies; rejecting conventional divides between high and low culture, audience and performer, text and context, they adopted the arts of improvisation, experimentation, and amalgamation as techniques for staging popular *encuentros*, or encounters, within and across various sites and contexts of struggle. On the other hand, recognizing the mobility, adaptability, and reproducibility of sonic texts, New Song activists used musical production and circulation as a means of popularizing political struggles, articulating political agendas, and expressing political solidarity.

This adoption of the sonic as a political and pedagogical tool was a structuring feature of La Peña del Sur's programming. In an interview from 2004 about his life's work as an artist and organizer, Stuart said of La Peña del Sur, "[It] was a place in which some very renowned [artists] could turn up, but also people who were just getting started."[43] Recalling what distinguished this project from other cultural centers in the Bay Area, Stuart remarked, "For me, a peña is more spontaneous, more experimental."[44] When asked the same question, cofounder Samuel Guía added that, in holding peña, "the process itself is the most important, not the product."[45] Here, both Stuart and Guía acknowledge how the peña as a historic institution influenced the structure La Peña del Sur's nightly proceedings. Pedagogy and popular encounter were privileged over virtuosity and individual talent. Interactive performance was privileged over an artist/audience divide. And La Peña was spontaneous and unpredictable; by design, the center was a nexus for the address of community emergencies (evictions, legal struggles, economic hardship, etc.) and political exigencies.

A typical night at La Peña del Sur opened with a short address by Stuart, the center's ongoing emcee. Stuart often used the opportunity to share his poetry in progress, and invited others to do the same. Much of his work integrated critiques of U.S. imperialism, the ongoing colonization of the Americas, and ever-shifting stages of capitalist expansion. Yet his spoken verse also ventured into expressions of queer desire, descriptions of same-sex interludes, and celebrations of homosocial encounter. Stuart performed his work in a way that unnerved some audience members because of a kind of feminized "flamboyance."[46] The softness of his gestures, the tenderness of his verse, and lilt of his voice defied the normative display of masculine authority and patriarchal leadership commonly invoked by New Song's male figureheads. According to Stuart, this capricious performance of text and embodiment was strategic; he initiated La Peña del Sur's nightly proceedings with an uncompromising reminder that queer desire was always already present in Latina/o American political communities, and it would not be disavowed at the center.

Following the "opening" of La Peña del Sur's proceedings, featured performers would take the stage. Unlike a typical concert, however, La Peña was conducted as an interactive endeavor. Divisions between performer and audience were dissolved. Peña participants often brought their own instruments and took to the stage alongside scheduled performers. Sets were determined as much by audience members as the performers themselves, as the former refracted the sonic encounter through chorus, clapping, and coaction. In short, La Peña was a participatory rather than passive encounter, constituted through the collective performance of anthemic song, sensual dance, and communal revelry. Central to its mission, these moments of collective (inter)action nurtured pleasures, friendships, and solidarities that fortified participants as they engaged in the challenging work of building coalition and initiating change.

While La Peña del Sur echoed many of the tenets of the Nueva Canción movement and its hallmark institution, the peña, the cultural center also adapted itself to the geopolitical contingencies of its context: its position in the urban global North, its location in a neighborhood in transition, and its *pueblo* of diverse migrant subjects. These differences of historical and geographic context enabled La Peña's cultural workers to confront some of the limitations of Nueva Canción discourse, which, in its privileging of particular "unities" failed to effectively grapple with how the colonial-capitalist system it so trenchantly critiqued is always-already constituted through relations of racial, gender, and sexual difference. As a nexus for the performance of sonic and visual cultures, La Peña del Sur convened an impressive range of artists and media representing divergent political interests and affiliations, aesthetic techniques and concerns, and generational trends. Yet, its organizers embraced the fragility and unpredictability of such conventions. Whereas historic Nueva Canción "encuentros" emphasized ideological continuity and presumed universal political agendas, La Peña del Sur was constituted and celebrated as a place of *(des)encuentro*: a site of convocation that, through musical performance and artistic exchange, embraced disorientation, discord, and disjuncture.[47]

As a place of (des)encuentro, La Peña del Sur became a site of both personal encounter and political fragmentation. It was a place where Farabundo Martí National Liberation Front (FMLN) poets collaborated with Mission Chicano youth to perform political rock en español, where Andean and Afro-Peruvian musicians came together to perform *huaynitos* and dance *festejo*, where internationally renowned musicians such as Los Folkloristas and Inti-Illimani became the audience of "undiscovered" talent of Mission youth, where queer performance installations brushed up against photo exhibits of *iglesias católicas*, where prison abolitionists gabbed with immigration reformists, where the local homeless folks ate free empanadas and toasted with the self-proclaimed intelligentsia. My use of the word *(des)encuentro*—which can loosely be translated as a failed meeting, a temporary mixup, or an ongoing disagreement—signals the inherent, productive contradictions of such a "contact zone."[48] It acknowledges both the inevitable losses, confusion, and failures of recognition that mark the "encounter" of sociosonic difference, as well as the coalitions that can be built on the foundations of such unlikely, disorienting, and often painful confrontations.

SUREANDO Y SUREADO: DESENCUENTROS CON LATINIDAD

In November 1992, roughly five months after La Peña del Sur opened its doors, the *New York Times* featured an article entitled "What's the Problem with 'Hispanic'? Just ask a 'Latina/o.'"[49] As the article suggests, the racialization of Latinas/os in the U.S. public sphere within the context of "new nativism" prompted, in both popular and academic circles, dynamic debates concerning the contours of U.S. Latinidad.[50] As racialized subjects, Latinas/os residing in the United States once again revisited an enduring contradiction of cultural and ethnic nationalism: the political urgency and efficacy of building coalitional political affiliation that contested the monolithic imposed racialized ethnic identity "Latina/o" while simultaneously addressing the various heterogeneities and tensions within and among migrant communities from Latin America. Would the institutionalization of "Latina/o" as an identity category effectively mitigate forms of what Angel R. Oquendo has referred to as "divisive racial dualism?"[51] Or, in "referencing millions of people currently living in the United States," does the term "Latina/o," as Suzanne Oboler has suggested, lump "millions of people of a variety of national backgrounds . . . into a single 'ethnic' category" without making allowances for "their varied racial, class, linguistic and gender divides?"[52]

These questions concerning both the imaginative possibilities and inherent contingencies of Latinidad as a political affiliation were territorialized in the community formation processes that occurred at La Peña del Sur. Here, I use the term *Latinidad* as defined by Ramón Rivera-Servera. For Rivera-Servera, "Latinidad . . . refers to the ethnic and panethnic imaginaries, identities, and affects that emerge from the increased intersections of multiple Latina/o communities . . . [it] articulates . . . a point of contact between Latina/os of diverse backgrounds who find themselves increasingly sharing common cultural material and lived experiences, be it from representations in the media—produced in the United States or imported from Latin American sources—or actual physical proximity to one another in places of work, residence, religious practice, or leisure."[53] Rivera-Servera's conception of Latinidad aptly references the ongoing negotiation of panethnic, intraracial political imaginaries, identities, and aesthetics that defined the performative, coalitional work endeavored by La Peña del Sur artists, activists, and patrons. Queer Latina/o scholars such as Rivera-Servera and Juana María Rodríguez have written extensively about the ways in which mobilizations of identity politics in the United States both enable moments of social transformation and enact modes of political effacement, interrogate practices of social differentiation, and recapitulate mechanisms of control and domination.[54] These tensions and negotiations were ever-present during La Peña's proceedings. Yet, unlike other cultural centers in the area, the contradictions within and limitations of the monolithic nationalist (e.g., "Peruvian") or internationalist (i.e., "Latin") frameworks in which Latin American cultural production is most often localized were actively interrogated and challenged. In lieu of recapitulating the dominant racial-regional divides that often inform popular and academic representations of Latin Americans, La Peña's programming committee staged cultural and aesthetic (des)encuentros designed to generate a unique convocational space where conflicting notions of the ethnic, the national, the transnational, and the popular could be debated and challenged within the Mission District immigrant community.

Critical to the orchestration of La Peña as a site of (des)encuentro were three geocultural techniques: juxtaposition, improvisation, and participation. The first of these was achieved through the programming of unlikely performance mash-ups. On October 24, 1992 La Peña del Sur headlined "Encuentro Chicano-Boricua," featuring Javier Pacheco from California and Ronald Rosario from Puerto Rico. This aural encounter brought together the aesthetic traditions and their attendant histories of two multiracial communities with a long-standing presence in the United States. The distinctive relations of U.S. imperial, racial capitalism expansion within Mexico and the Caribbean, and the migration patterns that these produced, have meant that multiple generations of migrants from these regions have principally lived and organized in distinctive regions of the United States, with the largest concentration of Chicanos in the Pacific and Southwest and Puerto Ricans in the North and Southeast. To date, both activist and academic communities have faced numerous challenges in bridging these coastal formations, as well as interrogating or disrupting the totalizing and exclusionary scripts that have informed their institutionalization. Here, the programming practice of juxtaposition not only brought these tensions to the fore; they likewise enabled the exploration of sound-based solidarities rooted in the identification of common historical and political ground through improvisational and participatory performance.

The "Ecuentro Chicano-Boricua" and others of its kind—"De los Andes y de Aztlán," "Trova del Caribe y del Cono Sur," and "Las Venas Abiertas" constituted moments of discord and disjuncture that embraced rather than negated differences of culture and class, nation and region, gender and sexuality, and race and ethnicity. Such (des)encuentros were mobilized as itineraries of departure rather that destination, and were thus guided by the political principles of active participation and improvisation; performances at La Peña were flexible, dynamic dialogues between audience and performer rather than passive acts of cultural production and consumption. Thus, while unlikely cultural and aesthetic pairings set the stage for the exploration of discord and disjuncture, audience participation—from singing, laughing, ad-libbing, clapping and dancing, to booing, yelling, and foot stomping, to the spontaneous addition of instruments and artists and song sets—worked to disturb normative boundaries of genre. As I argued in the introduction, such boundaries have often worked to impose and reify anticoalitional geopolitical divides through their alignment with state-sponsored forms of heteromasculinist racial nationalism.

The (des)encuentro of Peruvian musical cultures at La Peña exemplifies how such musical production can stimulate unique debates concerning the internally and externally imposed geopolitical boundaries of the global Southern nation. As I have discussed in previous chapters, the sociosonic projects of transnational Andean and Afro-Peruvian artists offer very different and, at moments, even competing challenges to dominant narratives of Peruanidad via transnational pan-Andeanism and Afro-diasporicism. For Andean musicians in the United States, the performance of regional rhythmic traditions such as huayno (referred to in Bolivia as *huayño*) were adapted to produce a pan-Andean regional affiliation that transgressed (inter)national boundaries while retaining the historical and geographic specificity expressed through melodic, linguistic, and instrumentational variation. Afroperuanismo, in turn, drew upon Black Brazilian, Cuban, and North American musical traditions to form its transnational sociosonic landscape, which encompassed delocalized traditions throughout the African diaspora in the Americas. In this manner, central to Afroperuanismo was a critique of the exclusionary aspects of anticolonial *indigenismo* as a response to colonial *criollismo*.

For Andean and Afro-Peruvian musicians living in the San Francisco Bay Area, La Peña del Sur came to function as an auditory contact zone, where local Andean bands such as Markahuasi, Kashua, and Inkarrí, and Afro-Peruvian groups De Rompe y Raja and Instituto Cultural Peruano engaged in sociosonic convocation.[55] It provided a place where diverse and divergent political agendas were debated alongside and often through the technologies of performance: rhythm, melody, instrumentation, and stylistic interpretation. Amidst the leisure and pleasure of performing, listening, and dancing, artists and attendees partook in challenging political conversations about what it means to be a Peruvian, South American, Latina/o, and migrant. This is not to suggest that such encounters inevitably resulted in immediate recognition or even gradual resolution; as cultural critic Josh Kun reminds us, "the consequences" of musical encounters are "never predetermined."[56] Rather, it is to emphasize how La Peña's musical confrontations performed the theoretical work that is the necessary precondition for political community formation: addressing what Juana María Rodríguez has aptly dubbed the "ghosts" of raced and gendered postcolonial nationalisms. At La Peña del Sur, this confrontation was staged via the (des)encuentros of dissonant sonic imaginaries of the local (coastal vs. highland), the regional (urban vs. rural), and the national-popular (Black and indigenous).

Nor were the cultural confrontations that took place at La Peña limited to addressing competing nationalisms internal to the global Southern nation. In the political moment of Proposition 187, the peña emerged as a site in which the intersecting and interarticulated politics of race, gender, sexuality, and nation were negotiated at the scale of the transnational immigrant community. If the unique structure of La Peña as a cultural institution made it accessible to the Mission community that it served, it likewise referenced the heterogeneity of the district's multigenerational, multinational Latina/o community and, consequently, the complexity of political organizing along ethnonationalist lines. For example, for all of La Peña's constituents, the ascendance of California's new nativism and anti-immigrant austerity politics were matters of utmost concern. However, while Proposition 187 was typically constructed in the popular media as an attack on Latina/o families, La Peña became a unique site of political mobilization for queer and feminist Latina/o interests.

La Peña hosted a number of visual art installations and informational workshops that drew attention to how the legislation's denial of health care and social services would disproportionately affect all women and queer men. On the one hand, Latina *feministas* of the La Peña community drew attention to the hazardous effects of denying immigrant women prenatal and gynecological care. On the other hand, queer Latino activists contested popular media portrayals of the AIDS epidemic as a "gay white disease," arguing, as Horacio Roque Ramírez has noted, that "while the epidemic was beginning to level off for white gays, it continued to impact disproportionately gays of color, including a large immigrant class."[57] In these debates concerning the racial, sexual, gendered, and (trans)national politics of Latinidad, what became clear to La Peña's performers, activists, and cultural workers was that any political agenda that centered on Latinidad as an ideological formation must necessarily attend to the places of heterogeneity that it referenced and or contested, from the raced and gendered body to the queer immigrant neighborhood to the transnational community.

ENCUENTROS CON LATINIDAD: SUREÑOS Y EL SUR GLOBAL

In his comprehensive exploration of how the heterogeneity of U.S. Latinidad relates to pan-Latina/o claims for political and economic recognition in the United States, historian and cultural critic Juan Flores offers the "Latino Imaginary" as a useful model for understanding U.S. Latina/o community formation. For Flores, the "Latino Imaginary" suggests "a conceptual space of pan-group aggregation that is too often and too easily confused with the official, demographic version. Not that calculation is itself foreign to an 'imagined' Latina/o community; in fact it is at this epistemological level that the very act and authority of counting and measuring become issues of vital social contestation. The 'imaginary' in this sense does not signify 'the real' as the immediately present and rationally discernable. It is the 'community' represented 'for itself,' a unity fashioned creatively on the basis of shared memory and desire, congruent histories of misery and struggle, and intertwining utopias."[58] In its emphasis on cultural production as the theoretical and political nexus of "pan-group aggregation," Flores's "Latino Imaginary" offers an insightful framework for understanding the community formation processes enabled through La Peña del Sur. While critical of imposed demographic categories, this "conceptual space" emphasizes the fluid and organic processes through which heterogeneous groups come together to identify what historian Ranajit Guha has referred to, in a different context, as historical and political "convergences."[59] And while historically and geographically specific, a Latina/o imaginary encompasses social, economic, and cultural relationships that extend beyond and often actively transgress the imposed political geographies of racialized community or sovereign nation.

La Peña del Sur became an unlikely site for the production of a Latina/o imaginary, tenuously linked by cultural practices and quotidian experiences that, for many of its participants, converged in the geographic imaginary of *el sur* (the South). In bringing together a wide range of "southernized" sonic cultures and political subjects, La Peña del Sur became a political crossroads for cultural practitioners and consumers at local, national, and international scales. Scheduled events and performances both reflected and depended upon the committed participation of the San Francisco Bay Area community; thus, the growth of the institution's participation and patronage—largely by word of mouth—only increased its political and geographic purview. In turn, the continued, casual collocation of historically and geographically dispersed sonic cultures in a small apartment on Twenty-Second Street threw into clear relief both the oppositional potential and the political urgency of drawing connections between the multiple scales of global Southernism in which La Peña's veterans, newcomers, and visitors were often situated.

The importance of drawing such local/global connections became particularly apparent in 1994, when La Peña hosted a series of artists and events that addressed some of the crucial geohistorical events of the year: the devaluation of the Mexican peso, the public debut of the Ejército Zapatista de Liberación Nacional (Zapatista Army of National Liberation, or EZLN), the signing of the North American Free Trade Agreement, the increased militarization of the southern border, and of course, the introduction of Proposition 187. In this sense, La Peña came to function as what cultural critic Josh Kun has called an "audiotopia": "a musical space of difference, where contradictions do not cancel each other out, but are thrown into relief . . . an auditory 'contact zone' where different narratives and boundaries clash and are irrevocably transformed."[60] The coordinated staging of these aesthetic and informational events achieved the important sociosonic work of an "audiotopia" by converting La Peña del Sur into a critical public forum. As a cultural institution both imagined and territorialized as a unique sociosonic place, it allowed for new interpretations of the local, regional, and international processes that shaped the lives of U.S. Latinas/os and Latin Americans throughout the global South.[61]

CONCLUSIONS

By way of conclusion, I want to reflect on some of the critical insights that La Peña del Sur, a cultural collective born of and at a bleak political juncture in California state politics, might offer to future immigrant rights activism in the United States. First, La Peña exemplifies the importance of cultural production as a means of combining localized sites and moments of leisure and play with urgent political and theoretical work. As Lisa Lowe has cogently argued, "Cultural productions emerging out of the contradictions of immigrant marginality displace the fiction of reconciliation, disrupt the myth of national identity by revealing its gaps and fissures, and intervene in the narrative of national development that would illegitimately locate the 'immigrant' before history or exempt the 'immigrant' from history."[62] The hypermobility of musical cultures allows for a particularly astute disarticulation of the imposed geopolitical boundaries and narrative fictions that Lowe describes. As the auditory (des)encuentros of La Peña del Sur demonstrate, musical production enables sociosonic linkages between the global and the local, the written and the oral, the historical and the present, the dystopic and the imaginative.

A second critical insight to be drawn from the history of La Peña del Sur is the importance of forging activist communities that rather than assuming stable or monolithic political affiliations maintain a constant commitment to addressing the contingencies of heterogeneity, contradiction, and difference. Here, I am reminded of Audre Lorde's astute theorization of difference as a source of strength rather than axes of fracture within processes of coalitional formation. "We have been taught either to ignore our differences, or to view them as causes for separation and suspicion rather than as forces for change. Without community, there is no liberation, only the most vulnerable and temporary armistice between an individual and her oppression. But community must not mean a shedding of our differences, nor the pathetic pretense that these differences do not exist. . . . Difference is the raw and powerful connection from which our personal power is forged."[63] As Lorde argues, and as the case of La Peña del Sur as a site of (des)encuentros effectively illustrates, it is only through returning to internal, as well as external contradictions of objective relations that any popular cultural movement can effectively be sustained.

A third important lesson to be gleaned from the history of La Peña del Sur concerns how, when, and where various political agendas can and should be imagined and activated. Throughout its near ten years of operation, La Peña organizers and participants engaged in heated debates concerning competing conceptions of sustainability as they relate to the limits and possibilities of institutionalization. On one side of the debate were those that favored the securing of a permanent, licensed locale in order to grow and expand La Peña del Sur. Proponents of La Peña's institutionalization argued that it would enable greater community participation and ensure the long-term sustainability of the venue. On the other side of the polemic were those who viewed La Peña del Sur's situatedness in the Mission District's informal economy as an opportunity to engage in modes of performance, dialogue, and exchange that circumvented disciplinary mechanisms of state power and the logics of racial capital accumulation and development. In the end, the latter constituency won out; La Peña remained an ephemeral, extraeconomic affair until it ended its chapter on Harrison Street. Those who view expansion and permanence as markers of political success might argue that the closing of La Peña del Sur's doors in 2001 represented a failure or loss for San Francisco's Latina/o community. But for activists such as Stuart, the La Peña project was an overwhelming political victory in that it made physical and ideological space for convocation, conversation, creativity, and coalition. In this sense, informality, ephemerality, and improvisation can be viewed as La Peña del Sur's greatest strengths, and its closure, an effect in shifting economic conditions and political urgencies. At the dawn of the new millennium, the demographics of the Mission District neighborhood dramatically shifted, owed to the combined effects of recession and gentrification. But La Peña's spirit lived on in the innumerable creative projects that it spurred and artists that it fostered, as well as in Stuart's subsequent sociospatial work. The director returned to Santiago, Chile, in 2001, where he would found another grassroots peña, Kolectivo Kahuín.

Taken together, these insights suggest the exigency of forms and processes of cultural production that, through an abiding commitment to destabilizing the material and embodied notions of difference imposed vertically and even horizontally, disarticulate the multiscalar discourses and policies that continue to racialize and gender U.S. Latinas/os as at best deviant and at worst, criminal. The situated model of political mobilization territorialized through La Peña del Sur suggests an alternative strategy of transscalar cultural activism. In this sense, La Peña del Sur makes both visible and audible the sociosonic geographies of opposition to which this book dedicates its attention.

EPILOGUE

Musical Pirates, Sonic Debts, and
Future Geographies of Transit

When fourteen-year-old Renata Flores Rivera of Huamanga, Ayacucho, re-leased "Chaynatam Ruwanki Cuyanaita" on YouTube in late July 2015, the budding chanteuse hardly anticipated that her soulful Quechua cover of Michael Jackson's "The Way You Make Me Feel" would garner widespread acclaim among media critics and listening publics across the globe. Yet within six weeks her locally produced video earned over one million views, positioning Flores as a rising star on the international stage as well as a for-midable voice for contemporary Andean youth. Filmed under the auspices of La Asociación Cultural Peruana SURCA, an organization dedicated to in-digenous youth empowerment through art, "Chaynatam" integrates the ge-neric and aesthetic influences of classic soul and R&B with the artistic and political aspirations of a new generation of anticolonial activists. The aim of this intergenerational collaboration, which enlisted the musical direction and support of Flores's mother, Patricia, and the translation assistance of her grandmother, Ada, was to generate a decisively unpredictable soundtrack for a municipally based yet nationally oriented campaign entitled "Los jóve-nes también hablamos Quechua" (Young people speak Quechua too).

"Chaynatam" proffers a filmic narrative that dramatically departs from the one popularized by the King of Pop. In stark contrast with the scenic backdrop of Jackson's 1987 video, which features a U.S. urban neighborhood in deindustrial decline, Flores's millennial remix is staged amidst a markedly remote yet equally austere political scene: the uninhabited ruins of Vilcashuaman, once a lively administrative center of the Incan empire. Monuments such as these commonly grace Peru's gift-shop postcards and tourist propaganda, inviting urban nationals and foreign travelers to visit the enduring, vacant landscapes of the nation's ostensibly ever-vanishing, ever-vanquished indigenous population. Yet Flores and her cohort disrupt this tropic colonial scene in myriad ways. Not only does their very presence at the "archaeological" site suture the fictive cultural gap between Peru's mythical heritage populations and contemporary indigenous communities; of equal significance is their unique sartorial and sonic swag, which breaks with the geotemporal logics of nationalist folkloric canons focused on the curated, regionalized preservation of tradition rather than its popular, strategic reinvention. "Chaynatam" opens with an orbital pan of the young musicians, who are dispersed asunder Vilcashuaman's plaza-cum-stage. Outfitted within the technical tools of the rock music trade—box amplifiers and standing mics, a sunburst electric guitar and classic Fender bass, the teen artists don a casual yet trendy wardrobe that might be described as highland grunge. Bassist and arranger Jorge Luis Flores sports aviator sunglasses, faded blue jeans, and a nondescript, loose-fitting black tee, while Renata rocks a tailored uniform-style miniskirt, chunky over-the-knee socks, an ultracropped denim jacket, and an oversized *chullo*.[1] This visual colocation of revered ancestral ties, contemporary youth culture, and global cultural flows might be described as a staging of what Walter Benjamin has called "messianic time," an emplaced collision of past, present, and future that unearths enduring contradictions, ruptures false binarisms, and, potentially, imagines alternative geotemporal orders. It is these seemingly dissonant images and events that set the stage for the sonorous storyline of the text, which at its core ruptures commonsense geotemporal alignments of sound, culture, and place.

While "Chaynatam"'s audio progression is both funky and fetching, Renata's velvety vocals and sultry scats are the clear focal point of the text, sounding the political interventions that animate the young artists' collaboration. For those familiar with the rhythmic genres typically recorded in Quechua, the Andean *huayno* and its contemporary cousin, Andean *cumbia* or *chicha*, female singers typically aspire toward high-pitched, dense, and evenly syncopated sounds. In contrast, Flores's vocal flourishes showcase her rich lower register, breathy breaks, and formidable range; in short, they re-sound the seemingly stable boundaries of cultural linguistic tradition so as to respatialize their canonical containment beyond the settler colonial tactics of exclusion and erasure. "I sing in Quechua as a voice of warning, because the language is being lost," commented Flores in an interview with the AFP (Agence France-Presse).[2] "Children and young people are afraid to speak it. . . . We did this [cover] in Quechua so the world sees that we have an identity and we are proud of our culture." Here, Flores references the diverse, multiscalar listening publics that her work boldly hails. In the regional and national spheres, Flores addresses the social stigma associated with speaking Quechua, which, as Peruvian anthropologist Marisol de la Cadena has cogently argued, is often the distinguishing factor between what it means to be indigenous (*indígena*) versus indigenous descended (*mestizo*). This undeniable connection between language ability and social mobility has deeply impacted intergenerational language transmission in the Andean region. As Elena Burga, head of Peru's Ministry of Education program to promote bilingual education, has observed, "For young people, Quechua is synonymous with backwardness and poverty, because the colonial mentality of discrimination, contempt, and racism still persists in Peru."[3] Conversely, through creative techniques of sounding and staging, Flores and her cohort contest both domestic and international perceptions of indigenous languages and cultures as antithetical to or incompatible with constructs associated with geotemporal dynamism—the "urban," "modern," or "cosmopolitan." Their strategic, reverse appropriation of Black American musical texts and genres, coupled with Quechua lyrics and the creative aesthetics of indigenous Andean youth, is a significant departure from, if not a trenchant critique of, the conventional narratives of tradition and authenticity that I argued in chapter 1 both "protect" and abstract highland musical cultures. If, as indigenous critics and other indigenous studies scholars throughout the Americas have argued, eternal condemnation to the past is a preeminent technology of (settler) colonial occupation and mestizo hegemony, then theorizing interrelations of culture, time, and place is a political struggle that is both urgent and enduring.[4] Flores and her collaborators are among a growing number of young musicians who engage in such struggles by sounding what we might call performance geographies of indigenous futurity—that is, networks of musical production and exchange that repudiate the geotemporal logics of capitalist development through the emplacement of alternative visions and innovative methods of aural encounter and transmission. As Curtis Marez has succinctly argued, while futurism represents "the projection of a particular, determinant future social order," futurity can be read as a disruptive "open ended desire for a world beyond the limits of the present."[5] Following Marez, we might read "Chaynatam" and other projects of its kind as manifestations of an Andean futurity that, through the creative use of virtual space, emergent sounds, and ever-evolving technologies, radically rearticulates how Andean indigeneity is imagined and lived, locally, nationally, and globally.

Much like the stories of South American musical transit narrated throughout this book, Renata Flores Rivera's YouTube–based cultural activism represents an unconventional tale of sonic production, aesthetic flows, and spatial politics. In this sense, it echoes the continual import and relevance of the key theoretical questions of this book: what does it mean to *place* sound at the center of narratives of social formation? How do our understandings of the interanimating relations of social, spatial, and sonic formation shift when we imagine the aural and the geographic as agential forces? The pursuit of these questions in the preceding pages was inspired by my political commitment to narrating a neglected history of hemispheric aural circulation, one attuned to quotidian, informal, and grassroots modes of sonic engagement and transmission. While often ephemeral or infrapolitical by design, the performance geographies archived throughout this book collectively represent an enduring history of struggle against the social and spatial circumscriptions of dominant media and labor regimes at both regional and international scales. They evidence how South American cultural workers have deployed sonic tactics of place making—from the use of creative staging techniques, to the construction of informal economies and improvisational performance venues, to the formation of transnational musicians' networks—to activate alternative geographies of culture, sociality, labor, and activism.

At the same time, while Flores's YouTube–based campaign is generally aligned with spatialized practices of musicking discussed thus far, its unique content, form, and mediation likewise signals the dramatic cultural, economic, and technological shifts that have occurred in the two decades since my interest in this project first emerged. Among the most striking consequences of these shifts are the ways in which impoverished artists and social actors of color—particularly women and other queer folk—have circumvented the constraints of physical travel by exploiting virtual platforms of performance and exchange to engage in grassroots organizing and solidarity struggles or, more simply, to eke out a living. When I began working with U.S.-based Andean street musicians in 1991, busking for tips and cassette sales was the primary means through which an almost exclusively male workforce of migrant musicians engaged in means of cultural and economic reproduction in the global North. The birth and expansion of the "Andean music industry" discussed in chapter 2 required physical infrastructure, commodities, and travel. The performance geographies forged by feminist cultural workers such as Yma Sumac, Victoria Santa Cruz, and Susana Baca discussed in chapters 1 and 3 represent histories of grassroots cultural activism that was undeniably pathbreaking, yet, they are likewise atypical. This is in no small part owed to the ways in which physical and social mobility are consistently if dynamically constrained by raced and gendered boundaries and structures that required these artists to engage in the bold and often perilous transgression of the normative geocultural bounds of domesticity, respectability, femininity, and so on. In short, throughout the twentieth century, the South American musical transits discussed herein have entailed distinctive material relations in that they required the production and exchange of tangible objects, routes of physical travel, and live relations of musicking.

Yet, the emergence of new media platforms and virtual venues has prompted provocative inversions in the geographies of sonic mediation within and between America del Sur y del Norte. Renata Flores Rivera is but one example of the innumerable Latin American artists engaged in a novel politics of musical change and exchange, in which aural appropriation, unlicensed reproduction, and other modes of sonic piracy are the dominant formats and methods of musical circulation. Today Peru is the hemispheric center of the production and dissemination of pirated media.[6] Ironically, in a region where impoverished communities of color have experienced the ongoing exotification, appropriation, and abstraction of their sonic art and collective musical repertoires, ongoing relations of geo-economic provincialization has enabled South American cultural workers to perform, record, and reproduce the work of global Northern artists with little risk of legal reprisal. This dramatic reorganization of aural geographies of production and consumption, together with the hyperreproducibility of digital platforms and the prevalence of virtual relations of performance and exchange, raises novel questions concerning emergent and future geographies of sonic reproduction and musical debt, capitalist relations, and cultural flows.

I want to briefly reflect on these issues via two final case studies relevant to the performance geographies of musical transit discussed in this book. The first revisits my discussion in chapter 1 of the popular Andean medley "El Cóndor Pasa." Here, I return to some of the thorny political questions that arise when incidents of musical appropriation are imagined and addressed via legal regimes of copyright infringement and protected creative property. The second case study focuses on the unlicensed reproduction and sale of audio recordings via Perú's extensive *piratería* networks. Against the international condemnation of these practices, I offer an alternative reading of Lima's piracy markets to raise questions about sonic archives, popular curation, and collective ownership. Taken together, I argue that these case studies narrate itineraries and relations of musical transmission that provocatively complicate putative cultural imperialist mappings and critiques of musical worlding. By interrogating some of the conventional racial-regional imaginaries and politicoeconomic strategies that inform dominant academic assessments of and legislative remedies to uneven aural relations, my aim is to conclude by initiating a dialogue concerning how we might meaningfully combine sound studies research with social justice agendas.

Let me begin by arguing that any discussion of South American geographies of musical production, consumption, and exchange cannot be pursued in isolation from a broader consideration of enduring and extant raced and gendered structures of coloniality and capital. For, entangled relations of appropriation, expropriation, and debt function as structuring logics for most global Southern cultural workers regardless of whether their individual or collective creative repertoires are "discovered," thieved, or "referenced" by global Northerners. Moreover, as the material geohistories detailed hitherto evince, such relations of property are inherently and irrevocably steeped in the logics of capitalism, white supremacy, and empire, such that their stabilization can only (re)entrench geographies of alienation, abstraction, and abandonment. Given this, I conclude by advancing a bold anticolonial, anticapitalist argument: that questions of protected authorship such as unlicensed musical reproduction or unacknowledged sonic debts cannot be effectively pursued as litigious matters of individual offense or dispute; rather, they must be conceptualized as expressions of structural antagonisms that can only find meaningful redress via broad-based, multiscalar social justice agendas. To make this case, I turn to my first anecdote.

I began this geohistory of South American musical transits with a discussion of the Peruvian composer, musician, and folklorist Daniel Alomía Robles, who arranged the acclaimed musical score "El Cóndor Pasa." A musical mélange of song fragments respectively representing the rhythmic and instrumentational mainstays of Peru's northern coastal, central desert, and highland regions, the ballad, I argued, was a sonic expression of the modernist aspirations of Lima's early twentieth-century mestizo nationalists. Robles's "El Cóndor Pasa" was first introduced to audiences abroad in the 1920s–1930s during a fourteen-year stint that the artist spent living and traveling in the United States. In 1933, the composer copyrighted the musical score with the U.S. Library of Congress, and then returned to Peru, where he would become the head of the nation's newly formed Ministry of Culture. In keeping with familiar sagas of sonic appropriation, the song failed to garner international renown until Paul Simon rereleased a recording of the ballad to U.S. and European audiences in 1969. Simon had "discovered" "El Cóndor Pasa" when he met the traveling pan–Southern Cone folkloric group Los Incas at a nightclub in Paris in 1965. A typical tale of musical outsourcing, Simon paid the performers to record a single-session musical arrangement of the ballad, and then overlaid his own original lyrics. The single was released with liner notes that designated the score a popular Peruvian folk song rather than the creative composition of Alomía Robles.

In 1970, Alomía Robles's son Armando Robles Godoy, a successful film director, filed a copyright lawsuit against Simon in the U.S. courts, which was decided in his favor. In an interview with Lima's *La Primera* newspaper in 2008, Robles Godoy recalls the legal dispute as a mere "misunderstanding," stating that because "Paul Simon is very respectful of other cultures," this musical transgression "was not carelessness on his part." Rather, Godoy places blame on street performers Los Incas, who "gave [Simon] the wrong information" when they misinformed him that "it was a popular tune from the 18th Century." Strikingly, Robles Godoy expresses criticism of and contempt for the practices of grassroots popularization that enabled South American artists of the Nueva Canción tradition to survive in exile while continuing to draw attention to their anti-imperial political cause.

He is quick to defend the global Northern superstar, however, despite (or perhaps due to) Simon's position as an international artistic and economic powerhouse.

Alternatively, one might note that Paul Simon's appropriation of "El Cóndor Pasa" rehearses a familiar history of masculinist imperialist nostalgia, in which white, global Northern artists have catapulted their careers via the appropriation or "rescue" of "far-flung" cultural traditions. At the same time, however, Robles Godoy's take on this all-to-familiar sonic scene is likewise telling as it evokes some pressing questions about the material and ideological limitations of dominant structures of artistic redress. In this case of musical appropriation, Simon paid his dues: his debt to the Robles family was settled in a U.S. courtroom according to the legal parameters of U.S. copyright law. But what of Alomía Robles's own complicity in sonic appropriation? Here we see that the frequency with which dominant world music geographies abstract specific relations of race, economy, and place not only impacts interactions between artists in the global North and global South. Rather, transnational accords concerning property mediation conjoin with colonial modes of knowledge production in a manner that empowers national elites such as Alomía Robles to participate in their own dialectics of "love and theft."[7] As both a respected academic and a government official, Alomía Robles has access to (inter)national channels of governance and networks of capital that enabled the state-sanctioned commodification of collective indigenous repertoires into his own individual intellectual property. In this case we see that the settling of musical debts via international copyright law demands both access and capitulation to the political logics and economic structures of colonial governance and capitalist expansion. In other words, the leveraging of such "protections" effectively naturalizes the vulgar conversion of collective Andean expressive forms into partitioned commodities with specified owners and quantified value—an unfolding of precisely the modes of cultural and capitalist dispossession that lie at the heart of the (neo)colonial enterprise.

In her provocative essay "Neoliberalism at the end of Liberal Democracy," Wendy Brown keenly distinguishes between neoliberalism as an economic strategy and neoliberalism as a political rationality.[8] While the former refers to a globalized capitalist mode of production governed by the principles of a radically free market, the latter names the insidious application of market values to all social institutions and interactions. To imagine that all dimensions of human life can be evaluated in terms of market rationality, Brown argues, is to recode structural antagonisms as matters of individual will, choice, and management. Following Brown, I want to problematize the notion that relations of musical appropriation and debt can be adequately represented as, or remedied through the legal and/or discursive condemnation of, individual acts of transgression or opportunism. As scholars of critical race, gender, and sexuality studies, we are all too familiar with such state-making tactics. Moreover, if, as Brown and others have argued, the heteropatriarchal racial state's legitimacy is tied to differential markers of market success, can the expansion of neoliberal modes of regulation and management effectively offer substantive, effectual recourse to such antagonisms?

It is with this question in mind that I turn to my second anecdote. During a research trip to Lima in the winter of 2003, I visited the National Archive with the intention of perusing the library's holdings on Peru's mid-century Black Arts Revival. After meeting with an archivist, I discovered that "Afro-Peruvian music"—and indeed, "Afro-Peruvian" were not catalogued search terms. Hours into a haphazard periodical search that yielded little, I began chatting with a fellow scholar from Lima. Upon describing my project to him, he recommended that I visit El Hueco (figure Epi.1), one of the city's largest piracy markets. "There you will find the stories that you are looking for," he advised.

Located on Avenida Abancay on the fringes of Lima's centro histórico, El Hueco—"The Hole"—earned its moniker from its unusual topography. Ironically, it is housed in an enormous artificial crater that was intended to serve as the foundation for a second National Ministry of Education building—a state project that was abandoned in its initial stages due to the economic collapse under the Alan García administration. Lying defunct, the chasmal abandoned lot was enclosed by two major transportation arteries and enjoyed substantial foot traffic. Twenty-one years later, when the mayor of Lima initiated a citywide campaign to evict *ambulates* (street peddlers) from the city's sidewalks, El Hueco emerged as a centralized site of informal commerce. Over the past two decades, the collective efforts of its vendors have produced an increasingly embedded locale, one that now boasts permanent stalls, public restrooms, and, occasionally, siphoned electricity. Its merchandise has varied over time; in the past, CDs, DVDs, office supplies, and small electronics made up its featured wares. More recently, sportswear

EPI.1 Centro Commercial El Hueco. Photo by the author.

and evangelical literatures have also gained commercial prominence. But, digital media remains the mainstay of El Hueco's commercial base.

Media piracy at El Hueco is a complex cultural formation that relies on interregional partnerships and transnational ties, ever-evolving infrastructural improvisation, and segmented processes of creative and waged labor. Approximately four hundred of the market's *puestos* (stalls) are dedicated to media sales. These kiosks vary in size and dimension, measuring roughly three feet deep by four to eight feet wide. Merchandise is densely packed in hand-hewn wooden shelves that extend anywhere from eight to fifteen feet high, wherefore a single stall may contain tens of thousands of items for sale. Pirated audio and visual materials, primarily sourced through the unlicensed reproduction of digital files obtained through online sharing platforms, are available in a wide range of formats: MP3, MP4, CD, DVD, BluRay, USB, and media cards. Because of the sheer volume of merchandise, most booths rely on complex organizational systems in which their stock is alphabetized within broad generic categories. Patrons can peruse the offerings of a particular seller via thick binders with photocopied jackets of available media. Some of El Hueco's *puestos* are staffed by *socios*—those with recognized occupancy rights obtained through decades of squatting and collective protest, while others are run by *empleados* (employees), the majority of whom are indigenous or indigenous descended women in their late teens and early twenties.

El Hueco's acoustic environment is loosely organized into distinctive sonic ecologies; media *puestos* are often clustered according to the musical genres in which they specialize, ranging from *cumbia andina*, *música folclorica*, and *reggaetón* to salsa, merengue, rap, hip-hop, R&B, and soul. Each stall boasts audio and/or audiovisual equipment (often powered by homemade battery packs due to frequent power outages) so that sellers can advertise their wares and patrons can sample or test them before finalizing a purchase. For the market flâneur, wandering through El Hueco is not unlike touring an interactive auditory museum; the concentrated breadth of musical texts produced in and across the Americas, along with their unique cultural and linguistic adaptations and their variant arrangements and interpretations, constitutes nothing short than a rich, popular archive of hemispheric musical transits.

El Hueco has often been represented as an archetypical example of Lima's extensive piracy circuits, which have earned significant international notoriety over the past decade. Peru has been identified as a principal international player in the production and distribution of pirated digital media in the Americas.[9] The BBC recently reported that 98 percent of all music transactions in Peru occur in the black market. The International Intellectual Property Alliance, a private-sector coalition of trade associations representing U.S. producers of copyright-protected content and materials, commissioned several investigative reports regarding the scale of Peru's unlicensed digital media trade. International copyright protection organizations such as the IIPA have urged Peruvian authorities to conduct regular raids of known pirate markets. Such sweeps occasionally occur; in 2012 when 150 police officers armed with riot gear and teargas attempted to temporarily shut down the market, the commercial center's well-organized vendors successfully fought them off with rocks and sticks. This is neither unusual nor surprising: in a nation like Peru, where the vast majority of economic activity occurs via informal transactions, market vendors have long since developed extralegal modes of organization, coalition, and conflict resolution, on which these "gray market" economies rely.[10]

EPI.2 Stocked El Hueco stall. Photo by the author.

Against such narratives that cast El Hueco as a marker of global Southern "incivility," "disorder," or "corruption," I want to suggest an alternative reading of Lima's piracy networks. El Hueco has served as a primary archive for my book project, as it and its slightly older predecessor, Polvos Azules, constitutes one of the largest sound recording collections in the nation. In the absence of state infrastructure and public services such as libraries and research centers, pirate markets such as these arguably function as important sites of collective knowledge production, digital curation, and artistic registry (figure Epi.2). For example, the fabrication of innovative compilations has served as a signature piracy practice dating back to the days of the cassette. Today, video and sonic compilations are overwhelmingly the most popular and ubiquitous of El Hueco's media offerings. These musical texts are curated and crafted by the *pirata* who, part artist, part audiophile, specializes in the creative assembly and layering of song and sound, theme and genre. A veteran vender with expertise in regional musics of Andes, for example, introduced me to a series of compilations that he and other sound artists had arranged under the thematic rubric "guitarra ayacuchana." Some were organized according to intergenerational genealogies, while others boasted broad stylistic samplings, and others still a juxtaposition of popular and obscure songs and artists. This is but one example of how piracy sound artists and venders fulfill both political and pedagogical functions for their aural publics: on the one hand, compilations often record and preserve modes and moments of indigenous cultural politics that are absented from state archives; on the other, they creatively express both lived and imagined experiences of labor, leisure, and longing.

Numerous national artists have acknowledged their indebtedness to piracy reproduction and circulation. Renowned Afro-Peruvian *cajonero* Rafael Santa Cruz, for example, credits pirate circuits for the national popularization of Black Peruvian Song.[11] While *Cumanana*—the first long-play album of Afro-Peruvian music recorded by Virrey Records in 1959—fell out of licensed circulation within a few years of its release, it has remained in consistent circulation since the 1970s via unlicensed modes of reproduction. This unlicensed distribution brought the music of the Black Arts Revival to a national audience. Similarly, Susana Baca attributes her recent popularity in Peru to the dissemination of her musical and pedagogical work via piracy networks; because her albums were recorded abroad, the cost of a single recording is nearly equivalent to half the average monthly income of a wage worker employed full time. Again, these are just two of numerous cases in which piracy practices have accomplished modes of popular archival work that sanctioned sites of knowledge production are unable or unwilling to perform.

The performance geographies chronicled heretofore illustrate how South American cultural workers have mobilized spatialized sonic practices—from the use of creative staging techniques, to the construction of informal economies and improvisational performance venues, to the activation of transnational musicians' networks—to negotiate the social and spatial circumscriptions of extant racial capitalist landscapes. Yet as the YouTube activism of sound artists such as Renata Flores Rivera and the proliferation of piracy networks throughout Peru both illustrate, the emergence of digital media, online file-sharing platforms, and virtual performance venues has prompted unique tensions and contradictions within sonic mediation landscapes in and between America del Sur y del Norte. Ironically, the contemporary consumption of musical culture demonstrates an inversion in the politics of sonic appropriation: Putumayo recordings are now available both at Whole Foods Markets for $14.95 and at El Centro Commercial El Hueco for 60 cents. Meanwhile, an industry that once prided itself on the unfettered (and unremunerated) expropriation and curation of "exotic" cultural forms is now lobbying for the stringent regulation of international musical flows. Given this, I want to conclude with a set of questions that converge around future geographies of transit. What would it mean to rethink questions of sonic appropriation and musical debt in a manner that decouples the (e)valuation of creative work and capitalist determinations of value? How might we create and sustain venues for musical production and exchange—a sonic commons—that refuses current structures of private property protection and regulation? How might such a reorganization of sonic relations concomitantly activate shifts in spatial hierarchies and geographies of difference?

The geohistories of struggle narrated throughout this book powerfully illustrate that contemplations of these imperatives must be rooted in multiscalar organizing agendas that resist settling for legislative models of individual redress and/or multiculturalist tales of individual success. They both model and compel the eradication of vulnerability, exploitation, and encumbrance as they are organized at regional and national scales via collective, transnational investments in infrastructure, services, and opportunities. And they remind us that, amid the dystopic emplacements of power and difference that structure our social worlds, even the most quotidian, improvisational, and ephemeral of performance geographies harbors the transformative potential to imagine and activate alternative modalities of site-making, subject formation, and social transformation.

NOTES

INTRODUCTION

1 "Soundscapes: La Nueva Canción."

2 An expanded discussion of the multiple ways in which "folklore" as a conceptual term and cultural terrain will follow in chapter 1. For an excellent discussion of the *Nueva Canción* movement, see Fairley, "La nueva canción latinoamericana"; Reyes Matta, "The 'New Song' and Its Confrontation in Latin America"; and Tumas-Serna, "The 'Nueva Canción' Movement."

3 Rios, "Andean Music, the Left, and Pan-Latin Americanism."

4 Simon and Garfunkel, "El Condor Pasa (If I Could)."

5 Here I build on Frances Aparicio and Cándida Jáquez's discussion of "musical migrations," which they define as a conceptual tool that "foregrounds the processes of dislocation, transformation, and mediation that characterize musical structures, productions, and performances as they cross national and cultural borders and transform their meanings from one historical period to another." Aparicio and Jáquez, *Musical Migrations*, 3.

6 This conceptualization of South America is indebted to the collective work of María Amelia Viteri, José Fernando Serrano, and Salvador Vidal-Ortiz. In the introduction to their dossier "¿Cómo se piensa lo 'queer' en América Latina?," the authors argue that the regional term "South America" can be understood to represent not a fixed geographic location but rather "a position in the production of knowledge." Viteri, Serrano, and Vidal-Ortiz, "¿Cómo se piensa lo 'queer' en América Latina?," 47.

7 For an excellent anthologized discussion of the relationship between the growing presence of Latin(o) popular music in the United States, hemispheric bodily and cultural migration patterns, and the commodification of Latin(o) popular music, see Aparicio and Jáquez, *Musical Migrations*.

8 Examples of such tactics include, for example, the reclaiming and re-signification of public space, emphases on spontaneous and do-it-yourself modes of convocation, and the elaboration of informal modes and networks of cultural and economic exchange.

9 Taken together, these dialectics of social mobilization and state revanchism prompted mass migration and exile throughout the Southern Americas, which

in turn sparked the formation of transnational networks of political community and cultural exchange.

10 Aparicio, *Listening to Salsa*; Hernandez, *Bachata*; Hernandez, "Dancing with the Enemy"; Cepeda, *Musical ImagiNation*; Fiol-Matta, "Pop Latinidad"; Rivera, *New York Ricans from the Hip Hop Zone*; Vargas, *Dissonant Divas in Chicana Music*; and Vasquez, *Listening in Detail*.

11 These exceptions include the following: Wade, *Music, Race, and Nation*; Lipsitz, *Dangerous Crossroads*; Johnson, *Spaces of Conflict, Sounds of Solidarity*; Whiteley, Bennett, and Hawkins, *Music, Space and Place*; Connell and Gibson, *Sound Tracks*; Guilbault, "On Redefining the 'Local' through World Music."

12 See, for example, Romero, "Black Music and Identity in Peru"; Feldman, *Black Rhythms of Peru*; León Quirós, "The Aestheticization of Tradition"; and Rios, "Andean Music, the Left, and Pan-Latin Americanism."

13 Although widely interrogated, the "culture industry" model of global production and consumption articulated within the work of Frankfurt School theorists Theodor Adorno and Max Horkheimer has remained foundational to contemporary critiques of the world music industry. For example, "cultural imperialism" is a common analytical frame through which scholars of popular music have tracked sonic circulations from the global South to the global North. This model applies "culture industry" logic within global networks of capitalist production and exchange, suggesting that the process of packaging and mass-producing musical traditions in the "third world" for consumption in the centers of global capital results in the depoliticization, homogenization, and corruption of local musical products and practices. For discussions of the cultural imperialism model, see, for example, Campbell Robinson, Buck, and Cuthbert, *Music at the Margins*; Frith, "The Industrialization of Popular Music"; Garofalo, "Whose World, What Beat"; Roberts, "'World Music' and the Global Culture Economy"; Taylor, *Global Pop*; and Tomlinson, *Cultural Imperialism*.

14 Rosaldo, *Culture and Truth*.

15 In their book, *AfroPop!*, Sean Barlow, Banning Eyre, and Jack Vartoogian characterize such interactions as an "endlessly creative conversation" between "local roots and international pop culture." Barlow, Eyre, and Vartoogian, *AfroPop!*, vii.

16 Mitchell, "Transnational Discourse."

17 Essays and monographs by scholars of popular music studies that have influenced my own thinking on the relationship between globalization, cultural production, and mass mediation include Chambers, *Urban Rhythms*; Chanan, "Global Corporations and 'World Music'"; Connell and Gibson, "World Music"; Frith, *World Music, Politics, and Social Change*; Feld, "Notes on World Beat"; Garofalo, "Whose World, What Beat"; Guilbault, "On Redefining the 'Local' through World Music"; Guilbault, "Interpreting World Music"; Lipsitz,

Dangerous Crossroads; Middleton, *Studying Popular Music*; Mitchell, *Popular Music and Local Identity*; and Taylor, *Global Pop*. Within the fields of cultural and media studies more generally, my thinking on the relationship between cultural production and mass mediation has been influenced by the following: Appadurai, *Modernity at Large*; Appadurai, "Disjuncture and Difference in the Global Cultural Economy"; Canclini, *Hybrid Cultures*; Clifford, *Routes*; and Jenkins, *Convergence Culture*.

18 Here I take issue not with the terms themselves, but their popular usage as "spatial metaphors" within music studies scholarship. In fact, Schaffer's conceptualization of "soundscape" and Mary Louise Pratt's theorization of "contact zones" are both examples of spatialized cultural theorization. See Pratt, "Arts of the Contact Zone"; Schafer, *The Soundscape*.

19 Geographers Neil Smith and Cindy Katz describe spatial metaphors as geographic terms that, through reliance on conceptions of absolute space, abstract rather than materialize connections between social and spatial formation. See Smith and Katz, "Grounding Metaphor."

20 Connell and Gibson, *Sound Tracks*, 1.

21 Notable exceptions to this trend include Connell and Gibson, *Sound Tracks*; Guilbault, "On Redefining the 'Local' through World Music"; Johnson, *Spaces of Conflict, Sounds of Solidarity*; Kelley, *Thelonious Monk*; Lipsitz, *Dangerous Crossroads*; Vargas, *Dissonant Divas in Chicana Music*; Woods, *Development Arrested*. My thinking on the relationship between cultural production and spatial formation more generally is deeply indebted to the work of Mary Pat Brady, Doreen Massey, Katherine McKittrick, and Ruth Wilson Gilmore. See Brady, *Extinct Lands, Temporal Geographies*; Massey, *Space, Place, and Gender* and *For Space*; McKittrick, *Demonic Grounds*; Gilmore, *Golden Gulag*.

22 Small, *Musicking*.

23 Here I take seriously Feld's claim that genealogies of academic musical typologies and approaches to the study of sound are deeply embedded in the global circulation of sound—that is, the relations and structures that contribute to its various mediations. See Feld, "A Sweet Lullaby for World Music."

24 Here I draw on Shana Redmond's concept of a sound "franchise," which she defines as "an organized melodic challenge utilized by the African descended to announce their collectivity and to what political ends they would be mobilized." Redmond uses the term to connote the overdetermined relations of coalitional performance, state power, capital, mass media." Redmond, *Anthem*, 4–5.

25 Lefebvre, *The Production of Space*; Brady, *Extinct Lands, Temporal Geographies*.

26 Brady, *Extinct Lands, Temporal Geographies*, 6.

27 Massey, *For Space*, 3.

28 McKittrick and Peake, "What Difference Does Difference Make to Geography?," 2.

29 Gilmore, "Fatal Couplings of Power and Difference," 16.

30 For rich and nuanced discussions of the relationship between globalization and spatialization, see Massey, *Space, Place, and Gender*, and *For Space*; Mitchell, "Transnational Discourse"; and Gilmore, "Race and Globalization."

31 Schmidt Camacho, "Ciudadana X."

32 Gauthier and Yúdice, "The Latin American Music Industry in an Era of Crisis."

33 Cresswell, *Place*, 19.

34 My thinking on place has been mostly deeply influenced by the work of Ruth Wilson Gilmore, Neil Smith, Cindy Katz, and Doreen Massey. See Smith, "Contours of a Spatialized Politics"; Smith and Katz, "Grounding Metaphor"; Massey, *Space, Place, and Gender*; Smith, *The New Urban Frontier*; Gilmore, "Globalisation and US Prison Growth"; Gilmore, "You Have Dislodged a Boulder"; Gilmore, "Fatal Couplings of Power and Difference"; Gilmore, *Golden Gulag*; and Massey, *For Space*.

35 Smith, "Contours of a Spatialized Politics," 64.

36 Examples of feminist and antiracist geographers that offer compelling examples of this argument include Brady, *Extinct Lands, Temporal Geographies*; Massey, *Space, Place, and Gender*; Gilmore, "Fatal Couplings of Power and Difference"; McKittrick and Peake, "What Difference Does Difference Make to Geography?"; and McKittrick, *Demonic Grounds*.

37 Ochoa Gautier, "Sonic Transculturation, Epistemologies of Purification," 808.

38 Ochoa Gautier, "Sonic Transculturation, Epistemologies of Purification," 808.

39 Aparicio and Jáquez, *Musical Migrations*, 9.

40 I am thinking of the work of Redmond, *Anthem*; Pacini Hernandez, *Bachata*; Aparicio, *Listening to Salsa*; Habell-Pallán, *Loca Motion*; Johnson, *Spaces of Conflict, Sounds of Solidarity Music*; Vargas, *Dissonant Divas*; Kheshti, *Modernity's Ear*; and Casillas, *Sounds of Belonging*.

41 Sterne, *The Sound Studies Reader*, 2.

42 Jay, *Downcast Eyes*.

43 Sterne, *The Audible Past*.

44 Ochoa Gautier, *Aurality*.

45 Ochoa Gautier, "Sonic Transculturation, Epistemologies of Purification."

46 Rice, "Listening," 99.

47 Vasquez, *Listening in Detail*, 27.

48 Vargas, *Dissonant Divas in Chicana Music*, xii–xiv.

49 Luta, "Live Electronic Performance."

50 Small, *Musicking*, 9.

51 Taylor, *The Archive and the Repertoire*, 15.

52 Clark, "Performing the Memory of Difference in Afro-Caribbean Dance"; Roach, *Cities of the Dead*; Delgado and Muñoz, "Introduction."

53 Of course, there are many exciting exceptions to this scholarly trend. Some exceptions that have influenced my own thinking include Lipsitz, *Dangerous*

Crossroads; Kun, *Audiotopia*; Vargas, *Dissonant Divas in Chicana Music*; and Redmond, *Anthem*.

54 Niaah, *Dancehall*.

55 In addition to Niaah's illuminating book, other works that have influenced my thinking on the relationship between performance and space include Nash, "Performativity in Practice"; Thrift, "The Still Point"; and Houston and Pulido, "The Work of Performativity."

56 Butler, *Gender Trouble*.

57 Houston and Pulido, "The Work of Performativity," 42.

58 Diamond, "Introduction," in *Performance and Cultural Politics*, 2.

59 A peña is a popular performance venue, often associated with leftist politics, where artists and audiences convene to eat and drink, dance, and engage in political discussion. For an in-depth discussion of the peña and its association with social justice struggles, see Jara, *An Unfinished Song*.

1. SOUNDING PLACE OVER TIME

1 Unless otherwise noted, translations of Spanish language texts are my own.

2 Raimundo López, "'El cóndor pasa' declarada Patrimonio Cultural de Perú."

3 Baudouin published under the pseudonym Julio de la Paz; De La Paz, *El cóndor pasa*.

4 The meaning of the term *criollo* varies across historical, geographic, and cultural contexts throughout the Americas. In this case, it refers to the elite mestizo class of the early twentieth-century republic that distinguished itself from its peninsular and indigenous counterparts by embracing a continental American identity.

5 My reading of De La Paz's *El cóndor pasa* is based on a reprinted edition that appears in José Varallarnos's *El Cóndor Pasa*.

6 Varallarnos, *El Cóndor Pasa*, scene 1, 132.

7 Spanish: "los amos . . . nos tratan como béstias." Cited in Varallarnos, *El Cóndor Pasa*, scene 1, 134. Spanish: "Así debe ser, Frank. Los amos han nacido para mandar, y nosotros para obedecerles." Cited in Varallarnos, *El Cóndor Pasa*, scene 1, 134.

8 Spanish: "Algo hay en mi mente que me dice que las vida no es así"; Spanish: "Parece que en sus venas ardiera la misma sangre imperiosa del amo." Varallarnos, *El Cóndor Pasa*, scene 1, 134.

9 Spanish: "El último cóndor que por acá pasaba, lo vi volar una noche sobre mi choza, perdiéndose en la altura. . . . Allí dentro estaba Mr. Mac King, María, tu madre, también estaba . . . pero yo no se si nuestro amor se lo llevó el cóndor en su vuelo trágico." Varallarnos, *El Cóndor Pasa*, scene 1, 134.

10 Spanish: "El pelo rojo que hay en mi cabeza, es el reflejo del incendio de odios que hay en mi sangre . . . los odio a los amos; porque desde compraron las

minas nos compraron también a nosotros como bestias de carga." Cited in Varallarnos, *El Cóndor Pasa*, scene 1, 133.

11 For a more comprehensive discussion of the zarzuela, see Paz Soldán, "Apuntes críticas"; Mejía, *El misterio del cóndor*; Varallarnos, *El Cóndor Pasa*.

12 Cornejo Polar, "El indigenismo y las literaturas heterogéneas"; Mariátegui, *Seven Interpretive Essays on Peruvian Reality*.

13 Cornejo Polar, "El indigenismo y las literaturas heterogéneas"; Scheben, "Indigenismo y modernismo."

14 Spanish: "pujantes sueños, voces y presencias" that coalesced in "forjando la Nueva Patria [*sic*]." Theater review by Argentinian critic Julia Bowland, cited in Perez Torres Llosa, "El cóndor pasa."

15 Spanish: "Los que presenciamos su estreno podemos afirmar que fue un verdadero éxito." Varallarnos, *El Cóndor Pasa*.

16 Basadre Grohmann, *Historia de la República del Perú*.

17 Sánchez, *Introducción crítica a la literatura peruana*, 1202.

18 Spanish: "un drama clásico en el indigenismo o, mejor, en el nuevo teatro peruano." Cited in Varallarnos, *El Cóndor Pasa*, 81.

19 Basadre Grohmann, *Historia de la República del Perú*.

20 More, "Daniel Alomía Robles en primera persona."

21 Spanish: "En esos tiempos predominaba la música italiana . . . No se conocía absolutamente nada de la música nativa." More, "Daniel Alomía Robles en primera persona."

22 Juan Sixto Prieto, cited in Paz Soldán, "Apuntes críticas."

23 For an extended discussion of Peru's indigenista movement, see Cornejo Polar, "El indigenismo y las literaturas heterogéneas."

24 Ochoa Gautier, "Sonic Transculturation, Epistemologies of Purification."

25 Thurner, *From Two Republics to One Divided*; Thomas E. Skidmore and Peter H. Smith, "The Transformation of Modern Latin America."

26 Quijano, *Nationalism and Capitalism in Peru*.

27 Mariátegui, *Seven Interpretive Essays on Peruvian Reality*. For an in-depth discussion of indigenismo at the turn of the century, see Gibson, "El indio en la formacíon económica nacional"; Kapsoli, *El Pensamiento de la Asociacíon Pro Indígena*; Kristal, *Una visión urbana de los Andes*.

28 As ethnomusicologist Aurelio Tello contends, this attention to the development of national symbols was an aesthetic trend that spread throughout the nascent Latin American nations: "La preocupación por crear un arte con sello propio, que encontrara sus raíces en la música prehispánica, en la canción popular, en el folklore [*sic*], o en las reminiscencias y reinvenciones de éstos, fue un hecho generalizado desde México hasta el Cono Sur, o viceversa" (The preoccupation with creating an art bearing an original stamp, that could find its roots in pre-Hispanic music, popular music, folklore, or in the reminiscences and reinventions of these, was a general trend extending from Mexico through

the Southern Cone, or vice versa). See Tello, "Aires nacionales en la música de América Latina como respuesta a la búsqueda de identidad," 4.

29 While the roots of the term "folklore" can be traced back to European romanticism and the mourned loss of the popular practices of a preindustrial peasantry, the heterogeneity of postcolonial Latin American societies has meant that the concept of "folklore" has been appropriated by both bourgeoisie cultural nationalists and antistatist oppositional cultures. For an in-depth discussion of folklore in postindependent Latin America, see Rowe and Schelling, *Memory and Modernity*.

30 Rowe and Schelling, *Memory and Modernity*, 4.

31 McClintock, *Imperial Leather*, 358.

32 Tello, "Aires nacionales."

33 Schwab, "El folklore, nuevo campo de estudio en América y la necesidad de su orientación histórica," 1.

34 Palma, *Tradiciones peruanas*.

35 Ochoa Gautier, "Sonic Transculturation, Epistemologies of Purification," 813.

36 Anderson, *Imagined Communities*.

37 Linell, *Approaching Dialogue*.

38 Ochoa Gautier, "Sonic Transculturation, Epistemologies of Purification," 814.

39 The artist's musical instruction began with classical training with Italian musician and composer Claudio Rebagliati. Yet, according to ethnomusicologist Rodolfo Barbacci, it was under the tutelage of Franciscan priest Gabriel Salas that Alomía Robles was awakened to his passionate commitment to the compilation of popular and folkloric melodies. See Rodolfo Barbacci, "Apuntes para un diccionario biográfico musical de Perú."

40 Pinilla, *La música en el Perú*, 139.

41 See Holtzman, "Catálogo de las obras de Daniel Alomía Robles," 25. In his monograph on the elusive ballad and the life and work of Alomía Robles, Varallarnos diplomatically references *El Cóndor Pasa* as "una obra musical *extraída* o *basada*, en su esencia, de las viejas melodías y cantares del folklore andino" (a musical work *extracted from* or *based in*, in its essence, in the ancient melodies and songs of Andean folklore) (emphasis mine). Varallarnos, "El Cóndor Pasa," 25.

42 Here I wish to note that conceptions of indigeneity and mestizaje are in many ways place based and shift according to one's physical and social location. In other words, Indians can become mestizos within a generation or even a lifetime through processes of displacement and migration; the adoption of distinctive cultural practices such as accent, musical taste, and dress; and so on. These processes, in turn, shape those of racialization and ethnic affiliation. For an excellent discussion of race and indigeneity in Peru, see De la Cadena, *Indigenous Mestizos*; For a comprehensive biography of Robles's life and work, see Holtzman, "Catálogo de las obras De Daniel Alomía Robles"; and Varallarnos, *El Cóndor Pasa*.

43 Ochoa Gautier, "Sonic Transculturation, Epistemologies of Purification."

44 Brückmann, *El Cóndor Pasa*, 176.

45 Brückmann notes the etymology of the term and indicates its historic function (Brückmann, *El Cóndor Pasa*, 176). *Pasacalle* is derived from the phrase "pasar por la calle" and historically referred to musicians who roved Spain's public roadways and plazas.

46 The charango is a ten-stringed Andean instrument of the lute family. Variations of it have been found throughout the Andes since the 1500s. While traditionally fabricated from an armadillo shell, today the charango is most often fashioned from wood.

47 The orchestral accompaniment to Baudouin's *El Cóndor Pasa* consisted of eight parts: *introducción, coro, yaraví, dúo, romanza, kashua, pasacalle, and plegaria.*

48 S.v. "Victor matrix G-2295, El cóndor pasa / Orquesta del Zoológico," *Discography of American Historical Recordings*, http://adp.library.ucsb.edu/index.php /matrix/detail/600001472/G-2295-El_condor_pasa, accessed October 20, 2015.

49 Cavour Aramayo, *Instrumentos musicales de Bolivia*; Romero, "La música tradicional y popular" and *Sonidos andinos*.

50 String instruments such as the charango and guitar orient the rhythmic genre of sonic texts like the rasgueo, or patterned rhythmic strum. The *hualaycho* is a smaller version of the charango.

51 The kena and siku are the mainstay of Andean wind instruments. The kena is a straight, end-blown flute made from bamboo. It is notched at one end and fingered much like a recorder. In some highland areas, the kena was originally fashioned from the bone of condor wings. Also a wind instrument, the siku is diatonically tuned and consists of two separate halves, each containing every other note of the musical scale. It is usually played between two musicians, with each taking half of the instrument (a practice often referred to as *trensar*, or braiding). Often mistaken for the European pan flute, sikus vary in size from a few inches to several feet in length. For more comprehensive discussions of Andean wind and percussion instruments, see Cavour Aramayo, *Instrumentos musicales de Bolivia;* Romero, "La música tradicional y popular"; and Romero, *Sonidos andinos*.

52 See Ortiz, *Cuban Counterpoint*.

53 Rivera Cusicanqui, "Ch'ixinakax utxiwa."

54 See Beverley, *Subalternity and Representation*.

55 Dorian, "La nación."

56 Spanish: "una obra hecha con amor a todas las cosas nacionales . . . rica en material de música incaica . . . pero armonizada con gran arte." Cited in A. J. P. Paz Soldán, "Apuntes críticas," xx.

57 Spanish: "el autor del folklore Peruano." Cited in Varallarnos, *El Cóndor Pasa*.

58 "Peruvian Music Given on N.Y.U. Campus," 8.

59 "Listening In," 20.

60 I use the term "pan-Andean" to connote the Andean region of Ecuador, Peru, and Bolivia, traveled by Alomía Robles.

61 Varallarnos, *El Cóndor Pasa*, 77. The title of this section contains lyrics excerpted from Simon and Garfunkel's "Citizen of the Planet" (Paul Simon, *Citizen of the Planet*, 2003).

62 Aviruká, "El Cóndor Pasa . . . 1930."

63 Rios, "La flûte indienne."

64 Heckman, "Reviews."

65 Pareles, "Review/Pop: A Voyage through the Decades with Paul Simon as the Guide," www.nytimes.com/1993/10/04/arts/review-pop-a-voyage-through-the -decades-with-paul-simon-as-the-guide.html?mcubz=3, accessed December 13, 2014.

66 Levitin, "Still Creative after All These Years."

67 "Paul Simon," n.p.

68 Zolov, *Refried Elvis*, 229.

69 Cited in Zolov, *Refried Elvis*, 228–30.

70 *Celia Cruz y Tito Puente en España*, 1971.

71 Katerí Hernández, "The Buena Vista Social Club," 62.

72 Lipsitz, *Dangerous Crossroads*.

73 Here I use the term "imperialist nostalgia" as defined by Renato Rosaldo. See Rosaldo, *Culture and Truth*.

74 PBS, "Buena Vista Social Club," www.pbs.org/buenavista/music/ry_cooder_bio .html, accessed December 16, 2010.

75 For an extensive discussion of the political economy of Peru in the context of contemporary global economic restructuring, see Carranza, *Globalización y crisis social en el Perú*.

76 In fact, Paul Simon's rendition of "El Cóndor Pasa" was recently made available as a polyphonic ringtone for cell phones. The Alomía Robles family did initiate litigation against Simon in the year following "El Cóndor Pasa"'s international release and ultimately, in the words of Daniel's son Armando Robles Godoy, "las cosas se pusieron en lugar: Alomía Robles fue el autor de la música y Simon de la letra" (things were cleared up: Alomía Robles was the composer of the music, and Simon of the lyrics). Zamalloa, "Declaran a 'El cóndor pasa' patrimonio cultural de Perú."

77 On April 14, 2004, "El Cóndor Pasa" was finally declared a national cultural patrimony by the INC. Riofrio, "Daniel Alomía Robles."

78 Rosaldo, *Culture and Truth*.

79 For a discussion of indigenismo and socialism in Lima's intellectual circles, see Thurner, *From Two Republics to One Divided*.

80 Martin, "Yma Sumac, Vocalist of the Exotic, Dies at 86."

81 Vargas, *Dissonant Divas in Chicana Music*; Vasquez, *Listening in Detail*.

82 Sumac's birthdate remains a matter of contest. In Peru, an unverified copy of

her birth certificate is cited to suggest that the artist was born on September 13, 1922; her petition for naturalization in the United States, however, lists her birthdate as September 10, 1923.

83 *Ollantay* is an epic drama originally written in Quechua. It first appeared in print in 1857, published by Johann Jakob von Tschudi, in Quechua and German. The first Spanish version appeared in Lima in 1868, published by José Sebastián Barranca.

84 Limansky, *Yma Sumac*, 17.

85 Limansky, *Yma Sumac*, 17.

86 Rios, "La flûte indienne," 3.

87 Limansky, *Yma Sumac*, 170; original review in *Variety*, June 16, 1943.

88 Rios, "Andean Music, the Left, and Pan-Latin Americanism"; Limansky, *Yma Sumac*.

89 Accounts of Cholita's relationship to Sumac and Vivanco are conflicting; some news sources refer to her as Yma's cousin, while others suggest that she was a relative of Moisés. A few sources have even intimated that Cholita might not have been a familial relation at all. While a definitive account is not available, it seems clear that the artist had a close relationship with the couple.

90 Poling, "Most Exciting Voice in the World," 19.

91 Interview with *Metronome Magazine*, 1956.

92 Totten, "Yma Sumac."

93 Sloan, "The Other World Music," 409.

94 For a description of the instruments, see Sloan, "The Other World Music," 415.

95 Kheshti, *Modernity's Ear*.

96 Sumac, *Voices of Xtabay*, liner notes.

97 Poling, "Most Exciting Voice in the World," 16.

98 Poling, "Most Exciting Voice in the World," 19.

99 Qtd. in Poling, "Most Exciting Voice in the World," 19.

100 Holden, "Reviews/Music: The Yma Sumac Mystique," www.nytimes.com/1989/02/26/arts/reviews-music-the-yma-sumac-mystique.html?mcubz=3, accessed December 15, 2014; Sherman, "Yma Sumac Returns to Roar of Crowd," 40.

101 Poling, "Most Exciting Voice in the World," 21.

102 Vargas, *Dissonant Divas in Chicana Music*.

103 Editorial review on Amazon.com, www.amazon.com/Miracles-Yma-Sumac-dp/B004MPAFOA/ref=sr_1_1?ie=UTF8&qid=1503202022&sr=8-1&keywords=yma+sumac+miracles, accessed December 14, 2014.

104 "Welcome to SunVirgin.com."

105 Rowe and Schelling, *Memory and Modernity*, 4.

106 See Massey, *Space, Place, and Gender*; Smith and Katz, "Grounding Metaphor"; Smith, "Contours of a Spatialized Politics."

107 Smith and Katz, "Grounding Metaphor."

108 By "place" I mean a particular historicogeographic articulation that gives mean-

ing to an ensemble of social relations. See Massey, *Space, Place, and Gender*; Smith, "Contours of a Spatialized Politics"; Smith and Katz, "Grounding Metaphor."

109 Anzaldúa, *Borderlands / La Frontera*; Brady, *Extinct Lands, Temporal Geographies*; Pratt, *Imperial Eyes*; Saldívar, *Border Matters*.

2. PUTUMAYO AND ITS DISCONTENTS

1 Kassabian, "Would You Like Some World Music with Your Latte?"

2 Putumayo, "About Putumayo World Music," www.putumayo.com/history/, accessed September 5, 2016.

3 "About Putumayo World Music."

4 "With the advent and expansion of the world music industry," Kheshti argues, "there has emerged a complex social process in which it is the consumer who is called on to sonically construct the other through listening." Dubbed by Kheshti "the aural imaginary," this process entails a remapping of the body through the performance of leadership, in which "the ear is interpellated as the main site for the signification of sonic affect and alterity." See Kheshti, "Touching Listening."

5 Vivek Tiwary, "Lifestyle Marketing," www.starpolish.com/advice/article.asp ?id+37?original=1, accessed July 16, 2015.

6 For a discussion of the "ingenuity" of Putumayo's business model and its impact on the industry, see Mohndec, "Private Sector," www.nytimes.com/2003/12/21 /business/private-sector-stumbling-into-a-world-of-music.html, accessed October 15, 2016.

7 Mohndec, "Private Sector."

8 Mohndec, "Private Sector."

9 In *Conscious Capitalism*, coauthors John Mackey (co-CEO of Whole Foods Market) and Raj Sisodia define conscious capitalism as "a way of thinking about business to ensure that it is grounded in a higher purpose to enhance its positive impact on the world." Schawbel, "John Mackey: Why Companies Should Embrace Conscious Capitalism," www.forbes.com/sites/danschawbel /2013/01/15/john-mackey-why-companies-should-embrace-conscious-capitalism /#3e2831505dd3, accessed July 17, 2015. Mackey argues that "when reinvented in this way, capitalism is an extraordinarily powerful system of value creation mutually benefiting all stakeholders." Schawbel, "John Mackey."

10 Here I reference Omi and Winant's conceptual term "racial project," which the authors define as "simultaneously an interpretation, representation, or explanation of racial dynamics and an effort to reorganize and redistribute resources along particular racial lines." Omi and Winant, *Racial Formation in the United States*, 24.

11 "Musicking" refers to "taking part in any capacity in musical performance,

whether by performing, by listening, by rehearsing or by practicing, by providing material for performance (what is called composition) or by dancing." Small, *Musicking*, 9.

12 Lipsitz, "Dangerous Crossroads."

13 A critique of this tendency is eloquently expressed in Lowe's *Immigrant Acts*, which argues that ethnic nationalism, while often an important articulation of political identity, can frequently efface ethnic and socioeconomic schisms and strains within racial/ethnic communities. See Lowe, *Immigrant Acts*. Over the last two decades, the efficacy of the nation-state as a paradigm has also become a matter of debate within the fields of cultural studies, Black diaspora studies, ethnic studies, political geography, and Latina/o studies as many scholars have called into question the adequacy of this analytical frame, arguing that it elides the mutual embeddedness of racism and nationalism (see Gilroy, *Ain't No Black*), and Robinson, *Black Marxism*), obscures uneven development (see Massey, *Space, Place, and Gender*), and fails to adequately account for the migration and displacement sparked by contemporary and historic globalization processes (see Gilroy, *Ain't No Black* and *The Black Atlantic*; Hall, "What Is This 'Black' in Black Popular Culture?").

14 Some notable exceptions to this trend include the work of Oliart and Lloréns, "La nueva canción en el Perú"; Ríos, "Andean Music, the Left, and Pan-Latin Americanism"; Romero, "La música tradicional y popular"; Turino, "Nationalism and Latin American music" and *Moving Away from Silence*; and Romero, *Debating the Past*.

15 For an excellent overview of world music scholarship and its debates, see Feld, *A Sweet Lullaby for World Music*; and Guilbault, "Interpreting World Music."

16 Putumayo, "About Putumayo World Music," www.putumayo.com/history, accessed July 16, 2015.

17 Ry Cooder's introduction of Cuban *son* to the global stage via collaboration of the Buena Vista Social Club (BVSC) is an excellent example of this narrative. U.S. media discourses depicted the virtual absence of *son* from the world music circuit prior to the BVSC project as an example of its virtual demise as an art form—a demise brought on by the socialist Cuban state's lack of attention to or support of its musical traditions. National magazines such as *Time* and *Newsweek* featured editorials that concluded the derisory cultural institutions and programs of the contemporary Cuban state could only be remedied through the heroic intervention of U.S. capital and resources. Of course, a closer examination of this fabulated account makes evident the political stakes of its interventionist subtext. For an excellent discussion of BVSC politics, see Katerí Hernández, "The Buena Vista Social Club."

18 For further discussion concerning the inequities of the world music industry in its relations of representation and capital, see Garofalo, *Rockin' the Boat*; Lipsitz, *Dangerous Crossroads*; and Mitchell, *Popular Music and Local Identity*.

19 Some important exceptions to this scholarly trend include Jocelyne Guilbault, *Zouk and the Governing Sound*; Peter Wade, *Music, Race, and Nation: Música Tropical in Colombia*; and Whiteley, Bennett, and Hawkins, *Music, Space and Place*.

20 Dorr, "Mapping 'El Cóndor Pasa.'"

21 Canclini, *Transforming Modernity*.

22 I draw upon social geographer Neil Smith's notion of scale. For Smith, scale connotes a "geographic resolution to the contradictory social processes of competition and cooperation." The production and reproduction of scale, in turn, express "the social and geographical contest to establish boundaries between different locations, places, and sites of experience." Smith, "Contours of a Spatialized Politics," 64.

23 For an extended discussion of the relationship between economic restructuring and mass migration in Latin America, see Rodríguez, "The Real 'New World Order.'"

24 Carlos Lara Yupanqui, interview with author, March 13, 2005.

25 *Música latinoamericana* is the name that the pan-Andean folk music popularized by 1970s Nueva Canción artists such as Quilapayún and Inti-Illimani acquired in Peru. See Oliart and Lloréns, "La nueva canción en el Perú." For a broader history of Andean musical circulations in the Southern Cone and Europe, see Rios, "Andean Music, the Left, and Pan-Latin Americanism."

26 Rios, "La flûte indienne."

27 The popularization of pan-Andean musics in Lima and La Paz are overlapping yet distinct histories. A major difference, for example, is the discursive regimes that have governed the multicultural, settler colonial state. In the coastal city of Lima, *criollismo* has figured as a dominant discourse, while in the Andean city of La Paz cultural *mestizaje* has functioned as a dominant strategy.

28 For an extended discussion of chicha, see Turino, "Somos el Peru [We Are Peru]."

29 Spanish: "fiestas familiares donde cada asistente contribuye a una causa con la cantidad que éste dentro de sus posibilidades." Cited in Núñez Jaime, "Wendy Sulca."

30 Spanish: "Mis padres siempre escuchaban folklore en la radio, y me llegó a gustar." Interview with Carlos Lara Yupanqui, February 2013.

31 Spanish: "Teniamos invitaciones para tocar en diferentes lugares . . . polladas . . . escuelas . . . tocar para la clase trabajadora, apoyando a los obreros. Tocamos en manifestaciones del partido izquierdista, eventos sindicales. Por eso se llamaba el grupo Liberacion." Interview with Carlos Lara Yupanqui, fall 2013.

32 The tiple is a plucked-string chordophone of the guitar family.

33 Vientos is a catch-all term for Andean wind instruments, including quena and zampoña.

34 Lionnet and Shih, "Introduction."

35 This information is drawn from the eight years (1991–99) that I spent working and traveling with Markahuasi, whose musicians during that time period
included Argúrio Buendía, José Cabezas, Freddy Franco, Sebastian Huamaní,
Carlos Lara, Pedro Linares, and Andrew Taher. Markahuasi's original band
members also included José and Carlos Hilario, who after three years in the
United States formed an independent group.

36 On the "racial state," see Omi and Winant, *Racial Formation in the United
States*; Gilmore, *Golden Gulag*.

37 For a detailed discussion of the increased militarization of the U.S. Southern border over the last two decades, see Dunn, *The Militarization of the U.S-
Mexico Border, 1978–1992*. For an excellent discussion of border-making as a
spatial process, see Nevins, *Operation Gatekeeper*. For a detailed discussion of
the ideological and economic rationalization and ramifications of California
Proposition 187, which denies "illegal aliens in the United States from receiving
benefits or public services in the state of California" and passed by an overwhelming voter majority in November 1994, see Calavita, "The New Politics
of Immigration." (California Proposition 227, which was legislated four years
later, required all public school instruction in the state of California to be conducted exclusively in English.) And for a comprehensive discussion of California's burgeoning carceral geographies, see Gilmore, *Golden Gulag*.

38 Omi and Winant, *Racial Formation in the United States*.

39 Smith, *The New Urban Frontier*, 207.

40 In addition to performing in public areas such as street corners and subway
stations, AMI musicians often promoted themselves as street festivals.

41 These generic "music of the Andes" CDs are generally wholesaled by propri-
etary artists but are distributed under a different title, cover, and musical author. There have in fact been several cases in which recordings of bands re-
maining in Bolivia, Peru, and Ecuador have been digitally remastered in the
United States and sold under a different banner. In most cases, these global
Southern musicians are without recourse.

42 See, for example, Octavio Paz's infamous essay "The Sons of Malinche" in the
Pulitzer Prize–winning essay collection *The Labyrinth of Solitude*. Critical
writings on the figure of La Malinche include Franceschini, *La Virgen de la
Guadalupe, La Malinche, and La Llorona*; and Franco, "La Malinche: From Gift
to Sexual Contract."

43 Here I am thinking specifically of the Afro-Bolivian rhythms *saya* and *taquirari*,
which are among the rhythms most commonly recorded and performed by
musicians of the Andean music circuit.

44 Plambeck, "As CD Sales Wane, Music Retailers Diversify."

45 Of the forty-two nations that make up the Organization for Economic Cooperation and Development (OCDE), Peru ranks fourth in the (inter)national

distribution of pirated materials. "Perú es el cuarto país que más disminuyó su piratería entre miembros de la OCDE."

46 Núñez Jaime, "Wendy Sulca."

47 Abalo, "El asombroso canto de una niña peruana"; Núñez Jaime, "Wendy Sulca."

48 *Pueblos jóvenes*, or "young towns," are the colloquial name for the shantytowns located in the desert outskirts of Lima. They are populated almost exclusively by Black, indigenous, and mestizo campesinos who have migrated to the capital in waves since the 1940s in search of economic opportunity, turning Lima into the fourth-largest city in the Americas. Like many other rapidly industrializing cities in the global South, Lima lacks the housing and infrastructure to absorb this population influx, forcing many to live in self-constructed homes erected on unincorporated government land. The settlements are often composed of temporary shelters or permanent homes that are under construction; many lack running water and other basic services though electricity is often available on a pirated DIY basis. Water delivery or services to these parts of Lima cost between six and ten times as much as it does in affluent parts of the city. See Lloyd, *The "Young Towns" of Lima*.

49 "Revista Rolling Stone califica de 'fenómeno hispanoparlante' a peruana Wendy Sulca."

50 Interview with Peruvian talk show host Jaime Bayly on "El Francotirador," transmitted on Punto Final de Frecuencia Latina, October 31, 2010.

51 Hundreds of spoof videos have been posted on YouTube, mocking Sulca's vocal register, clothing, song lyrics, and video content.

52 Here I use the term "carnivalesque" in the Bakhtinian sense, referencing modes of cultural production that deploy humor and excess to subvert stylistic conventions, audience expectations, and social norms. See Bakhtin, *Rabelais and His World*. Jeanne Rogge Steele asserts that "in addition to qualities of inversion, ambivalence, and excess, carnival's themes typically include a fascination with the body, particularly its little-glorified or 'lower strata' parts, and dichotomies between 'high' or 'low.'" See Steele, "Carnival, Resistance, and Transgression in the Workplace."

53 Quoted in Abalo, "El asombroso canto de una niña peruana"; see also Núñez Jaime, "Wendy Sulca."

54 I borrow the term "reproductivity" from Sara Clarke Kaplan, to emphasize the linkages between different forms and modes of gendered reproductive labor. Kaplan writes, "In one register, reproductivity names the ensemble of discourses, state and individual practices, and collective fantasies through which modern notions of race, gender and sexuality have been given form and meaning through the logics and language of reproduction. . . . In another register, reproductivity also refers to the material *work* of reproduction, including the

production of the material and immaterial vital resources of human life and the production and reproduction of labor power. Procreation, waged and un-waged domestic work, and sexual labor and leisure are thus all part of the labor of reproduction." S. C. Kaplan, *The Black Reproductive*, 12–13.

55 Fahsbender, "Wendy Sulca."

56 Theidon, "First Do No Harm."

57 Spanish: "No sólo canto de mi vida, también canto de la vida de las personas, para chicos y grandes, para los niños que quieren a su mamá, para los chicos que no tienen papá, porque fallecieron, porque sus padres se separaron o los abandonaron, o en 'Cerveza, Cerveza,' la historia de alguien que trabaja en un lugar oscuro como una mina, que perdió a su amor y bebe para olvidar, que sufre, o ha sufrido, y se toma su cerveza. De verdad, quiero que tomen en serio mi música." Cited in Fahsbender, "Wendy Sulca."

3. (INTER)NATIONAL STAGES

1 Susana Baca, interview with author, February 11, 2012.

2 Baca, interview with author.

3 Rowell et al., "An Interview with Susana Baca," 300.

4 Baca, interview with author.

5 By standards, I reference the frequency with which most of the collection's songs appear in pirated Afro-Peruvian compilations that have been in circulation since the 1970s.

6 Byrne and Evelev, liner notes to *The Soul of Black Peru*.

7 The term "Black Pacific" has been used to connote dramatically different geo-political imaginaries. I build on the work of music scholars Heidi Feldman and Jonathan Ritter to reference the African-descended populations that have in-habited South America's Pacific Coast since the early 1500s. See, for example, Feldman, "The Black Pacific"; and Ritter, "Chocolate, Coconut, and Honey."

8 Some notable exceptions include George Reid Andrews, *Afro-Latin America*; Heidi Feldman, *Black Rhythms of Peru*; Javier León, "Mass Culture, Commod-ification, and the Consolidation of the Afro-Peruvian 'Festejo'" and "Santa Lib-ertad"; Jonathan Ritter, "La Marimba Esmeraldeña," "Articulating Blackness in Afro-Ecuadorian Marimba Performance," and "Chocolate, Coconut, and Honey"; Vaughn, "Afro-Mexico," "Mexico in the Context of the Transatlantic Slave Trade"; Vinson and Vaughn, *Afroméxico*; and Vinson and Restall, *Black Mexico*.

9 Some important notable exceptions to the trend include the work of Heidi Feldman, Javier Leon, and Martha Ojeda. In addition to the texts cited in the preceding note, see Ojeda, *Nicomedes Santa Cruz*.

10 Gates, *Black in Latin America*, 97.

11 Clark, "Performing the Memory of Difference in Afro-Caribbean Dance," 42.

12 The zamacueca is a dance that originated among the African descended in the Peruvian Viceroyalty and that became the basis for the *marinera limeña*, the *marinera norteña*, *la cueca chilena*, and the *zamba argentina*. For a rich discussion of this artistic form, see Bailes Nacionales en Amancaes, *Historia de la Danza*.

13 According to the Institución Cultural Pachayachachiq, "The panalivio is a very old afroperuvian dance. It was created by African-descended [Peruvian] inhabitants brought from Spain to perform agricultural labor. It is said that panalivios were subversive songs through which slaves denounced their abuse and misery." Spanish: "El panalivio es una danza afroperuana muy antigua. Fue creada por habitantes de orige afro, traídos desde España como esclavos, para realizar tareas agrícolas. . . . Dícese que los panalivios eran cantos de sublevación con que los esclavos denunciaban abusos y penas." Facebook post by Institución Cultural Pachayachachiq, March 31, 2013, www.facebook.com /pachayachachiq/posts/174309326055650.

14 Feldman, "The Black Pacific," 206–31; Feldman, "African or Andean?"; Feldman, *Black Rhythms of Peru*."

15 Feldman, *Black Rhythms of Peru*, 1.

16 Feldman, *Black Rhythms of Peru*, 5–6.

17 León Quirós, "The Aestheticization of Tradition"; León Quirós, "Roots, Tradition, and the Mass Media"; León Quirós, "Mass Culture, Commodification, and the Consolidation of the Afro-Peruvian 'Festejo'"; León Quirós, "Santa Libertad."

18 León Quirós, "The Aestheticization of Tradition," xii.

19 A peña is a cultural center that features artists affiliated with anticolonial and antiracist cultural activism.

20 By "cultural institutionalization," I mean the respatialization of cultural forms within institutional settings such as research centers, libraries, universities, and popular media outlets—sites that, prior to the 1950s, had largely barred the inclusion of Black academics, artists, cultural texts, and related subjects of inquiry.

21 Robinson builds upon and expands the work of an earlier generation of Black scholars, including W. E. B. Du Bois's *Black Reconstruction* and C. L. R. James's *The Black Jacobins*, that placed analyses of race and culture at the center of historical study and political inquiry. See Robinson, *Black Marxism*. As Robin Kelley observes, these authors emphasize "the agency of African people" by debunking the notion that the enslaved and their descendants passively tolerated ongoing conditions of economic exploitation, structural racism, and other forms of social inequality. See Kelley, *Race Rebels*, 5.

22 Kelley, *Race Rebels*, 4. Rather than focusing on conventional political insti-

tutions and organized social movements, Kelley turns his attention to "the so-called margins of struggle," where what anthropologist James C. Scott has dubbed "hidden transcripts" are activated. Following Scott, Kelley emphasizes that "hidden transcripts"—repertoires of political dissidence expressed in and through everyday cultural practices such as music, dance, and storytelling— are often "infrapolitical"—that is, invisible by design. See Scott, *Domination and the Arts of Resistance.*

23 By contemporary theorizations of diaspora, I refer to engagements with the diasporic that are rooted in what postcolonial theorist Jenny Sharpe has described as "a discourse of travel rather than an ideology of return." See Sharpe, "Cartographies of Globalisation," 44. Gilroy's *The Black Atlantic* demonstrates that networks of bodily and cultural exchange were enabled historically through the structures and institutions of Western modernity (colonialism, the Middle Passage, chattel slavery, and industrial capitalism) and contemporarily through relations of neoliberal globalization (transnational corporatism, migrant labor networks, new media technologies, and so forth).

24 See, for example, the thoughtful critiques of applications of diaspora in Edwards, "The Uses of Diaspora"; Gunning et al., *Dialogues of Dispersal*; and Kelley, "How the West Was One."

25 Various Peruvian scholars and practitioners have made this argument regarding the spatial containment of Afro-Peruvian culture. Both Susana Baca and Rafael Santa Cruz mentioned this as part of the crucial shift that occurred in the 1960s—that Black Peruvian culture was performed, studied, and written about in public institutions rather than solely practiced and remembered in the private sphere. For scholars who have made similar arguments, see, for example, Cuche, *Poder Blanco y Resistencia Negra en el Perú*; Rodríguez Pastor, *Negritud*; and Santa Cruz Gamarra, "Folklore peruano: Cumanana."

26 McKittrick, *Demonic Grounds*, xii.

27 McKittrick, *Demonic Grounds*, xii.

28 A prolonged discussion of this project that Stephanie Smallwood has aptly referred to as transforming "captive Africans into Atlantic commodities" exceeds the perimeters of this chapter (Smallwood, *Saltwater Slavery*). However, it bears noting that my theoretical understanding of this process of human objectification is indebted to the work of U.S. scholars Orlando Patterson, Saidiya Hartman, Fred Moten, Stephanie Smallwood, and Sara Clarke Kaplan. While none of these social theorists engage case studies in the Spanish Americas, I read their work as formative of a useful conceptual terrain for theorizing ongoing entanglements between the (re)production of racial capitalism and the racial state, on the one hand, and the legacies of chattel slavery on the other. See S. C. Kaplan, *The Black Reproductive*; Hartman, *Scenes of Subjection*; Moten, *In the Break*; Patterson, *Slavery and Social Death.*

29 Bowser, *The African Slave in Colonial Peru*. For a detailed discussion of gender

and ethnicity among Peru's enslaved population during the Bourbonic era in Lima, see Arrelucea Barrantes, *Replanteando la esclavitud.*

30 For an excellent discussion of postmanumission Peru, see Rodríguez Pastor, *Negritud.*

31 Rodríguez Pastor, *Negritud.*

32 I use the term "geographers of difference" as a shorthand to reference a wide range of scholars that employ geographic methods and frames to theorize the relationship between social and spatial differentiation. Geographer John Agnew defines "place" as meaningful location. See Agnew, "Politics and Place."

33 McKittrick and Peake, "What Difference Does Difference Make to Geography?," 40.

34 See, for example, Smith, "Contours of a Spatialized Politics"; Massey, *Space, Place, and Gender*; and Harvey, "Space as a Key Word."

35 Agard Jones, "Bodies in the System," 183.

36 S. C. Kaplan, *The Black Reproductive*, 11.

37 McDowell, *Gender, Identity, and Place*, 10.

38 "En el censo no preguntarán la raza."

39 Quotation from "En el censo no preguntarán la raza."

40 Here I follow Saidiya Hartman's conceptualization of blackness as a mode of social relationality rather than of individual identity: "Blackness incorporates subjects normatively defined as black, the relations among blacks, whites, and others, and the practices that produce racial difference. Blackness marks a social relationship of dominance and abjection and potentially one of redress and emancipation; it is a contested figure at the very center of social struggle." See Hartman, *Scenes of Subjection*, 56–57.

41 Cuche, *Poder blanco y resistencia negra en el Perú*, 31.

42 Romero, "Black Music and Identity in Peru," 309.

43 Because census data reflected racial categories that were linked to civil status (enslaved, emancipated, etc.) it is difficult to discern the extent to which the racial category "Black" included people of mixed racial descent. See Maclean y Estenós, "Negros en el nuevo mundo," 146.

44 Romero, "Black Music and Identity in Peru."

45 León Quirós, "The Aestheticization of Tradition."

46 See, for example, Mariátegui, *Seven Interpretive Essays on Peruvian Reality.*

47 León Quirós, "The Aestheticization of Tradition"; N. Santa Cruz Gamarra, "Estampas de Pancho Fierro."

48 Here I describe the convergence of interanimating political struggles, including the proliferation of decolonization movements throughout African and Asian French and British colonies, the entrenchment of civil rights activism in the southern United States, the advent of postcolonial intellectualism throughout the Caribbean, and the rise of socialist and anti-imperialist movements in Latin America.

49 See, for example, Robinson, *Black Marxism*; Gilroy, *The Black Atlantic*; and, Kelley, *Race Rebels*.

50 I use the term "Black Arts Revival" to connote the multiples stages and forms on and through which Peru's mid-century Black cultural resistance struggles were waged. This historical reference periodically appears in the work of Heidi Feldman, Javier León Quirós, and Raúl Romero. See Feldman, *Black Rhythms of Peru*; León Quirós, "The Aestheticization of Tradition"; and Romero, "Black Music and Identity in Peru."

51 Santa Cruz, "De Senegal y Malambo," 24.

52 See, for example, Hall, *Policing the Crisis*; Robinson, *Black Marxism*; Gilroy, *The Black Atlantic*; and Gramsci, *Selections from the Prison Notebooks*.

53 Santa Cruz, "De Senegal y Malambo," 24.

54 Mariátegui, *Seven Interpretive Essays on Peruvian Reality*, 220–21.

55 McKittrick, *Demonic Grounds*, 3.

56 Taylor, *The Archive and the Repertoire*, 4.

57 Santa Cruz, "De Senegal y Malambo," 24.

58 Leon, "The Aestheticization of Tradition"; Santa Cruz, "Folklore peruano"; Santa Cruz Castillo, interview with author.

59 R. Santa Cruz, interview with author; Feldman, *Black Rhythms of Peru*.

60 Clark, "Performing the Memory of Difference in Afro-Caribbean Dance."

61 Clark, "Performing the Memory of Difference in Afro-Caribbean Dance."

62 As Clark's interrogation of Nora's bounded categories concomitantly demonstrates, knowledge production is implicitly spatialized: not only does the "where" of knowledge repositories shape their value within Western philosophical traditions, but memory keeping is a task that is located within the confines of raced and gendered contexts. Indeed, as Sara Clarke Kaplan has noted, Nora's use of "true memory" is always already racialized, given that he associates it most closely with "Jews of the diaspora," "peasant culture," and "ethnic minorities." See Kaplan, "Souls at the Crossroads," 8–9.

63 Santa Cruz Urquieta, discussion with the author, February 21, 2013; Santa Cruz Castillo, discussion with the author, February 12, 2013; and Feldman, *Black Rhythms of Peru*.

64 Santa Cruz Gamarra, *Descubrimiento y desarrollo del sentido rítmico*.

65 Taylor, *The Archive and the Repertoire*.

66 Santa Cruz Castillo, *El cajón afroperuano*.

67 Santa Cruz Gamarra, *Descubrimiento y desarrollo del sentido rítmico*.

68 Rowell et al., "An Interview with Victoria Santa Cruz," 521.

69 Santa Cruz Gamarra, *Descubrimiento y desarrollo del sentido rítmico*.

70 Santa Cruz Gamarra, *Descubrimiento y desarrollo del sentido rítmico*, 6.

71 Santa Cruz Gamarra, *Descubrimiento y desarrollo del sentido rítmico*, 5.

72 Lefebvre, *Rhythmanalysis*, 19.

73 My reading of "Me gritaron negra" is focused upon the performance of this text

that appears in *Black and Woman: Entrevista con Eugenio Barba, un documental de la Odin Teatret.*

74 Santa Cruz Castillo, *El cajón afroperuano.*

75 Extracted from a documentary series *Retratos de TV Perú*, "Victoria Santa Cruz, negro es mi color."

76 *Retratos de TV Perú*, "Victoria Santa Cruz, negro es mi color."

77 McKittrick, *Demonic Grounds*, x.

78 McKittrick, *Demonic Grounds*, x.

79 McKittrick and Peake, "What Difference Does Difference Make to Geography?," 2.

80 Brady, *Extinct Lands, Temporal Geographies*, 8.

81 I agree with Feldman's assessment that Santa Cruz's work symbolized an "unprecedented public staging of blacknessblacknessblackness that emphasized racial difference and Black pride." Here, I am interested in theorizing the political work of Santa Cruz's staging techniques—specifically, the respatializations that they accomplished. See Feldman, *Black Rhythms of Peru*, 55.

82 Taylor, *The Archive and the Repertoire*, 19.

83 I borrow the term "racial state" from Omi and Winant's *Racial Formation in the United States from the 1960s to the 1990s.*

84 Gramsci, *Selections from the Prison Notebooks.*

85 See A. Kaplan, *The Anarchy of Empire in the Making of US Culture*; S. C. Kaplan, "Love and Violence/Maternity and Death"; Nakano Glenn, *Unequal Freedom: How Race and Citizenship Shaped American Citizenship and Labor*; L. Romero, *Homefronts.*

86 Spanish: "Yo, primero creo que he sentido la necesidad de expresarme através [la música afroperuana] porque es algo que viví desde niña. Lo viví en . . . el hogar y en las casas de los parientes . . . Cuando nos llevaban a la casa de los parientes, entonces ahí había música . . . si estaba en mi casa, a mi mama le cantaba . . . y nos enseñaba a danzar . . . Entonces, fui creciendo y me expresaba en ese sentido." Baca, interview with the author, February 11, 2012.

87 Baca, interview with the author.

88 Spanish: "uno va creciendo, con toda la información que tiene, con . . . el escuchar otras músicas, el saber que en el mundo hay otros . . . hijos de Africanos que están por ahí . . . y que hacen determinada música. . . . yo escuchaba todo. . . . Y ya en mí había el simiente de sentir, eh, y que así como aquí había un pueblo Afro de descendientes, Africanos en otras partes también había. Y compartíamos lo mismo; la antifonía, ese sentido, la cadencia mezclada con las cosas . . . de los diferentes países, ¿no? Entonces, eso es la música, te hace renacer y imprime en ti." Baca, interview with author.

89 "Aquí era una cosa de copiar solamente . . . pero si se puede con la música Afroperuana hacer una música nueva." Baca, interview with author.

90 Feldman, *Black Rhythms of Peru*; Baca, interview with author.

91 David Byrne's debut solo album, *Rei Momo*, was released three years after Paul Simon's *Graceland*. The history of *The Soul of Black Peru* outlined here draws from Feldman, *Black Rhythms of Peru*, 429.

92 Feldman, *Black Rhythms of Peru*, 429.

93 "Luaka History," www.luakabop.com/history/.

94 Baca, interview with author.

95 Vasquez, *Listening in Detail*.ˮ

96 The *chacarera* is an Argentinian musical and dance form that shares its choreographic roots with the Peruvian *marinera* and the Chilean *cueca*. For a comprehensive discussion of the history of the genre, see Vega, *Panorama de la música popular Argentina*.

97 Gilroy, *The Black Atlantic*; Gates, *The Signifying Monkey*.

98 Peta describes la jarana as "una fiesta criolla de madrugada," which roughly translates as "a late-night criollo celebration." Interview with author, July 15, 2015.

99 Spanish: "Mis tíos eran músicos y siempre llegaban en la noche con la gente que ya salían de la peñas y iban a rematar a mi casa." Interview with author, July 14, 2015.

100 Spanish: "Nosotros aprendimos a tocar, eh, por oído. . . . La ventana que daba a mi cuarto, daba justo frente a la sala, que era dónde se ponían a tocar, a cantar, y a bailar. Entonces, nosotras nos trepábamos por esa ventana y agüeitábamos la fiesta y cuando menos se dio cuenta mi papá, empezamos a, a tocar."

101 Interview with author, July 15, 2014.

102 "Lalo Izquierdo y los 40 años de Perú Negro," August 9, 2009, Cañete: Arte y folklore negro del Perú, http://caneteartenegro.blogspot.com/2009/08/lalo-izquierdo-y-los-40-anos-de-peru_09.html, accessed July 20, 2015.

103 This invocation of "Black power" was not coincidental; Izquierdo was inspired by Black feminist cultural workers from the United States—particularly those affiliated with the Black Power movement—and, like many Revival practioners of the era, valued internationalist affiliation and transnational exchange. Interview with Kata.

104 Spanish: "No, yo no quiero [que toques cajon] porque . . . los hombres nomas tocan y están en las peñas. Tú eres mujer! ¿Qué vas hacer de madrugada en las peñas? ¿No? Nunca quiso . . . que yo tocara, cantara, ni nada. Que no me relacionara con las peñas porque generalmente uno se tiene que amanecer, tú sabes, el alcohol, el cigarrillo." Interview with author, July 14, 2015.

105 Interview with author, February 16, 2014.

106 Vargas, *Dissonant Divas*, 135.

107 Spanish: "Siempre ha sido difícil hacer música. Cuando eres mujer, lo primero que te dicen porque tocas cajón es 'marimacha.' Porque el cajón es un instrumento masculino. . . . La gente decía que aquella mujer que tocaba cajón era, como lo dicen aquí en el Perú, 'machona' o 'marimacha.' Siempre."

108 McDowell, *Gender, Identity, and Place*, 34–35.

109 A loose translation of the double-valenced phrase "¡A ritmo de mujer y punto!"

110 Spanish: "Eso es lo qué yo aprendí en Milenio. El amor a lo Afro. . . . Aprendí lo qué era el sentirme mujer, Afro descendiente, orgullosa, ¿no? Aprendí a quererme como Afro descendiente, ¿no? Pero lo más importante es aprender a aceptarme. Porque aquí lo primero que hacen aquí es insultarte, ah. Y tú todo el tiempo creces con los insultos encima."

111 See, for example, Quijano, *Nationalism and Capitalism in Peru*; Mignolo, *Local Histories, Global Designs*.

112 My own understanding of the significance of slavery as a practice of spatial invasion and expropriation on the scale of the body has been developed in conversation with Gina Dent, Ruth Wilson Gilmore, and Sara Clarke Kaplan, discussion with the author, 2006.

113 Of course, Paul Gilroy is perhaps the most well-known scholar within this rubric, but his "Black Atlantic" model of diasporic cultural production and exchange continues to inform much of the current work within the field of Black studies. See Gilroy, *The Black Atlantic*.

114 Edwards, "The Uses of Diaspora," 57.

115 Bowser, *The African Slave in Colonial Peru*, 11.

116 Bowser, *The African Slave in Colonial Peru*; Feldman, "The Black Pacific."

117 Feldman, *Black Rhythms of Peru*; Ritter, "Chocolate, Coconut, and Honey."

4. "YOU CAN'T HAVE A REVOLUTION WITHOUT SONGS"

1 La Peña del Sur was located in the lower Mission District on Twenty-Second Street at Harrison. During its period of operation, the Mission was a vibrant Latino neighborhood with substantial Mexican, Central, and South American, and U.S.-born Chicano/Latino communities. Following the Silicon Valley boom in the mid-1990s, however, white middle-class gentrification shifted the district's demographics dramatically. Today, none of the activists/cultural workers discussed in this chapter reside in the Mission area.

2 As referenced in the introduction, "musicking" is a term developed by Christopher Small to describe musical production as a dynamic, interactive process. See Small, *Musicking*.

3 According to Jan Fairley, the term *Nueva Canción* first circulated at the summer event "Encuentro de la Canción Protesta," hosted in Cuba from July 29 to August 10, 1967. Fairley rightly asserts that nueva canción is "used as an all-embracing term, an umbrella under which much music and many musicians shelter." Fairley, "La nueva canción Latinoamericana," 107. Rather, as Jane Tumas-Serna puts it, "More than a musical style, [nueva canción] signifies an ideological stance." Tumas-Serna, "The 'Nueva Canción' Movement and Its Mass-Mediated Context," 139. While the intellectual and artistic origins of

the movement were rooted in earlier periods, this "countersong" movement combined traditional Latin American folk genres and with politicized lyrics to unite students and the urban working and rural peasant classes. See also Reyes Matta, "The 'New Song' and Its Confrontation in Latin America." *Nueva Canción* spread across Latin America and the Caribbean in the 1960s and '70s, when musicians joined the indigenous, mestizo, and African mass uprisings that called for an end to state militarism and U.S. intervention. See Zolov, *Refried Elvis*.

4 Hong and Ferguson, *Strange Affinities*.

5 According to the queer spatial theorist Natalie Oswin, this turn began in the 1970s but did not enroot until the 1990s. Oswin, "Critical Geographies."

6 See, for example, Bell and Valentine, *Mapping Desire*; Nash, "Contesting Identity"; Nash, "Toronto's Gay Village (1969–1982)"; Nash and Bain, "'Reclaiming Raunch'?"; Nast, "Mapping the 'Unconscious'"; and Nast, "Queer Patriarchies."

7 See, for example, Bell and Valentine, eds., *Mapping Desire*; Binnie, "Coming out of Geography"; Valentine, "Queer Bodies and the Production of Space"; and Valentine, "Sexual Politics."

8 Oswin, "Critical Geographies and the Uses of Sexuality," 90.

9 A discussion of this relationship between white gay gentrification and the displacement of migrant communities can be found in the chapter "Out There: The Topography of Race and Desire in the Global City" in Manalansan, *Global Divas*. For a rich analysis of the relationship between gay gentrification, "public safety" initiatives, and the policing of communities of color, see Hanhardt, *Safe Space*.

10 Puar, "A Transnational Feminist Critique of Queer Tourism," 936.

11 For an excellent history of gay Latino activism in San Francisco's Mission District, see Roque Ramírez, "'That's My Place!'"

12 Oswin, "Critical Geographies and the Uses of Sexuality."

13 Oswin, "Critical Geographies and the Uses of Sexuality," 100.

14 Some notable exceptions include Hanhardt, *Safe Space*; Fajardo, *Filipino Crosscurrents*; Manalansan, *Global Divas*; McKittrick, *Demonic Grounds*; and Yuval-Davis, "Women and the Biological Reproduction of 'the Nation.'"

15 Hong and Ferguson, *Strange Affinities*, 2.

16 Somerville, "Queer."

17 Hong and Ferguson, *Strange Affinities*, 2.

18 Here I use the term "queer" as it is mobilized within feminist-of-color work, to connote modes of analysis and practice that examine the articulation of racial, gender, and sexual formation. In particular, my understanding of queer as an analytical maneuver is informed by the scholarship of Mary Pat Brady, Fatima El-Tayeb, Rod Ferguson, Sara Clarke Kaplan, Audre Lorde, Siobhan Somerville, and Deb Vargas, among others. See Brady, *Extinct Lands, Temporal Geographies*; El-Tayeb, *European Others*; Kaplan, *The Black Reproductive*; Lorde,

Sister Outsider; Somerville, *Queering the Color Line*; Vargas, *Dissonant Divas in Chicana Music.*

19 "About La Peña."

20 "About La Peña."

21 "About La Peña."

22 Casasús, "Alejandro Stuart."

23 Galo Paz, interview with author, June 14, 2014; Samuel Guía, interview with author, June 12, 2014.

24 "La Peña del Sur, una plataforma para el talento latinoamericano," 65.

25 For an extensive discussion of the politics of "new nativism" see Perea, *Immigrants Out!*

26 Alejandro Stuart and Samuel Guía, e-mail correspondence with author, June 13, 2012.

27 City and County of San Francisco Planning Department, "City within a City."

28 City and County of San Francisco Planning Department, "City within a City"; Martí, "The Mission District."

29 While these groups were by no means the only national/ethnic groups in the district, they were the most populous.

30 Roque Ramírez, "'That's My Place!'"; Roque Ramírez, "Claiming Queer Cultural Citizenship."

31 Galo Paz, interview with author, June 14, 2014; Samuel Guía, interview with author, June 12, 2014.

32 Alejandro Stuart, e-mail correspondence with author, October 28, 2009.

33 For a more in-depth discussion of these organizational strategies, see Fairley, "La nueva canción latinoamericana"; Tumas-Serna, "The 'Nueva Canción' Movement and Its Mass-Mediated Performance Context"; and Reyes Matta, "The 'New Song' and Its Confrontation in Latin America."

34 The term "reunión" can connote a meeting or a house party. Here, the concept is invoked in its dual senses, suggesting that leisure and social time might be combined with critical political work.

35 Advertisements for La Peña del Sur's weekly lineup were featured in *Horizontes*, the *Reporter*, *New Mission News*, and *Cambio*.

36 "La Peña del Sur, una plataforma para el talento latinoamericano," 65.

37 La Peña del Sur flyer, created by Alejandro Stuart, June 1995, Flyer Box M1382, MSS Photo 210, Stanford University Special Collections.

38 Paz, interview with author, June 14, 2014.

39 For an extensive discussion of the politics of "new nativism," see Perea, *Immigrants Out!*

40 Redmond, *Anthem*, 1.

41 Redmond, *Anthem*, 1–2.

42 Tumas-Serna, "The 'Nueva Canción' Movement and Its Mass-Mediated Context"; Fairley, "La nueva canción latinoamericana."

43 Casasús, "Alejandro Stuart."

44 Spanish: "Para mí una peña es más espontáneo, más experimental."

45 Guía, interview with author, June 12, 2014.

46 A number of *peña* goers that I interviewed used this term to describe Alejandro's stage personality.

47 In my use of the term *(des)encuentro* to describe the conjoined processes of convergence and divergence that La Peña del Sur signifies, I am drawing on Julio Ramos's deployment of the term in Ramos, *Desencuentros de lamodernidad en América Latina.*

48 Pratt, *Imperial Eyes.*

49 González, "What's the Problem with 'Hispanic'?," 6.

50 See, for example, Perea, *Immigrants Out!*

51 Oquendo, "Re-imaging the Latino/a Race."

52 Oboler, "Hispanics? That's What They Call Us."

53 Rivera-Servera, *Performing Queer Latinidad,* 22.

54 Rivera-Servera, *Performing Queer Latinidad*; Rodríguez, *Queer Latinidad.*

55 For example, on Saturday, November 26, 1994, La Peña del Sur hosted "Una Noche Peruana" with Andean, rock, and Afro-Peruvian performers.

56 Kun, *Audiotopia.*

57 Roque Ramírez, "Claiming Queer Cultural Citizenship."

58 Flores, *From Bomba to Hip-Hop*, 198.

59 In a reflection on the possibility of applying theoretical models developed in historically and geographically specific contexts to new sites and objects, Guha argues for the possibility of "convergence" as an analytical approach that does not presume similarity, but rather, shares a common orientation toward a particular horizon. See Guha, "Subaltern Studies."

60 Kun, *Audiotopia,* 23.

61 La Peña del Sur officially closed its doors in 1998, when Alejandro Stuart returned to Chile to reestablish his career as a photographer and *gestor cultural* (cultural promoter). Yet, the closure of La Peña was also owed to the skyrocketing housing and rental markets of San Francisco's Mission District, which rendered the financial survival of the project in that area no longer viable.

62 Lowe, *Immigrant Acts*, 9.

63 Lorde, "The Master's Tools Will Never Dismantle the Master's House," 111–12.

EPILOGUE

1 A *chullo* is a handwoven knit cap with earflaps worn by indigenous men throughout the central Andes.

2 Cortijo, "Peruvian Teen Aims to Revive Quechua."

3 Cortijo, "Peruvian Teen Aims to Revive Quechua."

4 Some incisive critiques of colonial temporalities and indigenous responses

to them include Jodi Byrd's *The Transit of Empire*; Marisol de la Cadena's *Earth Beings*; Maria Josefina Saldaña Portillo's *The Revolutionary Imagination in the Americas and the Age of Development*; and Audra Simpson's *Mohawk Interuptus*.

5   Marez, *Farm Worker Futurism*, 9.

6   "Perú es el cuarto país que más disminuyó su piratería entre miembros de la OCDE."

7   Lott, *Love and Theft*.

8   Brown, "Neo-Liberalism and the End of Liberal Democracy."

9   "Perú es el cuarto país que más disminuyó su piratería entre miembros de la OCDE."

10 Estimates for the size of Peru's informal economy range from 60 percent to 98 percent of the total national economy.

11 Interview with author, February 22, 2012.

BIBLIOGRAPHY

Abalo, Juan Pablo. "El asombroso canto de una niña peruana," *The Clinic*, March 27, 2009. www.theclinic.cl/2009/03/27/el-asombroso-canto-de-una-nina -peruana/.

"About La Peña." *La Peña.* http://lapena.org/about. Accessed July 27, 2016.

Agard Jones, Vanessa. "Bodies in the System." *Small Axe: A Caribbean Journal of Criticism* 17, no. 3 (2013): 182–92.

Agnew, John. "Place and Politics." In "The Geographical Mediation of State and Society," special issue, *Boston* 3 (1987).

Anderson, Benedict. *Imagined Communities.* New York: Verso, 1983.

Andrews, George Reid. *Afro-Latin America.* New York: Oxford University Press, 2004.

Anzaldúa, Gloria. *Borderlands / La Frontera: The New Mestiza.* San Francisco: Aunt Lute Books, 1987.

Aparicio, Frances R. *Listening to Salsa: Gender, Latin Popular Music, and Puerto Rican Cultures.* Middletown, CT: Wesleyan University Press, 2010.

Aparicio, Frances R., and Cándida Jáquez. *Musical Migrations: Transnationalism and Cultural Hybridity in Latin/o America.* New York: Palgrave Macmillan, 2003.

Appadurai, Arjun. "Disjuncture and Difference in the Global Cultural Economy. *Theory, Culture and Society* 7, no. 2 (1990): 295–310.

———. *Modernity at Large: Cultural Dimensions of Globalization.* Vol. 1. Minneapolis: University of Minnesota Press, 1996.

Arrelucea Barrantes, Maribel. *Replanteando la esclavitud: Estudios de etnicidad y género en Lima borbónica.* Lima: CEDET, Centro de Desarrollo Étnico, 2009.

Aviruká. "El Cóndor Pasa . . . 1930: Banda de la Marina de los Estados Unidos." YouTube Posted March 2014. www.youtube.com/watch?v=AEUz3Yv4mbY.

Bailes Nacionales en Amancaes. "2. De la Zamacueca a la Marinera." *Historia de la Danza* (2007): 153.

Barbacci, Rodolfo. "Apuntes para un diccionario biográfico musical de Perú." *Revista Fénix* 6 (1949): 420–21.

Barlow, Sean, Banning Eyre, and Jack Vartoogian. *Afropop! An Illustrated Guide to Contemporary African Music.* Edison, NJ: Chartwell Books, 1995.

Basadre Grohmann, Jorge. *Historia de la República del Perú (1822–1933)*. Lima: Empresa Editora El Comercio, 2005.

Belaúnde Terry, Fernando. *Peru's Own Conquest*. Lima: American Studies Press, 1965.

Bell, David, and Gill Valentine, eds. *Mapping Desire: Geographies of Sexualities*. New York: Psychology Press, 1995.

Beverley, John. *Subalternity and Representation: Arguments in Cultural Theory*. Durham, NC: Duke University Press, 1999.

Binnie, Jon. "Coming Out of Geography: Towards a Queer Epistemology?" *Environment and Planning D* 15.2 (1997): 223–38.

Bowser, Frederick P. *The African Slave in Colonial Peru*. Stanford, CA: Stanford University Press, 1974.

Brady, Mary Pat. *Extinct Lands, Temporal Geographies: Chicana Literature and the Urgency of Space*. Durham, NC: Duke University Press, 2002.

Brown, Wendy. "Neo-Liberalism and the End of Liberal Democracy." *Theory and Event* 7, no. 1 (2003).

Brückmann, Ernesto Toledo. *El Cóndor Pasa: Mandato y obediencia. Análisis político y social de una zarzuela*. Lima: Editorial San Marcos, 2011.

Butler, Judith. *Gender Trouble: Feminism and the Subversion of Identity*. London: Routledge, 2011.

Byrd, Jodi A. *The Transit of Empire: Indigenous Critiques of Colonialism*. Minneapolis: University of Minnesota Press, 2011.

Byrne, David, and Yale Evelev. *The Soul of Black Perú: Afroperuvian Classics*. Warner Bros, B000002MXM, May 30, 1995.

Calavita, Kitty. "The New Politics of Immigration: 'Balanced-Budget Conservatism' and the Symbolism of Proposition 187." *Social Problems* 43, no. 3 (1996): 284–305.

Campbell Robinson, Deanna, Elizabeth Buck, and Marlene Cuthbert. *Music at the Margins: Popular Music and Global Cultural Diversity*. Thousand Oaks, CA: Sage, 1991.

Canclini, Néstor García. *Hybrid Cultures: Strategies for Entering and Leaving Modernity*. Minneapolis: University of Minnesota Press, 2005.

———. *Transforming Modernity: Popular Culture in Mexico*. Austin: University of Texas Press, 1993.

Carranza, Víctor. *Globalización y crisis social en el Perú*. Lima: IFEA, 2000.

Casasús, Mario. "Alejandro Stuart: Tengo el archivo más completo de la nueva canción latinoamericana." *El Clarín*, March 26, 2015.

Casillas, Dolores Inés. *Sounds of Belonging: US Spanish-Language Radio and Public Advocacy*. New York: NYU Press, 2014.

Cavour Aramayo, Ernesto. *Instrumentos musicales de Bolivia*. La Paz, Bolivia: Producciones CIMA, 1994.

Cepeda, María Elena. *Musical ImagiNation: US-Colombian Identity and the Latin Music Boom.* New York: NYU Press, 2010.

Chambers, Iain. *Urban Rhythms: Pop Music and Popular Culture.* London: Macmillan, 1985.

Chanan, Michael. "Global Corporations and 'World Music.'" In *Repeated Takes: A Short History of Recording and Its Effects on Music,* 151–78. New York: Verso, 1995.

City and County of San Francisco Planning Department, "City within a City: Historic Context Statement for San Francisco's Mission District." November 2007.

Clark, VéVé A. "Performing the Memory of Difference in Afro-Caribbean Dance." In *Kaiso! Writings by and about Katherine Dunham,* edited by VéVé A. Clark and Sara E. Johnson, 320–40. Madison: University of Wisconsin Press, 2005.

Clifford, James. *Routes: Travel and Translation in the Late Twentieth Century.* Cambridge, MA: Harvard University Press, 1997.

Connell, John, and Chris Gibson. *Sound Tracks: Popular Music Identity and Place.* London: Routledge, 2003.

———. "World Music: Deterritorializing Place and Identity." *Progress in Human Geography* 28, no. 3 (2004): 342–61.

Cornejo Polar, Antonio. "El indigenismo y las literaturas heterogéneas: Su doble estatuto socio-cultural." *Revista de crítica literaria latinoamericana* 4, nos. 7/8 (1978): 7–21.

Cortijo, Roberto. "Peruvian Teen Aims to Revive Quechua, One Pop Song at a Time." Ayacucho (Perú), *Agence France-Presse,* September 2, 2015.

Cresswell, Tim. *Place: A Short Introduction.* New York: Blackwell, 2002.

Cruz, Celia, and Tito Puente. *Celia y Tito Puente en España.* Tico, B013U0Y7V4, 1971, Vinyl.

Cuche, Denys. *Poder blanco y resistencia negra en el Perú: Un estudio de la condición social del negro en el Perú después de la abolición de la esclavitud.* Lima: Instituto Nacional de Cultura, 1975.

De la Cadena, Marisol. *Earth Beings: Ecologies of Practice across Andean Worlds.* Durham, NC: Duke University Press, 2015.

———. *Indigenous Mestizos: The Politics of Race and Culture in Cuzco, Peru, 1919–1991.* Durham, NC: Duke University Press, 2000.

De La Paz, Julio. *El cóndor pasa.* Lima: Editorial Renacimiento, 1913.

Delgado, Celeste Fraser, and José Muñoz. "Introduction." In *Everynight Life: Culture and Dance in Latin/o America,* 9–32. Durham, NC: Duke University Press, 1997.

Diamond, Elin. "Introduction." In *Performance and Cultural Politics,* edited by Elin Diamond, 1–11. London: Routledge, 1996.

Discography of American Historical Recordings. "Victor matrix G-2295, El cóndor

pasa / Orquesta del Zoológico." http://adp.library.ucsb.edu/index.php/matrix
/detail/600001472/G-2295-El_condor_pasa. Accessed October 20, 2015.

Dorian, Julio. "La nación." In *Apuntes críticas (El Condor Pasa)*, edited by A. J. P.
Paz Soldán. La Paz, Bolivia, 1913.

Dorr, Kirstie A. "Mapping 'El Condor Pasa': Sonic Translocations in the Global
Era." *Journal of Latin American Cultural Studies* 16, no. 1 (2007): 11–25.

Dunn, Timothy J. "The Militarization of the US-Mexico Border, 1978–1992: Low
Intensity Doctrine Comes Home." MA thesis, University of Texas at Austin,
1995.

Edwards, Brent Hayes. "The Uses of Diaspora." *Social Text* 19, no. 1 (2001): 45–73.

Eisenberg, Andrew J. "Space." In *Keywords in Sound*, edited by Davis Novak and
Matt Sakakeeny, 193–207. Durham, NC: Duke University Press, 2015.

El-Tayeb, Fatima. *European Others: Queering Ethnicity in Postnational Europe*.
Minneapolis: University of Minnesota Press, 2011.

"En el censo no preguntarán la raza." *La Prensa*, May 13, 1961.

Estenssoro Fuchs, Juan Carlos. "Música y comportamiento festivo de la población
negra en Lima colonial." *Cuadernos Hispanoamericanos* 451–52 (January–February 1988): 161–68.

Fahsbender, Frederico. "Wendy Sulca: Habla la estrellita de YouTube." *Rolling
Stone, Argentina*, October 5, 2010. www.rollingstone.com.ar/1311790-wendy
-sulca-habla-la-estrellita-de-youtube.

Fairley, Jan. "La nueva canción latinoamericana." *Bulletin of Latin American Research* 3, no. 2 (1984): 107–15.

Fajardo, Kale Bantigue. *Filipino Crosscurrents: Oceanographies of Seafaring, Mas-
culinities, and Globalization*. Minneapolis: University of Minnesota Press,
2011.

Feld, Steven. "Notes on World Beat." *Public Culture* 1, no. 1 (1988): 31–37.

———. "A Sweet Lullaby for World Music." *Public Culture* 12, no. 1 (2000): 145–71.

Feldman; Heidi Carolyn. "African or Andean? Origin Myths and Musical Performance in the Cradle of Black Peru." *Diagonal: Journal of the Center for Iberian and Latin American Music* 2 (2009): 1–11.

———. "The Black Pacific: Cuban and Brazilian Echoes in the Afro-Peruvian Revival." *Ethnomusicology* 49, no. 2 (spring/summer 2005): 206–31.

———. *Black Rhythms of Peru: Reviving African Musical Heritage in the Black Pacific. (Music/Culture)*. Middletown, CT: Wesleyan University Press, 2007.

Fiol-Matta, Licia. "Pop Latinidad: Puerto Ricans in the Latin Explosion, 1999."
Centro Journal 14, no. 1 (2002): 27–51.

Flores, Juan. *From Bomba to Hip-Hop: Puerto Rican Culture and Latino Identity*.
New York: Columbia University Press, 2000.

Fox, Patricia D. *Being and Blackness in Latin America: Uprootedness and Improvisation*. Gainesville: University Press of Florida, 2006.

Franceshini, Norma M. Juarbe. "La Virgen de la Guadalupe, La Malinche, and La

Llorona: Technologies of Meaning and Appropriation." PhD diss., Ohio State University, 1998.

Franco, Jean. "La Malinche: From Gift to Sexual Contract." In *Critical Passions: Selected Essays*, edited by Mary Louise Pratt and Kathleen M. Newman, 66–83. Durham, NC: Duke University Press, 1999.

Frith, Simon. "The Industrialization of Popular Music." *Popular Music and Communication* (1987): 53–77.

———, ed. 1989. *World Music, Politics, and Social Change*. Manchester, England: Manchester University Press.

Garofalo, Reebee, ed. *Rockin' the Boat: Mass Music and Mass Movements*. New York: South End Press, 1992.

———. "Whose World, What Beat: The Transnational Music Industry, Identity, and Cultural Imperialism." *World of Music* 35, no. 2 (1993): 16–32.

Gates, Henry Louis, Jr. *Black in Latin America*. New York: NYU Press, 2011.

———. *The Signifying Monkey: A Theory of African-American Cultural Criticism*. New York: Oxford University Press, 1989.

Gibson, Carlos. "El indio en la formación económica nacional." *El Deber Pro Indígena* 1, no. 9 (1913).

Gilmore, Ruth Wilson. "Fatal Couplings of Power and Difference: Notes on Racism and Geography." *Professional Geographer* 54, no. 1 (2002): 15–24.

———. "Globalisation and US Prison Growth: From Military Keynesianism to Post-Keynesian Militarism." *Race and Class* 40, nos. 2–3 (1998–99): 171–88.

———. *Golden Gulag: Prisons, Surplus, Crisis, and Opposition in Globalizing California*. Berkeley: University of California Press, 2007.

———. "Race and Globalization." In *Geographies of Global Change: Remapping the World*, 2nd ed., edited by R. J. Johnston, Peter Taylor, and Michael Watts. Oxford: Blackwell, 2002.

———. "You Have Dislodged a Boulder: Mothers and Prisoners in the Post Keynesian California Landscape." *Transforming Anthropology* 8, nos. 1–2 (1999): 12–38.

Gilroy, Paul. *Ain't No Black in the Union Jack*. Chicago: University of Chicago Press, 1991.

———. *The Black Atlantic: Modernity and Double Consciousness*. Cambridge, MA: Harvard University Press, 1993.

González, David. "What's the Problem with 'Hispanic'? Just ask a 'Latino.'" *New York Times*, November 15, 1992.

Gramsci, Antonio. *Selections from the Prison Notebooks*. Edited by Quintin Hoare and Geoffrey Nowell Smith. New York: International, 1999.

Guha, Ranajit. "Subaltern Studies: The Projects of Our Time and Their Convergence." In *The Latin American Subaltern Studies Reader*, edited by Ileana Rodríguez and María Milagros López, 35–46. Durham, NC: Duke University Press, 2001.

Guilbault, Jocelyne. *Governing Sound: The Cultural Politics of Trinidad's Carnival Musics*. Chicago: University of Chicago Press, 2007.

——. "Interpreting World Music: A Challenge in Theory and Practice." *Popular Music* 16, no. 1 (1997): 31–44.

——. "On Redefining the 'Local' through World Music." *World of Music* 35, no. 2 (1993): 33–47.

——. *Zouk: World Music in the West Indies*. Chicago: University of Chicago Press, 1993.

Gunning, Sandra, Tera W. Hunter, and Michele Mitchell, eds. *Dialogues of Dispersal: Gender, Sexuality and African Diasporas*. Oxford: Blackwell, 2004.

Habell-Pallán, Michelle. *Loca Motion: The Travels of Chicana and Latina Popular Culture*. New York: New York University, 2005.

Hall, Stuart. *Policing the Crisis: Mugging, the State, and Law and Order*. New York: Holmes and Meier, 1978.

Hanhardt, Christina. *Safe Space: Gay Neighborhood History and the Politics of Violence*. Durham, NC: Duke University Press, 2013.

Hartman, Saidiya. *Scenes of Subjection: Terror, Slavery, and Self-Making in Nineteenth-Century America*. Oxford: Oxford University Press, 1997.

Harvey, David. "Space as a Key Word." Paper for Marx and Philosophy Conference, May 29, 2004, Institute of Education, London.

Heckman, Don. "Reviews: From Sebastian to Simon and Garfunkel to Pickett." *New York Times*, March 8, 1970.

Hernandez, Deborah Pacini. *Bachata: A Social History of Dominican Popular Music*. Philadelphia: Temple University Press, 1995.

——. "Dancing with the Enemy: Cuban Popular Music, Race, Authenticity, and the World-Music Landscape." *Latin American Perspectives* 25, no. 3 (1998): 110–25.

"History and Mission." Womensbuilding.org. http://womensbuilding.org/about /mission-history. Accessed July 27, 2016.

Holden, Stephen. "Reviews/Music: The Yma Sumac Mystique." *New York Times*, February 26, 1989. www.nytimes.com/1989/02/26/arts/reviews-music-the -yma-sumac-mystique.html?mcubz=3.

Holtzman, Rodolfo. "Catálogo de las obras de Daniel Alomía Robles." *Boletín Bibliográfico Universidad Nacional Mayor de San Marcos* 16 (1943).

Hong, Grace Kyungwon, and Roderick A. Ferguson, eds. *Strange Affinities: The Gender and Sexual Politics of Comparative Racialization*. Durham, NC: Duke University Press, 2011.

Houston, Donna, and Laura Pulido. "The Work of Performativity: Staging Social Justice at the University of Southern California." *Environment and Planning D: Society and Space* 20, no. 4 (2002): 401–24.

Hurtado Riofrio, Víctor. "Daniel Alomía Robles: 'Honor a Quien Honor Merece.'"

boletindenewyork. www.boletindenewyork.com/danielarobles.htm. Accessed July 27, 2016.

Institución Cultural Pachayachachiq. Facebook post, March 31, 2013. www
.facebook.com/pachayachachiq/posts/174309326055650.

Jara, Joan. *Victor: An Unfinished Song.* London: Jonathan Cape, 1983.

Jay, Martin. *Downcast Eyes: The Denigration of Vision in the 20th Century French Thought.* Berkeley: University of California Press, 1994.

Jenkins, Henry. *Convergence Culture: Where Old and New Media Collide.* New York: NYU Press, 2006.

Johnson, Gaye Theresa. *Spaces of Conflict, Sounds of Solidarity: Music, Race, and Spatial Entitlement in Los Angeles.* Berkeley: University of California Press, 2013.

Kaplan, Amy. *The Anarchy of Empire in the Making of US Culture.* Cambridge, MA: Harvard University Press, 2005.

Kaplan, Sara Clarke. *The Black Reproductive: Feminism and the Politics of Freedom.* Minneapolis: University of Minnesota Press, 2018.

———. "Love and Violence/Maternity and Death: Black Feminism and the Politics of Reading (Un)Representability." *Black Women, Gender and Families* 1, no. 1 (spring 2007): 107–11.

———. "Souls at the Crossroads, Africans on the Water: The Politics of Diasporic Melancholia." *Callaloo* 30, no. 2 (spring 2007): 511–26.

Kapsoli, Wilfredo. *El pensamiento de la Asociación Pro Indígena.* Cusco: Centro Bartolomé de Las Casas, 1980.

Kassabian, Anahid. "Would You Like Some World Music with Your Latte? Starbucks, Putumayo, and Distributed Tourism." *Twentieth-Century Music* 1, no. 2 (2004): 209–23.

Katerí Hernández, Tanya. "The Buena Vista Social Club: The Racial Politics of Nostalgia." In *Latino/a Popular Culture,* edited by Michelle Habell-Pallan and Mary Romero, 61–72. New York: NYU Press, 2002.

Kelley, Robin D. G. "How the West Was One: On the Uses and Limitations of Diaspora." *Black Scholar* 30, nos. 3–4 (fall 2000–winter 2001): 31–35.

———. *Race Rebels: Culture, Politics, and the Black Working Class.* New York: Free Press, 1996.

———. *Thelonious Monk: The Life and Times of an American Original.* New York: Simon and Schuster, 2009.

Kheshti, Roshanak. *Modernity's Ear: Listening to Race and Music in World Music.* New York: NYU Press, 2015.

———. "Touching Listening: The Aural Imaginary in the World Music Culture Industry." *American Quarterly* 63, no. 3 (2011): 711–31.

Kristal, Efraín. *Una visión urbana de los Andes: Génesis y desarrollo del indigenismo en el Perú: 1848–1930.* Lima: Instituto de Apoyo Agrario, 1991.

Kun, Josh. *Audiotopia: Music, Race, and America.* Berkeley: University of California Press, 2005.

"La Peña del Sur, una plataforma para el talento latinoamericano: Dos años de lucha cultural en el Barrio de la Misión." *New Mission News*, December 1997.

Lefebvre, Henri. *The Production of Space*. Oxford: Blackwell, 1991.

———. *Rhythmanalysis: Space, Time and Everyday Life*. New York: Continuum, 2004.

León Quirós, Javier Francisco. "The Aestheticization of Tradition: Professional Afroperuvian Musicians, Cultural Reclamation, and Artistic Interpretation." PhD diss., University of Texas, Austin, 2003.

———. "Mass Culture, Commodification, and the Consolidation of the Afro-Peruvian 'Festejo.'" *Black Music Research Journal* 26, no. 2 (fall 2006): 213–47.

———. "Roots, Tradition, and the Mass Media: The Future of Criollo Popular Music." *Musical Cultures of Latin America: Global Effects, Past and Present*, 163–73. Los Angeles: Ethnomusicology Publications, 1999.

———. "Santa Libertad: Teatro del Milenio and the Debate over Music and Social Consciousness in the Afroperuvian Community." *Diagonal: Journal of the Center for Iberian and Latin American Music* 2 (2006).

Levitin, Daniel. "Still Creative after All These Years: A Conversation with Paul Simon." *Grammy Magazine* 16, no. 1 (winter 1997): 16–19.

Limansky, Nicholas E. *Yma Sumac: The Art behind the Legend*. New York: YBK Publishers, 2008.

Linell, Per. *Approaching Dialogue: Talk, Interaction and Contexts in Dialogical Perspectives*. Vol. 3. Amsterdam: John Benjamins, 1998.

Lionnet, Françoise, and Shu-mei Shih, eds. *Minor Transnationalism*. Durham, NC: Duke University Press, 2005.

Lipsitz, George. *Dangerous Crossroads: Popular Music, Postmodernism, and the Poetics of Place*. New York: Verso, 1997.

"Listening In." *Washington Post*, September 20, 1923.

Lloyd, Peter. *The "Young Towns" of Lima: Aspects of Urbanization in Peru*. Cambridge: CUP Archive, 1980.

López, Raimundo. "'El cóndor pasa' declarada Patrimonio Cultural de Perú." April 13, 2004. *www.latinoamerica-online.info/cult04/musica06.04.html*. 2004-04-13.

Lorde, Audre. "The Master's Tools Will Never Dismantle the Master's House." *Sister Outsider: Essays and Speeches*, 110–13. Berkeley, CA: Crossing Press, 2007.

Lott, Eric. *Love and Theft: Blackface Minstrelsy and the American Working Class*. New York: Oxford University Press, 2013.

Lowe, Lisa. *Immigrant Acts: On Asian American Cultural Politics*. Durham, NC: Duke University Press, 1996.

Luaka Bop. "Luaka History." www.luakabop.com/history/. Accessed July 14, 2014.

Luta, Primus. "Live Electronic Performance: Theory and Practice." *Sounding Out!*, December 9, 2013. Web. https://soundstudiesblog.com/2013/12/09/live-electronic-performance-theory-and-practice/.

Mackey, John. "Why Companies Should Embrace Conscious Capitalism." *Forbes*, January 15, 2013.

Mackey, John, and Rajendra Sisodia. *Conscious Capitalism, with a New Preface by the Authors: Liberating the Heroic Spirit of Business*. Cambridge, MA: Harvard Business Review Press, 2014.

Maclean y Estenos, Roberto. "Negros en el nuevo mundo." Lima: PTCM, 1948.

Manalansan, Martin F. *Global Divas: Filipino Gay Men in the Diaspora*. Durham, NC: Duke University Press, 2003.

Marez, Curtis. *Farm Worker Futurism*. Minneapolis: University of Minnesota Press, 2016.

Mariátegui, José Carlos. *Seven Interpretive Essays on Peruvian Reality*. Translated by Marjory Urquidi. Austin: University of Texas Press, 1971.

Martí, Fernando. "The Mission District: A History of Resistance." Mission Anti-Displacement Coalition. December 2006.

Martin, Douglas. "Yma Sumac, Vocalist of the Exotic, Dies at 86." *New York Times*, November 4, 2008.

Massey, Doreen. *For Space*. London: Sage, 2012.

———. *Space, Place, and Gender*. Minneapolis: University of Minnesota Press, 1994.

McClintock, Anne. "Imperial Leather." In *Dangerous Liaisons: Gender, Nation, and Postcolonial Perspectives*, edited by Anne McClintock, Aamir Mufti, and Ella Shohat. Minneapolis: University of Minnesota Press, 1997.

McDowell, Linda. *Gender, Identity, and Place: Understanding Feminist Geographies*. Minneapolis: University of Minnesota Press, 2003.

McKittrick, Katherine. *Demonic Grounds: Black Women and the Cartographies of Struggle*. Minneapolis: University of Minnesota Press, 2006.

McKittrick, Katherine, and Linda Peake. "What Difference Does Difference Make to Geography?" In *Questioning Geography: Fundamental Debates*, edited by Noel Castree, Alisdair Rogers, and Douglas D. Sherman, 39–54. Malden, MA: Blackwell, 2005.

Mejía, Luis Salazar. *El misterio del cóndor: Memoria e historia de "El cóndor pasa. . . ."* Lima: Taky Onqoy Ediciones, 2013.

Middleton, Richard. *Studying Popular Music*. Philadelphia: Open University Press, 1990.

Mignolo, Walter. *Local Histories, Global Designs: Coloniality, Subaltern Knowledges, and Border Thinking*. Princeton, NJ: Princeton University Press, 2000.

Mitchell, Katharyne. "Transnational Discourse: Bringing Geography Back In." *Antipode: A Radical Journal of Geography* 29, no. 2 (April 1997): 101–14.

Mitchell, Tony. *Popular Music and Local Identity: Rock, Pop, and Rap in Europe and Oceania*. London: Leicester University Press, 1996.

Mohn, Tanya. "Private Sector: Stumbling into a World of Music." *New York Times*, December 21, 2003. www.nytimes.com/2003/12/21/business/private-sector -stumbling-into-a-world-of-music.html.

More, Ernesto. "Daniel Alomía Robles en primera persona." In *Peruanidad: Órgano antológico del pensamiento nacional*, vol. 2. Lima: Ministerio del Gobierno, Dirección de Propoganda e Informaciones, 1942.

Moten, Fred. *In the Break: The Aesthetics of the Black Radical Tradition*. Minneapolis: University of Minnesota Press, 2003.

Nakano Glenn, Evelyn. *Unequal Freedom: How Race and Citizenship Shaped American Citizenship and Labor*. Cambridge, MA: Harvard University Press, 2004.

Nash, Catherine. "Contesting Identity: Politics of Gays and Lesbians in Toronto in the 1970s / Identidad en conflicto: Políticas de gays y lesbianas en Toronto en los años 1970." *Gender, Place and Culture: A Journal of Feminist Geography* 12, no. 1 (2005): 113–35.

———. "Performativity in Practice: Some Recent Work in Cultural Geography." *Progress in Human Geography* 24, no. 4 (2000): 653–64.

———. "Toronto's Gay Village (1969–1982): Plotting the Politics of Gay Identity." *Canadian Geographer* 50, no. 1 (March 2006): 1–16.

Nash, Catherine Jean, and Alison Bain. "'Reclaiming Raunch'? Spatializing Queer Identities at Toronto Women's Bathhouse Events." *Social and Cultural Geography* 8, no. 1 (2007): 47–62.

Nast, Heidi J. "Mapping the 'Unconscious': Racism and the Oedipal Family." *Annals of the Association of American Geographers* 90, no. 2 (2000): 215–55.

———. "Queer Patriarchies, Queer Racisms, Inter-national." *Antipode: A Radical Journal of Geography* 34, no. 5 (2002): 874–910.

Nevins, Joseph. *Operation Gatekeeper: The Rise of the "Illegal Alien" and the Making of the US-Mexico Boundary*. New York: Routledge, 2002.

Niaah, Sonjah Stanley. *Dancehall: From Slave Ship to Ghetto*. Ottawa, Canada: University of Ottawa Press, 2010.

Núñez Jaime, Víctor. "Wendy Sulca: La niña que creció en YouTube." *El País* (España). January 15, 2013. http://blogs.elpais.com/periodista-en-serie/2013/01/wendy-sulca-la-nina-que-crecio-en-youtube.html.

Oboler, Suzanne. "Hispanics? That's What They Call Us." In *The Latino Condition: A Critical Reader*, edited by Richard Delgado and Jean Stefanic, 3–5. New York: NYU Press, 1998.

Ochoa Gautier, Ana María. *Aurality: Listening and Knowledge in Nineteenth-Century Colombia*. Durham, NC: Duke University Press, 2014.

———. "Sonic Transculturation, Epistemologies of Purification and the Aural Public Sphere in Latin America." *Social Identities: Journal for the Study of Race, Nation and Culture* 12, no. 6 (2006): 803–25.

Ochoa Gautier, Ana María, and George Yúdice. "The Latin American Music Industry in an Era of Crisis." In *Global Alliance for Cultural Diversity, Division of Arts and Cultural Enterprise UNESCO, Paris*, 1–13. November 2002.

Ojeda, Martha. *Nicomedes Santa Cruz: Ecos de África en Perú*. London: Tamesis Books, 2003.

Oliart, Patricia, and José A. Lloréns. "La nueva canción en el Perú." *Comunicación y Cultura* 12 (1984): 73–82.

Omi, Michael, and Howard Winant. *Racial Formation in the United States*. 2nd ed. New York: Routledge, 1994.

Oquendo, Angel R. "Re-imaging the Latino/a Race." In *The Latino Condition: A Critical Reader*, edited by Richard Delgado and Jean Stefanic, 60–71. New York: NYU Press, 1998.

Ortiz, Fernando. *Cuban Counterpoint: Tobacco and Sugar*. Translated by Harriet de Onís. Durham, NC: Duke University Press, 1995.

Oswin, Natalie. "Critical Geographies and the Uses of Sexuality: Deconstructing Queer Space." *Progress in Human Geography* 32, no. 1 (2008): 89–103.

Palma, Ricardo. *Tradiciones peruanas*. No. 860 (85)-3. Centro Editor de América Latina, 1971.

Pareles, Jon. "A Voyage through the Decades with Paul Simon as the Guide." *New York Times*, October 4, 1993.

Patterson, Orlando. *Slavery and Social Death*. Cambridge, MA: Harvard University Press, 1982.

"Paul Simon—In His Own Words." *Super Seventies RockSite!* www.superseventies .com/sspaulsimon.html. Accessed June 6, 2015.

Paz, Octavio, and Lysander Kemp. *The Labyrinth of Solitude: Life and Thought in Mexico*. Translated by Lysander Kemp. London: Penguin Press, 1967.

Paz Soldán, A. J. P. "Apuntes críticas." In *El Cóndor Pasa*. Lima, 1913.

Perea, Juan F. *Immigrants Out! New Nativism and the Anti-Immigrant Impulse in the United States*. New York: NYU Press, 1997.

Pérez Torres Llosa, Ricardo. "El cóndor pasa: Una visión de vida para meditar." *Suplemento Cultural de La Crónica*. Lima, 1979.

"Perú es el cuarto país que más disminuyó su piratería entre miembros de la OCDE." *Gestión*. March 5, 2013. http://gestion.pe/tendencias/peru-cuarto -pais-que-mas-disminuyo-su-pirateria-entre-miembros-ocde-2060640.

"Peruvian Music Given on N.Y.U. Campus." *New York Times*, July 25, 1930.

Pinilla, Enrique. *La música en el Perú*. Lima: Patronato Popular y Porvenir Pro Música Clásica, 1985.

Plambeck, Joseph. "As CD Sales Wane, Music Retailers Diversify." *New York Times,* May 30, 2010. www.nytimes.com/2010/05/31/business/media/31bestbuy .html?mcubz=3.

Poling, James. "Most Exciting Voice in the World: A Fiery Peruvian, Yma Sumac." *Colliers*, April 14, 1951.

Pratt, Mary Louise. "Arts of the Contact Zone." *Profession* 1 (1991): 33–40.

———. *Imperial Eyes: Travel Writing and Transculturation*. New York: Routledge, 1992.

Prieto, Juan Sixto. "El Perú en la música escénica." *Fénix. Revista de la Biblioteca Nacional del Perú*. Número 9. Lima, 1953.

Puar, Jasbir. "A Transnational Feminist Critique of Queer Tourism." *Antipode: A Radical Journal of Geography* 34, no. 5 (2002): 935–46.

Quijano, Anibal. *Nationalism and Capitalism in Peru: A Study in Neo-Imperialism.* New York: Monthly Review Press, 1971.

Ramos, Julio. *Desencuentros de la modernidad en América Latina: Literatura y política en el siglo XIX.* Mexico City: Fondo de Cultura Económica, 1989.

Redmond, Shana. *Anthem: Social Movements and the Sound of Solidarity in the African Diaspora.* New York: NYU Press, 2013.

"Revista Rolling Stone califica de 'fenómeno hispanoparlante' a peruana Wendy Sulca." *Andina del Perú para el Mundo.* October 6, 2010. www.andina.com .pe/agencia/noticia-revista-rolling-stone-califica-fenomeno-hispanoparlante -a-peruana-wendy-sulca-321168.aspx.

Reyes Matta, Fernando. "The 'New Song' and Its Confrontation in Latin America." In *Marxism and the Interpretation of Culture,* edited by Cary Nelson and Lawrence Grossberg, 447–60. Urbana: University of Illinois Press, 1988.

Rice, Tim. "Listening." In *Keywords in Sound,* edited by David Novak and Matt Sakakeeny, 99–111. Durham, NC: Duke University Press, 2015.

Rios, Fernando. "Andean Music, the Left, and Pan-Latin Americanism: The Early History." *Diagonal: Journal of the Center for Iberian and Latin American Music* 2 (2009): 1–13.

———. "La flûte indienne: The Early History of Andean Folkloric-Popular Music in France and Its Impact on Nueva Canción." *Latin American Music Review* 29, no. 2 (2008): 145–89.

Ritter, Jonathan Larry. "Articulating Blackness in Afro-Ecuadorian Marimba Performance." *Musical Cultures of Latin America: Global Effects, Past and Present* (2003): 143–53.

———. "Chocolate, Coconut, and Honey: Race, Music, and the Politics of Hybridity in the Ecuadorian Black Pacific." *Popular Music and Society* 34, no. 5 (2011): 571–92.

———. "La Marimba Esmeraldeña: Music and Ethnicity on Ecuador's Northern Coast." PhD diss., University of California, Berkeley, 1998.

Rivera, Raquel. *New York Ricans from the Hip Hop Zone.* New York: Palgrave Macmillan, 2003.

Rivera Cusicanqui, Silvia. "Ch'ixinakax utxiwa: A Reflection on the Practices and Discourses of Decolonization." *South Atlantic Quarterly* 111, no. 1 (winter 2012).

Rivera-Servera, Ramón H. *Performing Queer Latinidad: Dance, Sexuality, Politics.* Ann Arbor: University of Michigan Press, 2012.

Roach, Joseph. *Cities of the Dead: Circum-Atlantic Performance.* New York: Columbia University Press, 1996.

Roberts, Martin. "'World Music' and the Global Culture Economy." *Diaspora: A Journal of Transnational Studies* 2, no. 2 (January 1992): 229–42.

Robinson, Cedric. *Black Marxism: The Making of the Black Radical Tradition.* Chapel Hill: University of North Carolina Press, 1983.

Rodríguez, Juana María. *Queer Latinidad: Identity Practices, Discursive Spaces.* New York: NYU Press, 2003.

Rodríguez, Néstor. "The Real 'New World Order': The Globalization of Racial and Ethnic Relations in the Late Twentieth Century." In *The Bubbling Cauldron: Race, Ethnicity, and the Urban Crisis,* edited by Michael Peter Smith and Joe R. Feagin, 211–25. Minneapolis: University of Minnesota Press, 1995.

Rodríguez Pastor, Humberto. *Negritud: Afroperuanos, resistencia y existencia.* Lima: CEDET Centro de Desarrollo Étnico, 2008.

Romero, Lora. *Homefronts: Domesticity and Its Critics in the Antebellum United States.* Durham, NC: Duke University Press, 1997.

Romero, Raúl R. "Black Music and Identity in Peru: Reconstruction and Revival of Afro-Peruvian Traditions." In *Music and Black Ethnicity: The Caribbean and South America,* edited by Gerard Béhague, 307–30. New Brunswick, NJ: Transaction, 1994.

———. *Debating the Past: Music, Memory, and Identity in the Andes.* New York: Oxford University Press, 2001.

———. "La música tradicional y popular." In *La música en el Perú.* Lima: Patronato Popular y Porvenir Pro Música Clásica, 1985.

———. *Sonidos andinos: Una antología de la música campesina del Perú.* Lima: Pontificia Universidad Católica del Perú, Instituto Riva-Agüero, Centro de Etnomusicología Andina, 2002.

Roque Ramírez, Horacio N. "Claiming Queer Cultural Citizenship: Gay Latino (Im)migrant Acts in San Francisco." In *Queer Migrations: Sexuality, US Citizenship, and Border Crossings,* 161–88. Minneapolis: University of Minnesota Press, 2005.

———. " 'That's My Place!': Negotiating Racial, Sexual, and Gender Politics in San Francisco's Gay Latino Alliance, 1975–1983." *Journal of the History of Sexuality* 12, no. 2 (2003): 224–58.

Rosaldo, Renato. *Culture and Truth: The Remaking of Social Analysis.* Boston: Beacon, 1989.

Rowe, William, and Vivian Schelling. *Memory and Modernity: Popular Culture in Latin America.* New York: Verso, 1991.

Rowell, Charles Henry, et al. "An Interview with Victoria Santa Cruz." *Callaloo* 34, no. 2 (2011): 298–517.

Saldívar, José David. *Border Matters: Remapping American Cultural Studies.* Berkeley: University of California Press, 1997.

Sánchez, Luis Alberto. *Introducción crítica a la literatura peruana.* Lima: P. L. Villanueva, 1974.

Santa Cruz Castillo, Rafael. *El cajón afroperuano.* Lima: Cocodrilo Verde Ediciones, 2004.

Santa Cruz Gamarra, Nicomedes. "De Senegal y Malambo." *Caretas* 479 (June–July 1973): 22–24.

———. "Estampas De Pancho Fierro." *Expreso* (Lima), February 2, 1964.

———. "Folklore peruano: Cumanana." *Expreso* (Lima), May 24, 1964.

———. *Ritmos negros del Perú*. Lima: Editorial Losada, 1971.

Santa Cruz Gamarra, Victoria. *Descubrimiento y desarrollo del sentido rítmico*. Lima: Eyzaguirre, 2000.

———. "Me Gritaron Negra." In *Black and Woman: Entrevista con Eugenio Barba, un documental de la Odin Teatret*. www.youtube.com/watch?v=p6Frs9r DWx8. Accessed June 2015.

Schafer, R. Murray. *The Soundscape: Our Sonic Environment and the Turning of the World*. Rochester, VT: Destiny Books, 1994.

Schawbel, Dan. "John Mackey: Why Companies Should Embrace Conscious Capitalism." *Forbes*, January 15, 2013. www.forbes.com/sites/danschawbel /2013/01/15/john-mackey-why-companies-should-embrace-conscious -capitalism/#3e2831505dd3.

Scheben, Helmut. "Indigenismo y modernismo." *Revista de crítica literaria latino-americana* 1, no. 1 (1979): 115–28.

Schmidt Camacho, Alicia. "Ciudadana X: Gender Violence and the Denational-ization of Women's Rights in Ciudad Juárez, México." cr: *The New Centennial Review* 5, no. 1 (2005): 255–92.

Schwab, Frederico. "El folklore, nuevo campo de estudio en América y la necesi-dad de su orientación histórica." In *Actas y trabajos científicos del XXVII congreso internacional de Americanistas*. Lima: Librería e Imprenta Gil, 1939.

Scott, James C. *Domination and the Arts of Resistance: Hidden Transcripts*. New Haven, CT: Yale University Press, 1992.

Sharpe, Jenny. "Cartographies of Globalisation, Technologies of Gendered Sub-jectivities: The Dub Poetry of Jean 'Binta' Breeze." In *Dialogues of Dispersal: Gender, Sexuality and African Diasporas*, edited by Sandra Gunning, Tera W. Hunter, and Michele Mitchell. Oxford: Blackwell, 2004.

Sherman, Robert. "Yma Sumac Returns to Roar of Crowds." *New York Times*, March 24, 1975.

Simon and Garfunkel. "Citizen of the Planet." Columbia Europe, 2004. B00068C7WK.

———. "El Condor Pasa (If I Could)." Columbia Records, 1970. B00I80V6DE.

Simpson, Audra. *Mohawk interruptus: Political Life Across the Borders of Settler States*. Durham, NC: Duke University Press, 2014.

Skidmore, Thomas E., and Peter H. Smith. "The Transformation of Modern Latin America, 1880s–1990s." In *Modern Latin America*, 42–67. Oxford: Oxford University Press, 2001.

Sloan, Heather L. "The Other World Music: Percussion as Purveyor of Cultural Cues in Exotic Lounge Music." *College Music Symposium* 49 (2009): 409–26.

Small, Christopher. *Musicking: The Meanings of Performing and Listening*. Middletown, CT: Wesleyan University Press, 1998.

Smallwood, Stephanie E. *Saltwater Slavery: A Middle Passage from Africa to American Diaspora*. Cambridge, MA: Harvard University Press, 2008.

Smith, Neil. "Contours of a Spatialized Politics: Homeless Vehicles and the Production of Geographic Scale." *Social Text* 1, no. 33 (1993): 54–83.

———. *The New Urban Frontier: Gentrification and the Revanchist City*. New York: Routledge, 1996.

Smith, Neil, and Cindi Katz. "Grounding Metaphor: Towards a Spatialized Politics." In *Place and the Politics of Identity*, edited by Michael Keith and Steve Pile, 67–83. New York: Routledge, 1993.

Somerville, Siobhan. "Queer." In *Keywords for American Cultural Studies*, edited by Bruce Burgett and Glenn Hendler, 187–90. New York: NYU Press, 2007.

———. *Queering the Color Line: Race and the Invention of Homosexuality in American Culture*. Durham, NC: Duke University Press, 2000.

"Soundscapes: La Nueva Canción (The New Song Movement in Latin America)." Smithsonian Institute Folkways Recordings. www.folkways.si.edu/la-nueva-cancion-new-song-movement-south-america/latin-world-struggle-protest/music/article/smithsonian. Accessed September 16, 2015.

Steele, Jeanne Rogge. "Carnival, Resistance, and Transgression in the Workplace." *Corporate Communication: Theory and Practice*, July 28, 1994, 239.

Sterne, Jonathan. *The Audible Past: Cultural Origins of Sound Reproduction*. Durham, NC: Duke University Press, 2003.

———. *The Sound Studies Reader*. New York: Routledge, 2012.

Stuart, Alejandro. E-mail message to author, June 14, 2012.

Sumac, Yma. *Yma Sumac: Voices of Xtabay*. Capitol Records, B0070PD9VA, 1950, Vinyl.

Taylor, Diana. *The Archive and the Repertoire: Performing Cultural Memory in the Americas*. Durham, NC: Duke University Press, 2003.

Taylor, Timothy D. *Global Pop: World Music, World Markets*. New York: Routledge, 1997.

Tello, Aurelio. "Aires nacionales en la música de América Latina como respuesta a la búsqueda de identidad." *Hueso Húmero* 44 (2004): 210–37.

Theidon, Kimberly. "First Do No Harm: Enforced Sterilizations and Gender Justice in Peru." *openDemocracy*, April 29, 2015. www.opendemocracy.net/opensecurity/kimberly-theidon/first-do-no-harm-enforced-sterilizations-and-gender-justice-in-peru.

Thift, Nigel. "The Still Point: Resistance, Expressive Embodiment and Dance." In *Geographies of Resistance*, edited by Michael Keith and Steven Pile, 124–51. New York: Routledge, 1997.

Thurner, Mark. *From Two Republics to One Divided: Contradictions of Postcolonial Nationmaking in Andean Peru*. Durham, NC: Duke University Press, 1997.

Tiwary, Vivek. "Lifestyle Marketing." www.starpolish.com/advice/article.asp?id +377original=1. Accessed July 16, 2015.

Tomlinson, John. *Cultural Imperialism: A Critical Introduction*. London: Continuum, 2001.

Totten, Steven. "Yma Sumac: The Incan Princess and Voice of the Andes." *Sounds and Colors*, August 30, 2012. http://soundsandcolours.com/articles/peru /yma-sumac-the-incan-princess-and-the-voice-of-the-andes-15927/.

Tumas-Serna, Jane. "The 'Nueva Canción' Movement and Its Mass-Mediated Performance Context." *Latin American Music Review / Revista de Música Latinoamericana* 13, no. 2 (1992): 139–57.

Turino, Thomas. *Moving Away from Silence: Music of the Peruvian Altiplano and the Experience of Urban Migration*. Chicago: University of Chicago Press, 2010.

———. "Nationalism and Latin American Music: Selected Case Studies and Theoretical Considerations." *Latin American Music Review* 24, no. 2 (2003): 169–209.

———. "Somos el Peru [We Are Peru]: Cumbia Andina' and the Children of Andean Migrants in Lima." *Studies in Latin American Popular Culture* 9 (1990): 15–37.

Valentine, Gill. "Queer Bodies and the Production of Space." In *Handbook of Lesbian and Gay Studies*, edited by Diane Richardson and Steven Seidman, 145–60. London: Sage, 2002.

———. "Sexual Politics." In *A Companion to Political Geography*, edited by John A. Agnew, Katharyne Mitchell, and Gerard Toal, 408–20. Malden, MA: Blackwell, 2003.

Varallarnos, José. *El Cóndor Pasa: Vida y obra de Daniel Alomía Robles, músico, compositor y folklorista peruano*. Lima: CONCYTEC, 1998.

Vargas, Deborah. *Dissonant Divas in Chicana Music: The Limits of La Onda*. Minneapolis: University of Minnesota Press, 2012.

Vasquez, Alexandra T. *Listening in Detail: Performances of Cuban Music*. Durham, NC: Duke University Press, 2003.

Vaughn, Bobby. "Afro-Mexico: Blacks, Indígenas, Politics, and the Greater Diaspora." In *Neither Enemies nor Friends*, 117–36. New York: Palgrave Macmillan US, 2005.

———. "Mexico in the Context of the Transatlantic Slave Trade." *Diálogo* 5, no. 1 (2001): 5.

Vega, Carlos. *Panorama de la música popular Argentina: Con un ensayo sobre la ciencia del folklore*. Buenos Aires: Editorial Losada, 1944.

"Victoria Santa Cruz, negro es mi color." *Retratos de TV Perú*, TV Perú, 2008.

Vilches, Manuel. "Entrevista con Alejandro Stuart." www.latinoamericano.cl. Accessed August 12, 2013.

Vinson, Ben, and Matthew Restall, eds. *Black Mexico: Race and Society from Colonial to Modern Times*. Albuquerque: University of New Mexico Press, 2009.

Vinson, Ben, and Bobby Vaughn. *Afroméxico*. Fondo de Cultura Económica, 2004.

Viteri, María Amelia, José Fernando Serrano, and Salvador Vidal-Ortiz. "¿Cómo se piensa lo 'queer' en América Latina?" *Iconos, Revista de Ciencias Sociales* 39 (2011): 47–60.

Wade, Peter. *Music, Race, and Nation: Música Tropical in Colombia*. Chicago: University of Chicago Press, 2000.

"Welcome to SunVirgin.com." www.sunvirgin.com. Accessed November 5, 2015.

"What Is Nueva Canción?" Acción Latina. www.accionlatina.org/encuentro /nueva_cancion.html. Accessed July 14, 2006.

Whiteley, Sheila, Andy Bennett, and Stan Hawkins, eds. *Music, Space and Place: Popular Music and Cultural Identity*. Burlington, VT: Ashgate, 2004.

Woods, Clyde Adrian. *Development Arrested: The Blues and Plantation Power in the Mississippi Delta*. London: Verso, 1998.

Yuval-Davis, Nira. "Women and the Biological Reproduction of 'the Nation.'" *Women's Studies International Forum* 19, no. 1 (1996).

Zamalloa, Oscar. "Declaran a 'El cóndor pasa' patrimonio cultural de Perú." *ABC*, April 8, 2004. www.abc.com.py/edicion-impresa/suplementos/cultural /declaran-a-el-condor-pasa-patrimonio-cultural-de-peru-757089.html.

Zolov, E. *Refried Elvis: The Rise of the Mexican Counterculture*. Berkeley: University of California Press, 1999.

Note: Page numbers in italics indicate illustrations.